THE ULTIMATE PRACTICAL GUIDE TO

PRUNING
AND TRAINING

HOW TO PRUNE AND TRAIN TREES, SHRUBS, HEDGES, TOPIARY, TREE AND SOFT FRUIT, CLIMBERS AND ROSES

RICHARD BIRD

southwater

Dedication
To Hilary with lots and lots of love

This edition is published by Southwater,
an imprint of Anness Publishing Ltd,
108 Great Russell Street, London WC1B 3NA;
info@anness.com

www.southwaterbooks.com;
www.annesspublishing.com

If you like the images in this book and would
like to investigate using them for publishing,
promotions or advertising, please visit our
website www.practicalpictures.com
for more information.

A CIP catalogue record for this book is
available from the British Library.

Publisher: Joanna Lorenz
Executive Editor: Caroline Davison
Designer: Michael Morey
Illustrator: Liz Pepperell
Production Manager: Ben Worley

PUBLISHER'S NOTE

THE ULTIMATE PRACTICAL GUIDE TO
PRUNING
AND TRAINING

Contents

Introduction

Pruning is one of those garden tasks that you can ignore if you wish. However, this approach will only succeed for a while, because eventually the pruning work will accumulate and it will be a huge task to sort everything out. Gardeners' neglect of pruning is not so much through dislike or boredom – as with weeding, for example – but has more to do with a fear of the unknown. Pruning is often perceived as one of the black arts of gardening, a skill that some possess, while others do not.

Of course, as with all matters connected with gardening, it is simply a matter of experience. Sitting and thinking about the task in hand will not improve your technique, but getting out there and doing it will. We all make mistakes at first, but nature is very forgiving and it is not often that you kill a tree or shrub by making pruning mistakes, especially as most gardeners err on the side of caution when they first set out.

In this book we aim to provide the basic techniques that will give you the confidence to pick up your secateurs (pruners) and make a start. You will not need all the information in the book because it is doubtful whether you grow everything we cover, but it should act as a guide through many a season and many a change in your garden. Above all, it is important to have a go and see how your garden improves.

LEFT This impressive garden with its wide variety of trees, shrubs and climbers shows the benefits of careful pruning.

The principles of pruning and training

Pruning is one of those jobs that most gardeners either hate or are frightened of – or both! The fear is partly because while most garden operations seem to be common sense, cutting back a shrub or tree seems to be a drastic thing to do, which will leave disastrous evidence for everyone to see if something goes wrong. It is a bit like giving someone a haircut – you would rather leave it to the professional. The other job that is also considered tricky, propagation, is not a problem, because if the seeds do not come up or the cuttings fail, who is to know? Yes, pruning is definitely a tricky thing to attempt. Or is it?

Not a magic art
Shrubs and trees have been grown for thousands of years in gardens. People have been pruning them for all that time without causing their demise. In fact, pruning, like any other garden technique, has a logic

ABOVE A delightful crab apple tree, *Malus* 'Evereste', in full flower. It has benefited from being pruned for shape, as well as for flower and fruit production.

ABOVE This flowering currant, *Ribes sanguineum* 'Pulborough Scarlet', with its mass of brilliant flowers, is kept in shape and growing vigorous by good pruning.

behind it and with experience most gardeners soon learn to prune their plants without a second thought. Most of us have a limited range of plants in the garden so it is not as if you have to remember how to prune every plant that is available, just your own collection. Pruning is definitely not a magic art; everyone can soon learn to do it.

In the wild
In nature, of course, no one prunes plants. Horses may browse them and trim them tightly back, branches die and fall off, and occasionally lightning or wind lops off a branch or even fells a whole tree. Yet nearly all manage to recover. As, indeed, do roses from the modern fashion of pruning them with chainsaws. So,

ABOVE Crab apples are both decorative and useful as fruit in the kitchen. Pruning will improve the yield.

perhaps pruning is not such a delicate art that you can kill a plant if it all goes wrong.

So why prune?

If plants do not get much pruning in the natural world, why do they need it in gardens? There are several good reasons why we should prune, especially if you remember that we are growing plants in artificial conditions and that we want them to perform at their very best. Of course, you need not prune them at all if you do not want to. Many gardeners do not prune, but you may not get the best out of your plants. Having said that, there are many trees and shrubs that do not need any regular pruning. One of the attractions of conifers, for example, is that most require no attention at all. However, there is no doubt that if you do prune, your trees and shrubs will look much better for it. They will be shapely and productive, and will not have any dead or damaged wood to spoil their beauty.

ABOVE An attractive group of silver birches, *Betula pendula*, that might have benefited from a little more attention with initial training so that they grew more upright.

ABOVE This well-flowered hydrangea is looking at its best and has benefited from good pruning.

Reasons for pruning

Flower and fruit production – get the most out of your plants
Plant health – keep your plants healthy
Improved shape – keep the plants in the shape that you want
Control – do not let your plants take over and swamp everything

There are four main reasons for pruning. If carried out every year, the amount of work involved is often minimal and the results will greatly outweigh the effort.

Flower and fruit production

One of the main reasons for pruning is to increase the productivity of your plants. Most shrubs will produce more flowers if they are regularly pruned. Rose bushes, for example, will grow straggly if left to their own devices, with their flower power diminishing with every year that they are left unpruned. However, if they are regularly pruned so that they produce new growth, and trained so that they produce more flower buds, they will flower prolifically for many years. Some shrubs, such as *Chaenomeles*, will produce a lot more flowers if they are tightly pruned. Similarly, many trees and bushes will produce much more fruit if they are properly pruned. By maintaining an open plant, you enable the fruit to ripen properly.

ABOVE The layered habit of *Viburnum plicatum* is enhanced by a regime of careful pruning. This specimen has produced a large number of beautiful flowers.

Plant health

Allied to the above is the question of plant health. One of the first tasks when pruning is to remove all the dead and diseased wood. This helps keep the plant in tip-top condition and hence performing well. The very act of pruning involves looking closely at the plant, so you are likely to be much more aware of any problems. You can then take avoiding action by cutting out the diseased part. Pruning plants also prevents the branches from becoming overcrowded so that more air and light can enter, again helping to maintain a healthy plant. With shrubs in particular, it is often good practice to remove some old growth each year so that new, healthy shoots are produced, constantly rejuvenating the plant.

Improved shape

The shape of some plants, such as conifers, needs little improvement. However, there are many that benefit from being shaped: even conifers have occasional wayward branches that need removing if their elegance is to be maintained. In the most extreme cases, hedges and topiarized plants are very heavily and regularly cut to produce a very definite ornamental shape. Most other plants

ABOVE A shrub that has been renovated may look untidy for a while, but the benefits will soon show.

ABOVE Most people relish the idea of growing their own fruit. Pruning is part of the process and can help improve crops.

do not need this type of intense attention but many – hollies and cherry laurel, for example – benefit from the occasional shaping.

Control

Plants have a tendency to do their own thing which may not be what the gardener wants. The soil may be richer than the plant would experience in the wild and the competition from other plants is likely to be less, so some plants go mad and ramp away. To prevent them swamping other plants or upsetting a carefully planned display, they need to be cut back. Some plants increase by running below ground and producing suckers and these will need to be removed regularly before a miniature forest develops. Shade can also be a problem, and many shrubs that have outgrown their space will need cutting back to stop them overshadowing sun-loving plants. Many climbers have a tendency to rush up a wall and enter the gutters or eaves, and these also need controlling.

ABOVE Dead wood looks ugly as well as causing further health problems for the shrub. Careful pruning can help to improve the condition of the plant.

ABOVE Pruning will improve the health and productivity of your fruit trees, as well as the ripening process.

ABOVE Without good initial training, trees and shrubs can become misshapen and unattractive – as is the case with this camellia. Unless you feel that you can restore the shrub through renovation pruning, it is advisable to replace it with a new shrub.

Tools and equipment

These can be divided into four groups. There are those that perform the cuts, such as saws, secateurs (pruners) and knives; those that are used for clearing up, such as rakes, forks and shredders; safety equipment; and finally the means to gain access to taller plants, such as ladders and towers. They can further be divided into manual tools and mechanical ones, such as hedge trimmers and chainsaws.

Cutting equipment

The most essential tool is a good pair of secateurs. These should be kept sharp. Poor-quality ones, with blades that move apart when you cut, or blunt ones, will tear the wood as it passes through. They may also crush and bruise the wood. To a skilled user, a sharp knife can replace secateurs in certain instances. For thicker wood, a pair of long-handled pruners – secateurs with long handles – can be used, but you should avoid cutting through very thick wood; use a saw instead. Long-arm pruners are secateurs on an extension arm that can reach into tall shrubs or trees but are operated from ground-level.

Saws come in a variety of shapes and sizes. Small folding saws are the most useful for the small garden owner. These are usually very sharp and remain so for some years. Instead of sharpening, as one used to do, it is usual to buy a new one when it begins to blunt. Bow saws and even chainsaws may be necessary in larger gardens. Some of the folding saws can be attached to extension arms so that higher branches can be removed without the need for ladders.

Shears are useful for hand-clipping hedges or shearing over certain shrubs such as lavender or ground cover. They are generally

LEFT Shredders are invaluable for recycling prunings of various sizes. Instead of being burnt, they are cut into small enough pieces to be composted and used again in the garden.

used for topiary where curves and trickier corners are concerned. You can also use sheep-shearing shears, but these are not the easiest things to use and scissors are easier for really intricate pieces.

Power tools

In small gardens it may be unnecessary to use power tools, but in a larger one they can be a real boon. The crucial thing about such tools is to use them sensibly. Make certain that you know how to operate them and that you are well protected. If you are uncertain about your abilities, have any work that entails their use done by professionals. Chainsaws are probably the most dangerous tool and should be used only if you have taken a course on their use. It is also very important that power tools are kept in good condition. They should be maintained professionally at least once a year. The settings and running of the engine should be checked and the cutters sharpened. Do this in advance of when you will next need them.

You can get power secateurs but these are very expensive and really useful only if you have a very large orchard and have a lot of fruit pruning or a vast amount of roses to keep in shape.

Clearing up

Most tools needed for this, such as rakes, brooms, forks, wheelbarrows and carrying sheets, should be available as part of the general garden toolkit. Another piece of power equipment of general use to the pruner is the shredder, which will reduce all the waste to small pieces suitable for composting or mulching. Electrically powered equipment is cheaper but generally less powerful and less manoeuvrable; petrol-driven machines tend to be heavier but are more mobile and therefore more suitable for larger gardens.

You also need to exercise discretion if you opt to burn prunings. Bonfires should be lit at dusk and must be supervised at all times. Check with your local council to see if there are any legal restrictions on bonfires in your area.

BASIC TOOLS AND EQUIPMENT

Most gardeners can prune the majority of their plants with just a pruning saw and a pair of secateurs (pruners), but the larger the garden and the more varied the jobs, the larger the collection of tools you will need. It is well worth investing, for example, in a long-arm chainsaw or hedge trimmer if you have tall hedges or trees that need tackling.

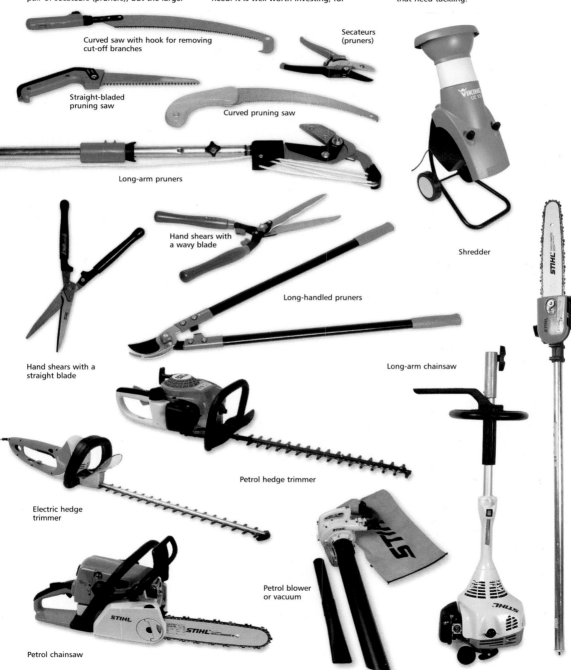

Curved saw with hook for removing cut-off branches

Secateurs (pruners)

Straight-bladed pruning saw

Curved pruning saw

Long-arm pruners

Hand shears with a wavy blade

Shredder

Long-handled pruners

Hand shears with a straight blade

Long-arm chainsaw

Electric hedge trimmer

Petrol hedge trimmer

Petrol blower or vacuum

Petrol chainsaw

Reaching up

There is a limit to how high you can safely reach, especially if you are using power tools. Stepladders can be used for trimming tall hedges as long as the ground is even beneath their feet. They can tip over if you lean out too far, but they do not lean into and deform the plant you are pruning. Ladders can slip sideways and should always be used with care. With trees, the rule is always to face the ladder into the centre of the tree. For hedges, lean the ladder against the hedge. If the hedge is a bit thin, strap a plank of wood to the top of the ladder to stop it sinking in too far.

It is safer to use a tower scaffold of some description. These are stable and stand on four adjustable legs, and some have wheels so they can be moved around. However, they are bulky, can be cumbersome to move when erected, and you will need somewhere to store them. Hedge trimmers and chainsaws are now available on extension arms so that you don't have to climb.

ABOVE Ladders can be used for simple tasks such as picking fruit, but more sustained and complicated work is best carried out on a platform.

ABOVE One or more legs can sink into the ground, toppling the step ladder, but special pads will prevent this.

ABOVE Special step ladders with a platform and a wide base make working on tall hedges both safer and easier.

Safety equipment

Observing safety precautions is very important if unnecessary accidents are to be avoided. The operator should always be fully protected, with ear protectors, goggles, hard hats, gloves and boots with steel toecaps all being very important. A hard hat that also includes a face shield and ear protectors is a very good idea. Providing bystanders with safety equipment should not prove necessary, as they should be kept well out of harm's way at all times. When you are wearing ear protectors, someone may approach you undetected, so always keep a sharp eye out. If your hat takes a heavy knock from a branch, replace it, as the impact may have impaired its strength.

BASIC SAFETY EQUIPMENT

Unfortunately, accidents in the garden are very common and the availability of mechanized tools to the general gardener has added to the possible dangers. It is essential that proper safety gear, such as hard hats and goggles, is worn when you are carrying out certain pruning jobs. It is worth reiterating that certain jobs are best left to professional companies.

Ear protectors

Eye protectors

Safety helmet

Safety gloves

Safety helmet with visor and ear protectors

Visor and ear protectors

Safety boots

Reinforced safety gloves

Reinforced rubber safety boots

Basic pruning techniques

Although different shrubs and trees may need different pruning techniques, the physical process of making the cuts is usually the same. Cuts are generally made with secateurs (pruners), or long-handled pruners for thicker growth, or a saw of some kind.

Clean cuts

There are several general principles that apply when you are using all types of pruning equipment. The first may seem obvious, but it is often overlooked. The cut must be clean and there should be no tears in the wood or bits left hanging around the cut. The one essential requirement for achieving this, besides the ability to use the tools properly, is for the tools to be sharp and well maintained. A pair of secateurs that crushes the wood, rather than cleanly cutting through it, can cause problems.

When pruning trees, be aware that branches can be heavy, so avoid cutting straight through one in such a way that the weight makes it fall before you have finished cutting, tearing back along the branch or even down the trunk.

ABOVE After sawing through a thick stem, tidy up the cut by paring round the edge, creating a neat bevel.

Avoid snags

The second basic principle is to avoid snags. Snags are the short pieces of wood that stick out beyond a branch or a bud. All cuts should be made tight against the stem or up to a bud if removing the end of a shoot. Any piece of wood sticking out will not only look ugly but will usually die back, leaving dead wood through which diseases can enter. On roses, for example, if you leave a snag when deadheading, the stem may die back not just to the next bud but further down the branch.

ABOVE Secateurs are used for cutting thin shoots and branches. They should be sharp, so that the wood is cut cleanly and not bruised.

Ends of shoots or branches

When you are removing the end of a shoot or a branch, a sloping cut should be made just above the nearest bud to the point at which you want to shorten the shoot. The cut should be sloped at 45 degrees away from the bud (be careful not to cut through the bud). If you do accidentally cut through the bud, it may be necessary to recut back to the next bud. If there are two buds opposite one another, make the cut directly across the stem just above the pair of buds.

ABOVE Use a proper pruning saw to cut thicker branches. Avoid using carpenter's tools, which are not suitable for pruning.

ABOVE Hedging shears are useful for cutting back large quantities of thin wood where the cuts do not have to be precise.

ABOVE Long-handled pruners are secateurs on long handles, and will cut through thicker wood.

ABOVE Most shears have a notch near the hinge, which is useful for cutting thicker wood when trimming hedges.

Removing a branch or stem

Always cut off a branch or heavier stem with three cuts. This will help prevent the branch splitting. The first cut is made some way out (about 30cm/12in or so) from the trunk, in an upward direction, about

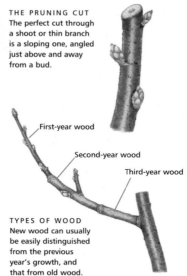

THE PRUNING CUT
The perfect cut through a shoot or thin branch is a sloping one, angled just above and away from a bud.

First-year wood

Second-year wood

Third-year wood

TYPES OF WOOD
New wood can usually be easily distinguished from the previous year's growth, and that from old wood.

a third of the way through. The second is made 8cm (3in) further along the branch and in a downward direction. As you pass the initial cut the branch will sag and split along to the second cut but will go no further. You can now cut straight through the remaining stub, close to the trunk.

Sealing wounds

Argument has raged for many years as to whether larger cuts should be sealed with some form of compound. Although some gardeners still stick to the practice, most now feel it is best to leave all cuts open to the air and weather. Trim round the cut with a sharp knife to remove any rough bark.

INCORRECT AND CORRECT PRUNING CUTS

Incorrect cut Do not make the cut too close to a bud. Aim to make the cut about a quarter of an inch above a bud.

Incorrect cut Do not cut too far above a bud, leaf or shoot because the remaining stub is likely to cause die-back.

Incorrect cut Do not slope the cut towards the bud as this is likely to cause rotting if water drains into it.

Incorrect cut All pruning cuts should be clean, with no bruising or ragged edges because these will allow disease to enter.

Correct cut The ideal cut is one that slants away, just above the bud. This will shed the rain away from the bud.

Correct cut When a pair of buds in involved, cut straight across the stem, just above the buds, without damaging either.

Ornamental Trees

Ornamental trees are among the easiest of woody plants to prune. Generally there is very little, if anything, to do. The only time there is real work is when they overgrow their allotted space or if they need repair work after a storm or high wind has blown off or damaged branches. Most of the work, and that rarely involves more than a few minutes, is in the initial stages, when the tree is first planted. It is important to ensure that the tree starts off growing the way you want it to.

The final shape is, of course, important. Most trees adopt their own shape but they may need a bit of initial help. For example, some trees develop a single, straight trunk, while others have multiple ones. *Amelanchier*, and some others, can have either, and this is where the training becomes important. Small weeping trees may also need a bit of special attention to ensure that they remain small and weeping. But even taking this into account, little work will be required, especially in small gardens where only one or two trees are involved.

LEFT An ornamental cherry tree in full flower, with an underplanting of daffodils. Cherries are usually easy to cope with because they need little pruning.

Buying young trees

As a general principle it is important to buy trees from a reputable supplier. It might cost a bit more but the quality should be good and many suppliers guarantee that if the plant fails within a certain period they will replace it.

What to look for

Always examine the tree thoroughly. Reject any trees that are diseased or are covered with some pest. Never buy a plant that is damaged. If the plant is pot-bound, i.e. the roots go round and round in a tight mass inside the pot, again reject it. Bare-root plants should not be desiccated and the roots should not be damaged.

Look for a plant that has a well-balanced structure and a healthy appearance. Avoid buying trees that have too much growth on them as these can be slow to establish. There is a balance between the amount of root and the amount of top growth it can support. In a nursery, trees have been intensively nurtured. Once planted out they have to fend for

ABOVE The most common way to acquire new trees is through nursery-produced stock that is sold in containers.

themselves to a certain extent and too much top growth during the initial stages will cause problems.

Most trees offered for sale will be one or more years old. The older, the more expensive, but they should be at least partially trained. Such a tree will not be too difficult to establish. A one-year-old is cheaper and easy to establish but takes longer to mature, but at least you can be in full control of its development and shape.

Be careful how you get your tree home. Damage can easily occur if you have a tall sapling sticking out of your sunroof, or if it is carelessly handled. Keep the tree in a cool spot prior to planting and water it well to make sure it does not dry out. Occasionally you may acquire a tree in a bare-rooted state. This is most likely to be as a gift from a friend as increasingly nursery-sold plants are in pots. Such trees should be put in the ground as soon as possible, even if it is only in a temporary position.

It is, of course, possible to grow your own trees from seed, cuttings, grafts or even divisions in some

cases. This will obviously take much longer than buying an established tree but there is a certain satisfaction in growing your own plants from scratch. Besides being cheaper, you also have the possibility of controlling the whole process to get what you really want.

ABOVE When buying trees and shrubs in containers, make certain that the roots have not become too congested within the pot.

ABOVE In general, trees can be grown on as they are, but occasionally they have wayward branches that need trimming.

Feathered trees

Virtually any single-stemmed tree can be feathered. Some feathered trees have a clearly defined shape, whereas others tend to have a more wayward appearance, which is part of their charm. As an extreme example, oak trees (*Quercus*) can have a very regular upright appearance or they can be allowed to grow with a twisted, irregular silhouette. Conifers are perhaps the most obvious example of feathered trees, with their almost pure cone-shapes.

Planting

Plant the tree in well-prepared soil with its roots spread out and not wound round or crammed into the hole. Do not prune the roots unless they are damaged, in which case just remove the damaged parts. The tree should be supported by a short stake that is inserted before the tree is put

ABOVE Conifers very rarely need much pruning. They look better if allowed to take on their natural shape.

TRAINING A FEATHERED TREE

Choose either a maiden whip or a young feathered tree that has an even structure and an intact leader. The leader is important if you want your tree to have a straight trunk. It is possible to train a replacement leader on some trees.

YEAR ONE On planting, remove any dead or wayward branches, especially those that cross or rub against others.

YEAR TWO In general, very little pruning is required other than keeping the shape balanced and the trunk clear.

into the ground. This ensures that you do not accidentally damage unseen roots when you hammer the stake into the soil.

Formative pruning

The aim is to produce a healthy, well-shaped tree. First remove any dead branches or any that have been damaged during transportation or planting. This will help maintain the plant's health. The next task (which is partly cosmetic and partly to do with health) is to remove branches that cross or rub against each other or grow at too sharp an angle to the trunk. This not only improves the tree's appearance but also ensures that no wounds open up. Any other badly placed branches can also be

removed, especially round the base of the plant. It is best in most trees (except conifers) to have a clean, visible length of trunk, even if it is only short. The tree should now be straight with well-spaced, healthy branches.

Next year, repeat the above process. Be careful to remove any vigorous upright shoots that have developed, as these can compete with the leader, either to give the tree a split head or turn it into a multi-stemmed one.

Trees suitable for feathering

Lawson cypress (*Chamaecyparis lawsoniana*)	Larch (*Larix*) Spruce (*Picea*) Thuya (*Thuja*)

Standard trees

Any tree that grows with a bare lower trunk is suitable for training into a standard. Training may even be unnecessary because some trees will develop this habit naturally.

Training a standard tree

These are essentially the same as feathered trees except that more of the lower branches are removed so that the lower part of the trunk can be clearly seen. Although the term "standard" usually refers to a tree with a clear trunk, it is also often used to refer to a tree that has grown to a natural shape and size rather than one that has been dwarfed in some way.

The shape is perhaps not quite as "pure" as in the case of a feathered tree. Feathered trees normally have only one central leader, whereas a standard may have one or it may divide at some point on the trunk and have several. The degree of natural division often depends on

HOW TO TRAIN A STANDARD BIRCH TREE

1 (*left*) Most birch trees develop a natural shape and there is not much pruning required to keep them looking their best.

2 (*above*) However, if there are any wayward branches, as at the bottom of this particular tree, then they should be cleanly removed.

the situation in which the tree is being grown. For example, an oak tree growing among other trees will often grow tall and slender with just the one leader, but in isolation it will branch out and have a much more

rounded shape. In the garden, the leader can be allowed to develop, giving a tall elegant tree, or it can be cut back to produce a branched-head standard, which has a rounder shape. In many cases the tree will

TRAINING A SINGLE-STEMMED STANDARD

Tall trees that have a single stem can look slim and elegant in the garden. It is essential that the central leader grows

without being pruned or broken. If it does break, a new leader must be trained in its place if this is possible.

YEAR ONE Remove some of the lowest side shoots to partially clear the trunk, and cut back by a half those that will be removed next year.

YEAR TWO ONWARDS Follow the same procedure as for the previous year until the lowest branches are reached and take out any crossed-over shoots.

TRAINING A BRANCH-HEADED STANDARD

Branch-headed standards are rounder and have a more solid appearance than single-stemmed standards. Here, the

leader is removed, as are any branches that attempt to replace it, creating a good framework of branches.

YEAR ONE The procedure is the same as for a single-leader standard except that the leader is taken out where the topmost branch reaches the trunk.

YEAR TWO ONWARDS Continue to remove the lower side-shoots until the bottom branch is reached, and take out any misplaced shoots.

ABOVE The well-cleared trunk of this beautiful birch tree draws attention to the distinctive silvery bark for which it is valued.

Tree suitable for training as standards

Maple (*Acer*)	Tulip tree
Chestnut	(*Liriodendron*)
(*Aesculus*)	Crab apple (*Malus*)
Alder (*Alnus*)	Pine (*Pinus*)
Birch (*Betula*)	Poplar (*Populus*)
Hornbeam	Cherry (*Prunus*)
(*Carpinus*)	Almond
Indian bean tree	(*Prunus dulcis*)
(*Catalpa*)	Pear (*Pyrus*)
Ash (*Fraxinus*)	Oak (*Quercus*)
Laburnum	Willow (*Salix*)
(*Laburnum*)	Rowan (*Sorbus*)
	Lime (*Tilia*)

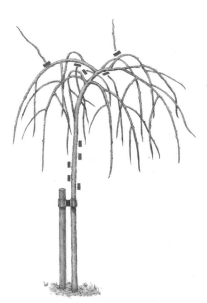

PRUNING A WEEPING STANDARD
Keep the trunks of weeping standards clear of shoots, and remove any shoots that spoil the shape by not weeping nicely.

automatically try to replace this lost leader. In such a case, the gardener will need to be vigilant and prune each new leader out to maintain the desired shape. Conversely, developing a tree with a single leader requires training one main shoot, while others are restrained.

Training a weeping standard

Weeping trees are highly regarded as ornamental plants in the garden. There are basically two types of weeping standard. One comprises trees such as the weeping willow, which have a natural weeping shape. The other type is artificially created.

Ground-spreading plants are grafted on to a standard trunk some distance from the ground so that they spread into the air rather than across the soil, often, when bare, creating a shape like the ribs of an open umbrella.

The natural weeping trees are essentially treated in the same way as standard trees. Pruning can be restricted to removing any dead, injured, weak or crossing wood.

The grafted weepers may need a bit more attention. Unlike the natural weeping trees, which need to put on upward growth in order to obtain their tree-like shape, the grafted varieties need to have any vertical shoots removed. At the same

time, any new growth on the trunk below the canopy should be removed. They also have a tendency to become somewhat tangled and congested, so remove crossing or weak growth. As all the growth is concentrated in the canopy while the trunk remains relatively thin, it is obviously important to make sure at this stage that the tree is well supported with a strong stake.

ABOVE This weeping standard is becoming too thick and some of the branches will need to be thinned out.

Trees suitable for training as weeping standards

Weeping maple (*Acer palmatum* 'Jiro-shodare')
Weeping alder (*Alnus incana* 'Pendula')
Weeping birch (*Betula pendula*)
Weeping hornbeam (*Carpinus betulus* 'Pendula')
Weeping ash (*Fraxinus sylvatica* 'Pendula')
Weeping holly (*Ilex aquifolium* 'Argentea Pendula')

Weeping laburnum (*Laburnum alpinum* 'Pendulum')
Weeping ornamental cherries (*Prunus* cvs)
Weeping pear (*Pyrus salicifolia* 'Pendula')
Weeping willow (*Salix babylonica*; *S. caprea* 'Kilmarnock'; *S. × chrysocoma*; *S. matsudana* 'Pendula'; *S. pupurea* 'Pendula')
Weeping sorbus (*Sorbus aucuparia* 'Pendula')

Multi-stemmed trees

Some trees naturally form multiple trunks (although some gardeners would argue that a tree with multiple trunks is a shrub). In many, if not most cases, trees with multiple stems can also develop as more conventional trees with a single trunk that divides some way above the ground. *Amelanchier* is a good example. The multiple stems may be natural or artificially produced, both in the wild and in the garden. Any feathered tree that is broken off, by accident or design, just above ground level will probably produce multiple stems. There are also trees, such as plum, that produce suckers, and these by their very nature produce more than one main stem.

Formative pruning

The initial pruning is relatively simple. If you have bought a young single-stemmed tree, you have to bite the bullet and throw most of it away! Cut through the main stem just above ground level, or at whatever height you want the

ABOVE This *Acer palmatum*, bursting into leaf, shows very clearly the beauty of its multiple stems.

TRAINING A MULTI-STEMMED TREE

Multi-stemmed trees tend to look rather like overgrown shrubs. Indeed, they are often regarded by gardeners as shrubs rather than trees. They can vary from having just two or three stems to what amounts to a thicket.

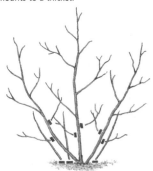

YEAR ONE Cut through the trunk of a suitable feathered tree at the height at which you want the multiple stems to start.

YEAR TWO After a year, select the most suitable stems in order to create a balanced tree and remove the rest.

YEAR THREE Continue to train the individual main stems by removing any dead wood or any branches that cross or rub against each other.

division of the trunk to begin. Once new growth appears from the base, select the required number (three or more) of shoots and remove the others. This will form the basis of your tree, so select the strongest growing shoots, which will make a balanced tree. Continue to train these as you would a tree with a single stem, removing diseased, dead, weak or crossing growth.

Not all trees will shoot from the base after such drastic action, but a surprising number will. However, you should be selective, as not all trees look best with multiple stems.

Trees suitable for training with multiple stems

Maple (*Acer*)
Alder (*Alnus*)
Serviceberry (*Amelanchier*)
Strawberry tree (*Arbutus*)
Hornbeam (*Carpinus*)
Judas tree (*Cercis*)
Magnolia (*Magnolia*)
Sumach (*Rhus*)
Sweet chestnut (*Castanea*)
Willow (*Salix*)
Wingnut (*Pterocarya*)

ABOVE Multi-stemmed trees can be perfect for the larger garden. This is the rare but beautiful *Pterocarya stenoptera*.

Young evergreens

The initial training of an evergreen tree is not a great deal different to that of deciduous trees.

Training young evergreens

Conifers are generally dealt with as if they were feathered trees. In other words, only dead, injured or diseased wood is removed, along with any badly placed shoots or a competitive leader. Generally they are developed so that they are clothed with branches to the ground, but the bottom ones can be removed to leave a bare trunk, as with standard trees. Many conifers naturally make a

beautiful cone shape, or, as in the case of some pines, their own distinct shape. Some are naturally weeping.

Broadleaved evergreens such as hollies (*Ilex*) are also pruned in similar fashion although they can, in many cases, be more drastically cut and turned into multi-stemmed trees, either dividing at ground-level or at any height above it. They are more suitable for shaping than conifers, giving you the chance, for example, of creating a tree with a wide crown to cover an eyesore. Evergreens are generally much denser than deciduous trees and throw a

Evergreens suitable for training
Conifers (most)
Winter's bark (*Drimys winteri*)
Eucalyptus (*Eucalyptus*)
Eucryphia (*Eucryphia*)
Hoheria (*Hoheria angustifolia*)
Holly (*Ilex*)
Magnolia (*Magnolia grandiflora*)
Holm oak (*Quercus ilex*)

deep shade as opposed to a dappled one. For even denser growth it is possible to shorten the side shoots to make them bush out.

TRAINING A YOUNG EVERGREEN

It is possible to train evergreen trees into a variety of different shapes in the same way as you would train deciduous trees. However, most conifers are trained as single-stemmed standards.

YEAR ONE Very little pruning is required, although the bottom branches need removing if you want a bare trunk.

SUBSEQUENT YEARS Apart from the removal of any crossing or dead branches, there is again very little pruning required.

ABOVE Young conifers rarely need any training, and look better if clothed to the ground with branches.

Established pruning

With proper initial training most trees are set up for life and apart from a regular check-up rarely need much attention. It is possible to ignore their pruning totally and the tree will still thrive, much as they all do in the wild. However, a healthy tree is a far safer one as well as a prettier one, and so it is worth spending a short while each year checking any trees over.

The three Ds

The one gardening task that must be carried out at least once a year is a survey of all the trees in the garden in order to check that there is no dead, diseased or damaged wood. Any that is found should be cut out and the wounds cleaned up. It is probably a good idea to check at the end of the growing season, in autumn, and again after the winter during which strong winds and frost may have caused damage to your trees.

ABOVE Unusual trees, such as this weeping cherry, need special attention or they will lose the quality that makes them such an attractive feature in the garden.

Fallen branches should have the snags cut off and any tears should be cleaned with a sharp knife to remove all fragments of loose wood. Any heavy branches that are to be removed should be cut off in sections to prevent splitting and tearing. There is no need to dress wounds even from cuts left by the removal of large branches.

ABOVE Many trees produce suckers from the base of the trunk. These should be cut out as tightly to the trunk as possible.

ABOVE It is essential that any dead, damaged or dying wood should be removed from your trees. Autumn and winter storms can be a cause of damage that will need dealing with in the spring. Here, a pair of long-handled pruners is being used to remove a dead branch.

ABOVE Clean any larger cuts with a sharp knife to remove any ragged or torn bark.

ABOVE Usually little pruning is required for trees, but it is likely to help if any crossing or over-crowding branches are removed.

Unwanted growths

Most trees at some point produce branches that cross others, creating congestion and often wounds where the bark of one rubs against that of another in the wind. Any such crossing wood should be removed. If you are creating a branch-headed standard then it is also a good idea to thin the timber in the centre of the tree so that air and light can circulate.

Many trees from time to time throw out wayward growths – an odd stem will suddenly shoot off into space – spoiling the shape of the plant. These should be removed at some point within the shape of the tree. Similarly, if the tree is a variety with variegation or non-standard foliage, it may occasionally throw out reverted stems, with leaves that are plain green, like those of the parent species. These should be removed back at their point of origin.

Some trees produce water (or epicormic) shoots. These are shoots that appear around wounds where, for example, a branch has been removed or where a lawn mower has

ABOVE Variegated trees can throw out shoots on which the leaves revert to their original green. Remove these when you see them.

DEALING WITH EPICORMIC SHOOTS

1 Some trees – lime (*Tilia*) in particular – produce what are known as water or epicormic shoots on their trunks.

2 The best way of dealing with them is to rub them out with your fingers as soon as you see them.

REMOVING A LARGE TREE BRANCH

1 Make a cut about 20–25cm (8–10in) out from where the final cut will be on the underside of the branch. Cut about a third of the way into the branch.

2 Make a cut about 10cm (4in) nearer the position of the final cut, cutting until the branch snaps. The initial undercut prevents the wood splitting or bark from stripping.

3 Position the saw for the last cut to avoid damaging the swollen area at the base of the branch. The cut will heal in a couple of seasons. No wound painting is necessary.

damaged the bark at the base of the trunk. Cut these out at their base. If the tree has been grafted, then any shoots that appear from below the graft union should be removed, even if they look as though they might be in the ideal place, as these will be different from the rest of the tree. Similarly, suckers often appear from below ground. These may come from a grafted rootstock or just as a natural suckering habit. Unless you want to develop a multi-stemmed tree, these should all be removed back at their point of origin. Dig below soil level, if necessary.

Controlling size

In an ideal world it would be nice to allow trees to grow to their full potential, but there are often factors, such as a lack of space, which dictate that the tree should be kept to a certain size. In some cases this may simply be a question of removing a few side branches, perhaps even spoiling the shape. In other cases, it may mean reducing the size of the whole tree. One technique is known as dropcrotching: all the branches are reduced in length, so that the original outline of the tree is kept the same but much reduced in size. This should be done before the tree reaches its ultimate size, while the branches are still quite young, so that the shaping will not be too unsightly. Repeat every two or three years. Do not cut too deeply back into the tree or it may never recover its shape.

Letting in light

It has already been mentioned that it can sometimes be beneficial to open up the canopy to let in more light and air, particularly with fruiting trees. In addition, you may wish to grow other plants below trees, and too dense a shade will often prevent this. In order to let in more light (and, indeed, water in the form of rain), rather than remove the whole tree it

ABOVE In gardens where space is limited or where there is close planting, established pruning is required to control the size of a tree and so prevent it from smothering other plants.

ABOVE Working with ladders can be dangerous for those not used to them. This stepladder with a wide base is a much safer option.

is often possible to remove some of the lower branches. This is often done with oak trees, the shape of which is not unduly spoilt by such pruning. It allows grass and other plants to be grown beneath them.

Feeling their age

As with humans, trees age. In oaks, this may well be only after several hundred years, but it might be only after 30 in the case of birches. There are several problems associated with this. One is the development of stags' heads. This is most noticeable in oaks but can also occur in other trees. Some of the branches die, leaving them bare and stripped of bark (often looking like a stag's horns, hence the name). In some cases this makes the tree look venerable, but others will simply look diseased and unsightly. The tree is usually perfectly healthy, and the removal of the branches will return the tree to its normal appearance.

The other problem is that branches may start to sag and fall away. A similar and more frequent occurrence is when the trunks of multi-stemmed trees start to fall apart. These can be braced if the tree is an important one. This is best done by experienced professionals, as an inadequately braced tree may fall on somebody with dire consequences all round.

Safety

Ladder work may be necessary when pruning tall trees. If you do not feel confident or have not had the necessary experience of cutting large branches from a tree, especially those that are some way from the ground, call in a tree expert. It may cost money but not lives. If you do the work yourself, wear adequate safety gear, especially a hard hat.

ABOVE Most fully grown trees, such as these ornamental cherries (*Prunus*) or the birches (*Betula*) in the background, need little in the way of pruning.

Renovation pruning

When you take over an old garden, or acquire a new one which was part of a field or wood, there may be old trees in it that have been neglected or never been pruned. You may well be forced to decide whether to take the trees out and start from scratch, or try to renovate them. Trees take a long time to grow to maturity and leave a large gap when felled, so if possible it is best to try to bring them back to their former glory. There may also be preservation orders on the trees, so it would be illegal to remove them without permission. It may even be illegal to carry out major renovation without permission, so it is always best to check before you start.

Prune it step by step

Your aim with a neglected and overgrown tree is to turn back the clock and do all the things that should have been carried out in previous years. The best time to rejuvenate an old tree is in the late autumn or early winter. Start, as always, by removing any dead, diseased or damaged wood. This should remove quite a bit of material and allow you to begin to see the structure of the tree. Next remove any water or epicormic shoots along with any weak growths, especially those that have developed in the centre of the tree. Where branches cross over or rub against other branches, cut them out. The tree should now begin to look the way it should.

Examine the tree closely to assess whether there is still any overcrowding and whether anything else needs to be removed. Perhaps the tree has been regularly "pruned" by somebody who has simply gone over the outside of the tree

RENOVATING AN OVERGROWN TREE

1 (*left*) Some trees, such as this contorted hazel, can become overgrown and need to be renovated in order to bring back their shape and interest.

2 (*above*) Start the renovation by removing all the dead and damaged wood. This will allow you to see what remains much more clearly.

3 (*left*) Next thin some of the branches to reduce the congestion, especially towards the middle of the tree. Remove old and weak growths first.

4 (*above*) The dead stub shows how poor pruning can cause die-back, as the previous cut was made too high. Cut tightly back as shown here.

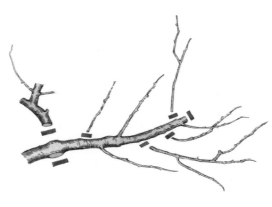

PRUNING KNOBBLY SPURS If a tree has been severely cut back over a number of years, the ends of the branches become a mass of spurs. Cut these back drastically to one or two in order to return the tree to its original shape.

TREE RENOVATION TECHNIQUES

In general, most ornamental trees can be left to their own devices, but sometimes it is essential to remove the lower branches or thin the crown in order to allow more light and rain to reach any plants that are growing under the tree.

CROWN RAISING More light can be obtained below a tree by removing some of the lower branches so that the light comes in under the canopy.

CROWN THINNING An alternative method is to thin out some of the branches from the crown so that dappled light filters its way through the canopy.

removing the new extension growth on the tips of the branches, so that it has thickened up around the perimeter, a bit like a hedge. You will have to reduce and thin this growth drastically to bring the tree back to something resembling a normal appearance.

Not all trees like to be pruned hard all in one go, as it can often kill them. It is usually better to prune them over a number of years, taking out just a bit each time. This means that the tree will look untidy over this period, but this is better than a dead tree.

Aftercare
Renovation is a drastic treatment for any tree, so make certain that it is fed and kept watered during any dry spells the following summer. Mulching will help to preserve soil moisture.

Safety
A lot of the pruning work on an overgrown tree inevitably takes place well above the head of the gardener, usually on ladders. If you do not feel confident to carry out this work yourself, then employ a specialist firm who will have had a lot of experience in dealing with this kind of renovation work. This is particularly important if you need, for example, to take out a dead crown from a large tree.

ABOVE Overgrown trees will inevitably contain a lot of dead and damaged wood. This should be one of the first things to be removed.

ABOVE If a tree has been neglected, there are likely to be branches that cross over or rub against others. These should be removed.

Pruning conifers

Conifers are very popular trees and shrubs, forming an architectural backbone to the garden that varies only slightly from season to season. They are also relatively easy to grow and require little attention once they have been planted. Unfortunately, many gardeners do not realize that they must be treated differently from their deciduous relatives. How often do you see a row of dead coniferous trees where the owner has decided that they have grown too large and so has lopped off half of each tree, only to discover that it was the wrong thing to do?

Cutting into old wood

Most conifers are very reluctant to put out new shoots from old wood, so cut back only into the new growth. Cutting back into the older wood creates a bald patch, and removing too much can result in the death of the tree. If you want to control the height, either ensure in the first place that the tree you buy will reach only the height you want it to, or be prepared to treat it like a hedge and clip it regularly once or twice a year, removing only some of the new growth.

What to prune

Having placed restrictions on pruning of conifers, there are still

ABOVE Many garden conifers have a beautiful natural shape and, given enough space in which to grow, require very little pruning.

ABOVE One task that always needs doing is the removal of dead branches. Cut back to good wood. Growth will spread to fill the gap.

tasks that need to be carried out. As always, any dead, dying, damaged or diseased wood should be cut out, preferably as far back as possible. Also remove any odd growths that stick out beyond the required shape. Do not leave these for too long or they may grow too vigorously and leave a hole when you remove them. Similarly, on variegated conifers, there may be some reversion

(plain green leaves), and this needs to be removed or it will gradually dominate to the detriment of the variegation. As we have already mentioned, a light clipping to keep the size and shape is generally the best strategy, but this is really only necessary with trees where the shape is very important, such as with pure cone shapes or slim columnar trees.

Pruning conifers

Most conifers will stand a little light pruning as long as you restrict yourself to the new growth. In general, this will apply only if you are cutting the tree to a shape, as in topiary, or creating a hedge. If done every year, this will also help to restrict its size. However, once a conifer has reached maturity, there is little that can be done to reduce its size except in the following examples. These will tolerate being cut back into old wood. One of the most common garden conifers, the Lawson cypress, *Chamaecyparis lawsoniana*, will not break from old wood, so do not attempt to prune it except for a light trim to retain size and shape.

Cephalotaxus	*Sequoia*
Cryptomeria	*Taxus*
Cunninghamia	*Torreya*

PRUNING TECHNIQUES FOR CONIFERS

1 If it is necessary to prune conifers, cut the shoots well back into the tree, so that their removal does not show.

2 Dead wood will always spoil the appearance of a conifer and should be removed as soon as possible.

3 Conifers do not need much pruning, but new growth can be clipped over to restrict the size of the tree. Do not cut into old wood.

4 Rather than shear over the tree and cut some leaves in half, it is neater to pinch out the growing tips to restrict growth.

Tying in

As trees get old and large, snow and sometimes wind can pull a branch out of place so that it sticks out sideways. This is a problem with shaped trees that have several main stems or near-vertical branches. If removed, these will leave a large gap that is unlikely to be refilled with new shoots. The only solution is to pull them back into position and tie them in place. Protect the bark with wadding (batting) so that the wire or rope does not chafe. If large branches are involved, you may need professional help.

If the tree is hopelessly distorted, it is often advisable to start again with a new tree. A conifer in such a poor state is very difficult to renovate and can look distinctly ugly if left as it is.

REMOVING A COMPETING LEADER

1 If a young conifer has two competing leaders, one of them should be removed to restore its single-stemmed shape.

2 If the new leader is not growing strongly upright, tie a cane to the main stem. Tie the leader to the cane to encourage vertical growth.

ABOVE Some conifers take on a regular shape, and these may need occasional pruning to keep the outline.

Felling trees

There are some tasks that most gardeners will only occasionally come across and perhaps never at all. The main one is the felling of a tree. This is not an easy task at the best of times, but toppling a large tree in a small garden without damaging anything in the process is very tricky indeed.

Can you do it?

Felling trees is really a job for the professional. Even if the way is clear, if the tree is by a lawn for example, it is still a skilled job to get it to drop exactly where required. If it is growing among other trees or shrubs, or stands near fences or buildings, it can be more of a problem. Such trees usually need to be taken down branch by branch, which involves quite a lot of clambering around in the tree. Apart from all the skills that this requires there is also the question of equipment. Not many gardeners have chainsaws capable of dealing with a tree and although you can hire them, they are dangerous

ABOVE One tree has fallen into another and it will be a tricky job, involving climbing into the tree, to get it down safely.

tools to use. They should be employed only if you have taken a course in their use and safety.

Professional tree surgeons do this kind of work all the time and, if they

are a good team, will know precisely how to get the tree down without damaging property or themselves. They will also be insured in case anything goes wrong.

Employing tree surgeons

Always ensure that you are employing people who have been properly trained and belong to a professional association. Check that they are fully insured. If you have no need for the wood or have not got the facilities for its disposal, make certain that they will remove it. Nowadays they will often mechanically shred the brushwood and this is worth keeping and composting to use as a mulch.

Shy away from anyone knocking on the door and offering to take the tree down. It may seem a bargain at first, but such people are rarely skilled enough to do the job properly and if anything goes wrong you could be faced with a very large compensation bill because they are bound not to be insured.

ABOVE This is not the kind of job for the average gardener; a skilled professional who knows what he is doing is required for this work.

ABOVE Removing tall trees in a restricted space without causing damage is highly skilled and must be left to the professionals.

FELLING A SMALL TREE

1 Small trees, such as this birch, that are situated in a clear space may well be within the capabilities of most gardeners, but do not tackle this job if you are in any doubt.

2 Start by making a sloping cut at 45 degrees on the side of the tree that is facing the direction in which you want it to fall. Go into the tree by between a quarter and one-third.

3 Follow this initial cut with a horizontal cut just below it, so that the two cuts eventually meet and you are able to remove a wedge of the trunk.

4 Remove the wedge from the trunk. This should ensure that when the tree is cut through, it will fall in the direction that you want it to.

5 Start sawing on the other side of the tree opposite the horizontal cut. As the saw nears the removed wedge of wood, the tree will fall forward.

6 Step back smartly as the tree falls, just in case it springs back as it hits the ground. Now you simply need to remove the stump from the ground.

What can you tackle?

If you are experienced in this area you can at least deal with small trees, especially multi-stemmed ones that are not too tall and heavy. But do not undertake this work unless you are confident of your abilities.

Before cutting, ensure that the ground is clear and that you can get away if anything goes wrong. For a clear fell, cut a notch on the side in the direction you want the tree to fall and then cut through from the other side level with this notch. The tree will start to topple in the right direction just before the trunk is cut through. Once it is down, dig up the remaining stump.

Before starting to fell, make certain that you can move back without tripping over and that the tree will not hit anything that can deflect it, and so land somewhere you did not want it too. Trees are large objects when on the ground, so ensure you have enough space.

Coppicing and pollarding

These two traditional techniques have generally dropped out of use both in the countryside and in gardens. Valuable both economically and aesthetically, they provided an important source of material for basket-weaving and fence-making, and enabled the growth of larger trees in a small space as well as producing good foliage.

Principles

Coppicing is the cutting back almost to ground level of all the main shoots of a multi-stemmed tree. These then regenerate and another set of main shoots develops, only for these to be removed as well. The wood may be thin and wispy, as in the case of willow, which is coppiced each year for weaving material, or quite thick and tall, as in sweet chestnut (*Castanea*), which is coppiced for poles on a cycle of up to 14 years.

ABOVE Willows growing next to water are frequently coppiced or pollarded in order to provide material for basket-making and garden use.

Trees suitable for coppicing and pollarding

Ailanthus (*Ailanthus*)
Alder (*Alnus*)
Hornbean (*Carpinus*)
Sweet chestnut (*Castanea*)
Indian bean tree (*Catalpa*)
Hazel (*Corylus*)
Eucalyptus (*Eucalyptus*)
Ash (*Fraxinus*)
Paulownia (*Paulownia*)
Oak (*Quercus*)
Willow (*Salix*)
Elder (*Sambucus*)

Pollarding is exactly the same except the cutting takes place at some height above the ground. Historically, this was done so that animals could not reach the new shoots. Again, the pollarding is done every year for thinner wood but at longer intervals for thicker material. Oak trees were pollarded so that the timber could be used for construction and firewood.

Modern uses

In the modern garden, the technique can still be used for the same purposes, particularly on willow to provide plant supports and other garden structures. It can also be

HOW TO COPPICE

1 Many plants with decorative stems in winter, such as this *Rubus*, should be coppiced in spring, before or just as they come into leaf.

2 Cut out all the stems close to the ground. Some of the more shrubby plants need to be cut just above the previous year's cut.

3 Make all the cuts clean and slightly angled to allow rain to run off. Take this opportunity to remove any weeds growing in the centre.

POLLARDING A LARGE TREE

1 This specimen is typical of a tree that has been regularly pollarded. All the branches are rising from the top of the trunk, rather like unruly hair.

2 Remove all the branches, using either a pair of strong long-handled pruners or a saw. At this stage it does not matter if some of the stubs are rather long.

3 Tidy up the pruned cuts by sawing through the base of each of the branches The new shoots will eventually appear round the edge of these cuts.

used on hazel in order to provide sticks to support peas as well as herbaceous and annual plants. Some trees, such as elder (*Sambucus*) or eucalyptus, also respond by

ABOVE Removing branches before felling a tree is akin to pollarding, and anything of this size must be tackled by a professional.

producing large or attractive colourful foliage if they are regularly coppiced. It can also be used to reduce the size of trees, for example to restrict the growth of an Indian bean tree (*Catalpa*).

Techniques

For coppicing, grow the tree as a multi-stemmed form. Once the poles have reached the required size, cut them off near the base with a saw in late winter to early spring. The cuts should be slightly sloped to allow rainwater to run off. Trim the bark neatly round the edge of the cut.

For pollarding, choose a tree with a main stem and plenty of side branches. Once it has become established, cut through the trunk above the group of shoots at the height at which you wish to form the head. Remove all other shoots below the main cluster. The trees

should subsequently be pollarded every one to three years in late winter by removing the shoots back to almost 1cm (½in) from the trunk.

ABOVE Coloured winter stems are achieved by coppicing every spring. It takes only a short while for the tree to recover.

Pleaching

Pleaching is a highly decorative form of pruning. It essentially produces a row of trees in which the branches are interlocked in a horizontal plane above a certain length of bare trunk, in effect making an elevated hedge. There are several variations on this. In some versions, parallel hedges are also trained across to form a horizontal or domed roof, while in others there is not only a roof but also ends, creating a room. In some versions, the side walls come right to the ground, although it is more normal to have them on stilts, as it were. In many areas of Europe, the trees are pleached just to produce a thin, horizontal roof, which protects the town squares from the glaring sun.

ABOVE Very attractive walkways can be achieved by pleaching trees, as this large pergola supporting a laburnum in full flower demonstrates.

Principles

The aim is to train the branches horizontally along wires or battens until they meet and intermingle with those of their neighbours. Side shoots from these main branches are kept to a minimum, just enough to clothe the structure with leaves. Once established, pleached trees are no more difficult to maintain than a hedge, although they do need cutting from a ladder.

Structure

The initial structure consists of stout vertical poles between which are stretched horizontal wires or wooden lathes. The verticals should be at about 2.5m (8ft) intervals, but this is only a rough guide as it is best to divide up the given space equally rather than have an odd distance somewhere in the line. The two end poles can be at the same distance as the others or can be reduced to half the distance from their neighbours. Fasten the battens or wires at 60cm (2ft) intervals. If you use wires, make certain that they are taut. Using tensioning screws or bolts that can be tightened as the wire stretches is a good idea.

ABOVE These pleached trees shown in winter reveal how they create both the sides and roof of a covered walkway that has now been filled with shrubs.

Trees suitable for pleaching

Hornbeam (*Carpinus*)
Beech (*Fagus*)
Holly (*Ilex*)
Laburnum
Lime (*Tilia*)* Possibly the most popular

Formative pruning

Plant trees at each of the posts, except the first and the last. These should be three- or four-year-old trees with a good structure of side shoots, the lowest being roughly level with the bottom wire. The general principle is to train the leader vertically until it reaches the top and then take it sideways. At the same time, remove all other side shoots except those that lie next to a wire or batten. Gradually allow these side shoots to grow sideways until they meet those of the next tree. See the illustrations on the right for a more detailed analysis of the pruning cuts.

Established pruning

Once the pleached trees are established and the hedge or tunnel is completed, then the supports can be removed. Subsequent pruning is as for any other hedge. Aim to keep the growth tight and well clipped. Remove any new shoots pointing in the wrong direction that may appear on the trunks.

ABOVE A walkway of young trees that have been allowed to grow together instead of being pleached, but which give the same effect.

TRAINING PLEACHED TREES

The essence of pleaching is to create what is, in effect, an aerial hedge. The branches of the trees are encouraged to grow until they become intermingled, but they are grown entirely in one plane. This creates an eye-catching garden feature.

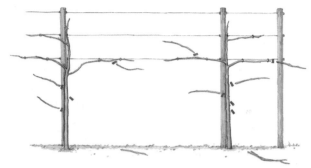

YEAR ONE Train the young trees against firmly planted posts with taut wires between them. Remove the bottom side shoots and tie the remainder into the wires, one to each wire.

YEAR TWO Continue to tie the new shoots to the wires as they appear. Tie in the existing side branches as they grow. Remove any other side shoots.

YEAR THREE OR LATER Interweave the side branches as they meet. Remove any extra side shoots from the main trunk and any from the main branches that go in the wrong direction or cause crowding.

Ornamental Shrubs

Shrubs are the backbone of a garden. They provide structure and form, as well as continuity throughout the seasons. Most flower at some point during the year but they are often grown just for their foliage, which may be decorative, act as a background to other plants, or provide a screen to what lies beyond.

Many gardeners simply turn a blind eye to pruning and let the shrubs get on with it. This policy often works for a limited number of years, but after a while the shrubs begin to outgrow their allotted space, as well as becoming leggy and full of dead wood. Unpruned, shrubs often lose their flower power and the number of blooms diminishes over the years. Regular pruning is not an arduous task and it certainly produces healthier and more productive as well as better-shaped shrubs.

Gardeners often tremble at the thought of pruning shrubs, but it is not at all complicated and the necessary skills are quickly learnt. Besides, you only have to know how to prune your own plants, not all the thousands of different ones that are in cultivation, so it soon becomes such a routine operation as cutting a hedge or mowing a lawn.

LEFT Ornamental shrubs form the backbone of any garden design, but should be pruned to control their shape and size to ensure that they continue to fit harmoniously together.

Initial training

Many shrubs that you buy from garden centres and nurseries are already trained to a basic shape, and these usually need little more than to be planted. But sometimes they need a bit of attention, especially those that have been lifted as seedlings or layers from your own or a friend's garden.

Buying shrubs

The same principles that apply to buying trees also apply to shrubs. In the first place, always buy healthy plants that are neither diseased nor harbouring pests. Never buy a sickly plant or one whose roots are wound into a tight ball. Try to choose a plant with well-balanced growth, avoiding anything that is drawn or too leggy. Do not automatically

ABOVE *Indigofera* is an attractive flowering shrub but one that benefits from good pruning. Left unpruned, its beauty diminishes.

select the largest plant on display as large plants in containers will not necessarily grow away quickly and fill their allotted space. Medium or even smaller ones will grow away faster and can soon overtake a larger one as they have a more balanced root to top-growth ratio.

Container and bare-root plants

Most shrubs are purchased in containers and can be planted at any time of year, as long as they are not allowed to dry out or scorch in hot sun before they have time to establish. However, a number of specialist nurseries, especially those dealing with roses and those who supply mail-order plants, provide them "bare-root". Bare-root plants are dug from nursery beds and sent to the customer, as the name suggests, with bare roots, i.e. not potted up in compost (soil mix). These are usually grown in rows in the nursery and are not necessarily given much in the way of initial pruning. They may need a bit more attention once they are planted. The advantage of bare-root shrubs is that

ABOVE Initial pruning helps to shape the shrub so that it makes the maximum impact. This *Deutzia elegantissima* would always be welcome.

ABOVE This *Viburnum opulus* is at the height of its powers and is a mass of flowers. Initial training helps to increase its flowering capacity.

they are usually cheaper, as they have not been handled or processed as much as containerized ones. Bare-root plants are usually only sold from mid-autumn to mid-spring, which is the best time for planting them.

Initial pruning and training

The aim of shaping any shrub, apart from topiary, is to let it achieve its natural habit. When shrubs are received from the nursery, most will already be trained in this fashion. Some may be badly formed, however, and need some remedial treatment as soon as they are planted. Remove any weak growth and if necessary cut out any crossing branches. If the shrub is to be dense and rounded in shape, cut back the shoots to a strong bud or pair of buds so that they branch out. As the shrub begins to grow it is likely to produce new growth from the base. Make certain that this is evenly spaced and cut out any crossing branches. Other than this, if a good specimen has been purchased in the first place, there should be no need for further pruning.

PLANTING AND PRUNING A YOUNG SHRUB

1 Prepare the soil well around the whole planting area so that the roots settle down quickly and produce a healthy plant.

2 Most shrubs are planted at the same depth as they were originally grown, either in their nursery bed or in the container in which they were purchased.

3 Some shrubs are already pruned, so they need no attention at all. Other shrubs have broken branches, weak growth and other defects that need correcting.

4 Remove any flowered wood back to a strong bud or to a strong new shoot.

5 Sometimes there are old dead stubs left from previous pruning sessions, or wood that has become broken in transit. You will need to remove these.

6 Often there will be inward-pointing shoots on the new shrub that are rubbing, or soon will rub, against other branches. You also need to cut these out.

7 The pruned plant should have a well-balanced, open basic framework from which the rest of the shrub will grow.

Established pruning

Once a shrub is fully established and growing away happily, it will need regular attention to keep it healthy and in shape. Many shrubs only need minimal treatment (a few can even be left to their own devices), but most need at least some attention.

Types of shrub

For pruning purposes, shrubs are usually divided into several categories: those that need no or minimal pruning (*Daphne, Ceanothus, Magnolia*), those that flower on the current year's growth (*Buddleja, Lavatera*), those that flower on the previous year's growth (*Forsythia, Philadelphus*) and those which are evergreen (*Elaeagnus, Osmanthus*). The main difference between the needs of the different categories is the timing of pruning and the amount required.

When to prune

Pruning is an ongoing activity, spread throughout the year, although the majority can be done in winter and spring. There is an old garden adage that says you should do things when you think of them, but although unlikely to kill the plant, pruning at the wrong time of year could at least curtail its flowering for the following season. For example, if you prune in the winter a shrub that flowers on the previous year's wood, you are likely to remove all the shoots that have flowering potential. These need time in the previous year to develop that wood and so should be pruned as soon after flowering as possible. Many of them, such as forsythia, are early flowering, leaving plenty of time for growth. The shrubs that flower on new wood are ones such as buddleja, which flower around mid- or late summer, once they have had a chance to produce new growth. These are usually best

ABOVE Not all shrubs need to be cut hard back. This *Ceanothus thyrsiflorus* only needs the longer new growth to be cut back by about a third after flowering.

pruned in the early spring. Evergreens usually only need minimal pruning, in spring.

Minimal pruning

In most cases, all that is needed is to look for and cut out any dead, dying or diseased wood. Some of these shrubs also benefit from being lightly trimmed over to reduce the length of the new growth, but only to prevent the shrub getting too large or outgrowing its position. If the shrub does get too large for its position, you can try cutting it back heavily. But often these shrubs will

Shrubs that need little or no pruning

Amelanchier	Daphne mezereum
Aronia arbutifolia	Enkianthus
Berberis	campanulatus
Callicarpa	Magnolia
bodinieri	Nandua (sacred
Calycanthus	bamboo)
Clerodendron	Phlomis
trichotomum	Rhododendron
Clethra alnifolia	(azalea)
Corylopsis	Salix helvetica
Crataegus	Salvia (sage)
(hawthorn)	Stephandra
Cytisus (broom)	Thymus (thyme)

Reversion

Sometimes shrubs with variegated leaves, most frequently evergreens, throw up a shoot which has reverted to the original green leaves of the parent species. If this shoot is ignored, it will gradually take over the whole bush and the variegation will be lost. So it is essential to cut out this green shoot at the base.

The reverse sometimes happens, where a green bush throws up a variegated shoot. If this is an interesting colour or pattern, it may be worthwhile taking a cutting and rooting it to see if you can produce a whole shrub with this variegation. This is how a lot of variegated plants are originally produced. Plain cream shoots that occasionally appear on variegated hollies are usually the result of cold weather. These cannot be used for propagation, as they lack chlorophyll.

Shrubs flowering on old wood

Corylus (hazel)	(beauty bush)
Cotinus (smoke bush)	*Philadelphus* (mock orange)
Forsythia	*Ribes*
Hydrangea	*sanguineum*
Kerria (Jew's mantle)	(flowering currant)
Kolkwitzia	*Rubus* (bramble)

Shrubs flowering on old and new wood

These two categories of shrub are basically treated in the same way, the only major difference being the timing. Firstly, remove any dead, damaged or diseased wood. Take out any branches that cross over others. These may be rubbing against each other or just producing congestion, preventing the circulation of air and light. Any thin weak growths that are not going to produce healthy shoots should also be taken out. You can

not make new growth from old wood, so you may have to remove it altogether and start again. Occasionally you may need to cut out an individual shoot that has suddenly decided to grow faster than the others and spoils the shape of the shrub.

PRUNING SHRUBS THAT FLOWER ON THE PREVIOUS SEASON'S GROWTH

1 The best time to prune is soon after flowering. Count the number of stems and decide which third look the oldest (these will usually be the thickest and darkest).

2 Cut back the oldest third just above ground if the branches rise from ground level or to a stump near the base if there is thick old wood. Cut just above a new shoot near the plant base.

ABOVE If this forsythia is pruned after it has flowered in the spring, then plenty of replacement shoots will grow during the summer to flower the following year.

PRUNING SHRUBS THAT FLOWER ON THE CURRENT SEASON'S GROWTH

1 Many shrubs, such as this hardy fuchsia, flower on the current season's growth. In spring, all the older material that flowered the previous year will have to be cut out.

2 During the spring this old growth is cut back – as far as the ground in the case of the fuchsia. In other shrubs it may just be back to the first sound bud or shoot.

3 Once growth starts again, new shoots appear and quickly grow to flowering size. These require no further pruning until the following spring.

promote new healthy growth by removing some of the older wood. Old shoots, which are usually easy to identify, should be removed to the base, but if they are already producing vigorous new growth from just above the base, cut just above these new shoots. Take out a few of these older stems so that the bush retains its shape and appearance. If necessary, you can remove up to a third of the bush annually, so that over a three-year period a new shrub is formed. Normally it is only necessary to do this every few years, when the shrub has become congested or tired. Finally, look at the shrub to assess its shape and see if any of the remaining shoots need trimming to improve its overall appearance. It may be that some of the longer stems need cutting back to contain its size.

Evergreens

Most evergreens need very little pruning other than the routine removal of any dead, dying and diseased wood. They may need to be lightly trimmed over each year in order to maintain the size if that is important in the context of your garden. If the foliage is variegated, as in the case of some hollies, it is also important to remove any shoots that revert to the original green.

Shrubs flowering on new wood

Buddleja	Hypericum
Caryopteris	calycinum
Cassia	Indigofera
Ceanothus 'Gloire	Lavatera
de Versailles'	Leycesteria
Ceratostigma	Potentilla
Fuchsia	Sambucus (elder)

ABOVE Potentillas can be kept neat by being trimmed over after flowering. Apart from taking out the odd old stem to keep the plant vigorous, little other pruning is required.

Evergreen shrubs

Abelia	Garrya
Azara	Hebe
Berberis	Laurus nobilis
Buxus (box)	(bay)
Camellia	Mahonia
Ceanothus	Osmanthus
Choisya ternata	Photinia
(Mexican	Pieris
orange	Pittosporum
blossom)	Prunus
Convolvulus	lusitanicus
cneorum	(Portuguese
Cotoneaster	laurel)
Daphne	Rhododendron
Elaeagnus	Sarcococca
Escallonia	Skimmia
Euonymus	(Christmas box)
fortunei	Viburnum tinus

PRUNING EVERGREEN SHRUBS

1 Evergreen shrubs usually need little pruning, but sometimes, as in the case of this bay (*Laurus nobilis*), they may need to have their shape checked or improved.

2 After you have removed any dead or damaged wood, look at the top of the shrub and cut back any straggly stems in order to improve its shape.

3 Remove any long stems well back into the bush, as these could grow away and completely distort the shape of the plant.

4 Then, complete the pruning by trimming back any wayward shoots near the base of the plant. The finished bush looks much tidier.

Deadheading

Most flowering shrubs benefit from deadheading. A plant requires a lot of energy in order to produce seed for reproduction. By removing the faded flowers, seeding is prevented and this energy is diverted into the new growth, sometimes producing a second flowering, which is always welcome. Another reason for deadheading your shrubs is that many of them look decidedly unsightly when they are covered with dead flowers, particularly those that have white flowers. As well as looking ugly themselves, dead flowers also tend to detract from the impact of those that are still at their best: remove the dead ones and then the look of the remainder will be greatly improved. Simply cut the flowering stem back to the first leaves as the flowers begin to fade.

ABOVE Dead flowers not only look ugly but also detract from the remaining flowers. They will sap the plant's energy, so remove them.

Renovation pruning

It is not uncommon to be faced
with a shrub that has not been
pruned for many years, and is now
in desperate need of renovation.
Although the task may look
daunting, it should not be
a problem provided you take a
systematic approach.

Clearing the way

The first stage, as with all pruning
jobs, is to remove the dead wood.
Next, take out any damaged, diseased
or otherwise dying wood. In an
overgrown shrub this often amounts
to a great deal of material. Once it
has been removed, the shrub already
looks better and you can now see the
framework you have to work on.
Also remove any suckers around the
plant. A neglected sumach (*Rhus*),
for example, is likely to produce
quite a number of suckers and these
should be removed below ground
level where the shoot joins the root.

If the shrub is badly diseased,
it is best to remove it completely
and start again, as it is highly
unlikely that you will be able to
resurrect it successfully.

RENOVATING AN OVERGROWN SHRUB Most shrubs can be renovated by removing dead
wood and some of the oldest stems, as well as reducing the length of the remainder.

Reinvigoration

Remove any weak growth and any
branches or stems that rub against
or cross over other branches. The
next thing to do is to try to
reinvigorate the shrub. Remove some
of the old wood to stimulate fresh
new growth. Generally, several of the
oldest main stems should be cut out
completely or cut back to any new

REMOVING SUCKERS

1 Some shrubs form a thicket as suckers grow around the base of the
plant, often from the roots, but also from the base of the trunk.

2 Suckers should be removed by cutting them close to the trunk, or
underground, close to the roots.

growth starting from near the base. Up to one-third of the oldest wood can be taken out. Repeat this process over the next three years until the shrub has completely regenerated itself. Some shrubs, such as *Ceanothus*, are reluctant to produce new growth from old wood. In this case, either omit this stage or remove the plant entirely and put a new one in its place.

Shaping up

A shrub that has been heavily pruned in this way is likely to be rather straggly and it may be necessary to reduce the remaining branches so that a better shape is achieved. The amount that can be removed will vary from shrub to shrub, but it can be up to about a half. However, some, such as *Ceanothus*, should only be trimmed over to remove the previous year's growth, as they will not reshoot from old wood.

Cutting down to the ground

There are some shrubs that can be simply cut to the ground and they will start again. Lilac (*Syringa*), elder

ABOVE Many shrubs that have grown straggly, such as this lavender, will not reshoot easily from old wood and should be replaced with new plants.

(*Sambucus*) and hazel (*Corylus*) are examples. Remove some of the top growth initially, so that the weight is removed from the main stems, then cut these off at about 15–30cm (6–12in) from the ground. If it is a grafted shrub, be certain to cut above the graft.

ABOVE With shrubs such as spiraea, you can remove one or two of the oldest shoots each year to promote the growth of new shoots.

Replacing

There are some shrubs that are virtually impossible to regenerate. If you cut back into the older wood, no new growth will appear and the plant will die. The best way to cope with this is to ensure that the shrubs are properly pruned in the first place and therefore do not become in need of renovation. However, if you inherit such overgrown plants when you move to a new garden, the only way to cope with them is to dig them out and replace them.

HOW TO RENOVATE A SHRUB

1 The first job when renovating any shrub is to cut out any dead branches or shoots right back to sound wood.

2 You need to remove any damaged wood, through which diseases can enter, as well as any dead wood.

Pruning for foliage effect

Some shrubs are grown mainly for their decorative foliage. It is possible to let these grow in the normal way and just give them a light pruning: they will still produce interesting foliage and will also produce flowers, often attractive ones, such as on the smoke bush (*Cotinus*). If, however, they are cut right back, the leaves will be larger and often of a more intense colour, giving the plant a more striking appearance.

What can be cut back?

Elder (*Sambucus*), *Rosa glauca* and the smoke bush (*Cotinus*) are all good examples of shrubs that benefit from a drastic pruning regime. *Eucalyptus gunnii* can become a very tall tree but if cut right back and treated as a shrub it produces very interesting juvenile foliage, which is much in demand by flower arrangers. Another interesting range of shrubs are those with decorative young stems. *Cornus stolonifera*, *C. alba* and the coloured-stemmed *Rubus* are good examples of these.

ABOVE A cotinus in full flower. If hard pruned in spring, the foliage will be larger and more colourful, but the flowers will be sacrificed.

Pruning for foliage

The most attractive foliage tends to appear on new growth, so all the old growth is removed, usually in late winter. This means that plenty of new shoots are produced in spring. All the plant's energy is thus put

Shrubs pruned for attractive foliage	
Berberis	Philadelphus
Cotinus (smoke	coronarius
bush)	'Aureus'
Eucalyptus	Rosa glauca
gunnii	Sambucus (elder)

into the production of leaves and very little or none into flowers. Hence, the leaves are big and there are no flowers. Once the shrub is established it is surprising just how much growth is put on in one year. Although cut to the ground in spring, an elder (*Sambucus*) can grow 2.5–3m (8–10ft) in a season. This can be repeated for as many years as you like. If you decide that you want a larger shrub or want it to flower, just stop cutting it back each year.

It is normal to cut it to within about 30cm (12in) of the ground, but as the plant ages so the basal stems can be left longer. However, it is possible to treat it as a pollard

HOW TO PRUNE FOR FOLIAGE

1 Elder (*Sambucus*), like the cotinus above, can be pruned hard if you would like to have good foliage effect, or pruned lightly if you prefer the flowers.

2 Cut back all the previous year's growth to a strong bud within 30cm (12in) or so of the ground. This may seem drastic but the shrub will rapidly recover.

3 After many years of this treatment, the pruning will be too far from the ground and some stems should be cut back each year, almost to the ground.

to create a taller bush, perhaps at the back of a border where you want the foliage to be above the surrounding plants.

Pruning for stems

Decorative, coloured stems are at their best in the winter, when, of course, they can be most clearly seen and add interest to an otherwise barren garden. If the shrubs are left unpruned, they become large and the stem colour is confined to the short growths at the tips of the branches. However, if they are regularly cut to

the ground each year, they will throw up a mass of thin shoots, each a strong colour – bright yellowish green, for example, in the case of *Cornus stolonifera* 'Flaviramea', and red in *C. alba* 'Sibirica'. The shoots are cut to the ground in spring, after which they quickly shoot and are fully grown by the following winter. These shrubs are unlikely to flower.

Some shrubs, such as the various brambles (*Rubus*), are grown entirely for their stems because the flowers are insignificant. The advantage of cutting these back in spring is not

only to provide good stems the following winter, but also to make it much easier to weed and generally tidy up around them.

Shubs pruned for attractive winter bark

Cornus alba 'Sibirica'	*Rubus thibetianus*
Cornus stolonifera 'Flaviramea'	*Salix alba* subsp. *vitellina* 'Britzensis'
Rubus cockburnianus	*Salix fargesii*
	Salix irrorata

PRUNING FOR COLOURFUL STEMS

1 The winter stems of *Salix alba* subsp. *vitellina*. Left unpruned, the stems will get higher and the coloured part shorter.

2 Cut back some of the older wood to reduce congestion and rejuvenate the plant from the base. Use a saw on this thicker wood.

3 Remove any dead branches and shoots right back to sound wood. Use a saw for thicker wood and clean up the cuts.

4 By now you should be left with the basic framework of the shrub and have some idea as to how it will look next year.

5 Cut back any remaining last year's shoots to a good strong bud. This may seem drastic, but the shrub will soon recover.

6 If the shrub is at the front of a border or has another shrub behind it, aim to keep it lower, almost to the ground.

ABOVE Winter colour in cornus and salix stems. The tall shrubs in the background are losing their colour by becoming too large.

Topiary

There has been a very long tradition of shaping shrubs and trees into decorative forms that are at total variance with their natural shapes. The gardener imposes a very strict pattern on their growth, either by forcing the shrub into a shape by wiring it on to formers or by clipping existing branches to make and retain a shape. The shapes can vary from simple geometric ones, such as balls or pyramids, which work particularly well in formally designed gardens, to free-form designs, such as birds or animals, which can often be of a witty or whimsical nature. Living sculpture does a lot to enliven a garden, creating immediate interest and focal points that draw the eye. Topiary can be free-standing or incorporated into hedges and even archways. It can be used in containers, perhaps in matching pairs placed at strategic places such as near entrances or at the top or bottom of flights of steps.

Topiary is not difficult in itself, but the freer-form shapes may well need an artist's eye and hand to make them really effective. There are a few basic techniques, which are easy to learn, but perhaps the most difficult aspect is the patience that is required while waiting for the shrub to grow into shape.

Since topiary has to hold its shape for as long as possible without daily or weekly pruning, the shrubs employed have to have special qualities that make them suitable. Theoretically, almost any shrub could be used, but in reality there are only a handful that are really good for the job.

LEFT In the late Piet Bekaert's garden in Belgium, the artist's house sits at the centre of a visually arresting geometrical framework of topiary, clipped hedges and trees.

Pruning and training simple topiary

Topiary is not difficult but needs a steady hand and a keen eye. The tools are those that you would use for pruning or hedging, namely a pair of secateurs (pruners) and hedge clippers, preferably hand ones as these are easier to control.

Selecting shrubs

Evergreen shrubs that are slow-growing and have compact growth, such as yew (*Taxus*) or box (*Buxus*), are the best types to use. It is also an advantage to use shrubs that have small leaves, again such as box, as it is easier to obtain a smooth finish with these. However, shrubs with larger leaves such as holly (*Ilex*) or bay laurel (*Laurus nobilis*) are suitable for simple shapes such as balls. Shrubs for topiary can be already fully grown, and then "carved" into shape, but they are best grown especially for the purpose and gradually clipped into shape as they grow.

ABOVE Cones are among some of the easiest shapes to construct, even if they take a few years to grow. They always look effective and draw the eye.

Creating a simple shape

To create a simple shape such as a ball, cone or pyramid, start when the plant is relatively small and clip it into a smaller version of the shape you desire. Gradually increase the size as the plant grows. This approach will create many multi-branched shoots, which will become very dense and will not only hold the shape well, but will look better. If you wait for the plant to reach the intended size and then start cutting, it will take many years before it thickens out and becomes a solid shape, if it ever does. Once the plant reaches the size you want, cut it into its final shape, preferably using a former so that it is completely regular.

Spirals

These have sufficient presence to be used individually, but they also work well as matching pairs, perhaps flanking a front door or another entrance, and they can even be planted in small groups to great effect. Spirals differ in form quite dramatically, from full-bodied figures with voluptuous curves to those with slender coils which look like a leafy garland twisted around a bare pole.

ABOVE A basic spiral made from box. Box is a good, compact shrub that holds its shape well and does not require a great deal of clipping.

ABOVE This relatively complicated shape is made possible by using a former, which will eventually become hidden.

ABOVE It is possible to construct complicated geometric shapes that always catch the eye.

ABOVE These perfectly rounded box hummocks enhance both the shape of the pool and the serenity of the formal garden in which they are situated.

The slender-coiled kind can be tricky because they demand more skill from the topiarist and take longer to train than the full-bodied kind, which can be clipped almost instantly. You will often see them grown from relatively quick-growing conifers such as juniper, thuja and chamaecyparis. They also tend to be quite expensive to buy. However, some of these swirling forms are not as difficult to create as you might think. Box is ideal for clipping small to medium-size spirals in containers, but yew is better for producing large specimens grown in the ground.

When training a spiral, you can put your own stamp on to the design because there are several variables. At one extreme there is the squat snail shell, which has broad coils and only a shallow-cut groove. This means that the coils lie on top of each other with no gaps. Imagine attaching a string to the tip and pulling upwards to separate the coils slightly: you then have the next variant, whereby the coils are set at a more pronounced angle. This angle, coupled with the width of the coils, suggests varying degrees of motion, from lazy turns to dynamic twists. Sometimes a spiral groove is clipped into a column instead of a cone, and you can also create near-horizontal coils clipped to resemble a gentle helter-skelter.

Whatever shape you decide on, do not worry if your spiral is not

ABOVE Topiary can also be great fun. Your imagination is the only limit when it comes to ideas. Avoid too many wacky shapes in one garden, however, as it can become boring.

mathematically perfect or if an existing topiary begins to drift from the original design, with a pronounced lean or unravelling top. Topiary often ends up being quirky or eccentric.

Standard trees and shrubs

There are two types of standard. One consists of usually prostrate or low-growing shrubs that are grafted on to the trunk of an upright-growing shrub. This type is generally purchased already trained. The other type involves training just one central stem by removing other competing stems and then pinching out any side shoots, just leaving those on the top to develop into a rounded bush. Good subjects for this treatment are the firethorn (*Pyracantha*) and the bay laurel (*Laurus nobilis*). Once fully grown, both types need regular trimming to keep their shape. In general, such standards are grown simply as balls, for example the popular bay laurels often seen flanking doorways or paths, but they can also be cut into more complex shapes.

With a shape such as a simple globe, dome, cone or stylized bird held at the top of a slender stem, the topiary standard is certainly elegant. Whatever the design, topiary standards will add a touch of style to your garden. Consider them as potted sculptures for the terrace, rising up above a sea of planting in the border or paired with an identical twin to frame a gateway. Many gardeners have experience of making standards using quick-growing tender perennials such as fuchsias and marguerite daisies (*Argyranthemum*), and the same techniques are used for creating standards of box, bay, holly and so on.

Suitable shrubs

Bay (*Laurus nobilis*)
Box (*Buxus sempervirens*)
Firethorn (*Pyracantha*)
Holly (*Ilex*)
Ivy (*Hedera*)
Privet (*Ligustrum ovalifolium*)
Shrubby honeysuckle (*Lonicera nitida*)
Yew (*Taxus baccata*)

Maintenance

Cut the topiary as required to keep the shape with a smooth outline. Use a former for precise geometric shapes to ensure that the outline is kept regular. Formers can be constructed from lengths of wood or from a sheet of wood cut to shape. Freer shapes such as spirals can be cut by winding a length of string down the shrub, then cutting to this. Trim complicated shapes by following the shape of the former within the plant.

TRAINING A TOPIARY CONE

1 Choose a relatively small, young plant which has evenly spaced branches. It should have a clear upright stem at the centre. Push a cane into the pot to guide the training.

2 Use hand shears to shape the branches. Work from the top, keeping a smooth and regular outline that widens out at the bottom of the plant.

3 Allow the plant to increase in size, but continue clipping the branches to keep the cone shape. This will create many multi-branched shoots that will hold the shape well.

CLIPPING A DOUBLE BALL

1 Buy a mature, dense, bushy plant with a clear upright stem at the centre. It must be the correct height for the final standard as it will fill out rather than grow taller.

2 Using secateurs (pruners) remove all the branches from the centre of the stem, making clean cuts. Leave enough shoots at the top and bottom to shape the double balls.

3 Start shaping the bottom ball by shortening the side shoots to form a rough ball. Cut out the shoot tip of the leading growth to encourage side shoots to form.

4 Shape the top ball in the same way, cutting the main shoot tip and pinching out the other shoot tip buds. Make sure the top remains securely attached to the supporting cane.

5 Use shears to clip to the final shape. Flip the shears over so that the blades follow the curve of the ball. Continue to pinch off any leaves or shoots that appear on the stem.

6 Until it is well-established, it is advisable to place the standard in a sheltered spot away from direct sunlight and wind. This mature standard looks striking against a beech hedge.

Pruning and training more complex shapes

While simple shapes, such as spheres and obelisks, can be very pleasing, particularly in formal situations, more complex shapes, such as animals or birds, add a touch of excitement, and even danger, to the art. Perhaps it is not something for the faint-hearted but until you try it you won't really know whether you can do it or not. A little artistic flair and imagination help, but many examples have been created by gardeners who would certainly never consider themselves as artists or sculptors.

Deciding what to do

The first difficulty is choosing a subject. The best place to look for inspiration is at existing topiary. Some gardens are famous for it and they are well worth a visit. Take a notebook and make sketches from different angles. If possible, take a look inside and see if there is any supporting structure. Another source, albeit only two-dimensional, is pictures in books and magazines, both of topiary and of everyday objects that could be subjects for topiary. Finally, you could pay a visit to the local garden centre and see what pre-shaped formers they have.

ABOVE This miniature knot garden is an unusual design. It need not be as complicated as it looks. Imagination and a steady hand are basically all that is needed.

Shrubs

With most forms of topiary, slow- and compact-growing shrubs are the best to choose. These hold their shapes better and tend to grow at an even pace all over the shape. Avoid large-leaved shrubs as these are difficult to cut into complex shapes.

Making complex shapes

The first task after planting your shrub is to build a former and erect it over the shrub. This can simply be a number of sticks or rods wired together, one for each main limb of the topiary. Attach branches to these as they grow, and then gradually trim them as they fill out so that the overall shape is formed. Another method is to make the complete shape out of chicken wire and then prune back the emerging branches about 2.5cm (1in) or so outside it. Keep pruning regularly at this distance so that the shrub bushes out and thickens, eventually filling out the shape completely. Although it is not to be generally

CLIPPING A PIG FREEHAND

1 Ingenuity and creativity are two of the key elements in producing interesting pieces of topiary. Seeing a pig in this box shrub is a stroke of genius.

2 You must have a clear idea of what you are doing before you start clipping. You should work out where all the main elements are going to go.

3 The finished pig makes an eye-catching feature in this winter garden. Unlike a marble sculpture, if you do make a mistake while clipping, you can wait until it grows again.

CLIPPING A TOPIARY BIRD IN A NEST

1 Choose a squat, bushy plant with plenty of dense foliage. Select suitable stems for the head and tail of the bird and tie these together with raffia or string.

2 Set the tail at the desired angle, using string and a tent peg in the ground. Using shears, start shaping the bird by clipping out the foliage between the tail and head stems.

3 Trim the foliage at the sides to create the curve of the bird's body. Shake out the bush as you work to release clippings that may be caught behind others.

4 Using secateurs (pruners), you can then go on to shape the head and neck of the bird. To train the beak, simply twist a small length of garden wire around the soft wood.

5 Again using shears, cut away branches at the bottom of the plant to form the nest. Remember to feed and water the topiary regularly to encourage recovery.

6 The finished bird in a nest looks effective in a terracotta pot placed in a simple setting – here, in front of a beech hedge. The tail is beautifully silhouetted against the backdrop.

recommended, some people start with an existing, full-grown shrub and just sculpt away. At first this can look a bit bare and sparse in places but new leaves and shoots will soon grow and it will thicken out to the shape required.

Maintaining complex shapes

Once you have achieved the shape you require it is essential that you keep pruning it to that shape. If you leave it too long, shoots will lengthen, often at different rates. If you simply shear off 15cm (6in) all over, you will end up with a

ABOVE After spending so much time creating your topiary specimen, you will want to ensure it is well kept and maintained.

distorted shape. Leave the former inside and, using this as a guide, try to cut back to a regular distance over the whole topiary.

If, for some reason, you miss a year's trimming you may have a monumental task to get it back into shape. It pays to take photographs from different angles so that you have an accurate idea of what it was like. Alternatively, a drawing with measurements will help you find your way back to the original. Often, you can just make out the line of the older wood which indicates the original shape.

Quick topiary

In general, most topiary is created from slow-growing shrubs such as yew or box as these are dense and retain their shape well. However, the downside of using such plants is that it may take several years for them to reach their ultimate shape and possibly more for them to thicken up to make a solid sculpture. One way of speeding up the process is to use a fast-growing climber instead, such as ivy (*Hedera*).

Ivy for speed

One of the reasons topiaried ivy is so quick to create is that it only covers the outside of the framework and does not have to form a dense mass – a bit like making a hollow papier-mâché head as opposed to carving one in solid wood or marble. Although ivy is fast growing, it is also good at holding its shape and therefore does not need too much attention once the shape is formed.

Formers

This form of topiary has become popular, and garden centres and nurseries have responded by offering a good range of differently shaped formers over which to grow the ivy. The better-quality ones are made from thick wire or even steel, while cheaper ones are available made from chicken wire. There is a vast range of designs, varying from geometric shapes to animals. Most have strong

TRAINING AN IVY BALL

1 Place one wire hanging basket on a flower pot for balance. Line the inside with moistened moss and fill with compost (soil mix).

2 Repeat the process with a second basket. Place the two basket frames firmly together and tie with wire twists.

3 Using a sharpened peg or cane, poke holes in the moss and plant ivy cuttings in a circular direction, starting from the top.

4 Once you have planted most of the cuttings, hang the basket and finish the underside of the topiary ball, filling in any gaps.

TRAINING AN IVY CONE

1 Plant seven small ivy plants with long trails (here, *Hedera helix* 'Ardingly') around the edge of the pot at even intervals.

2 Take your chosen topiary frame and gently place it in the pot, securing it carefully with your hands in the soil.

3 Carefully tease out each trail of ivy, and wind them up the sides and around the struts of the frame. Secure them with ties.

4 Pinch out the growing tips and tuck in the ends; this will encourage side shoots and bushiness. Trim when needed.

TRAINING AN IVY HEART

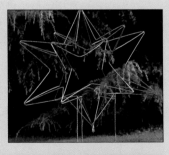

1 You can make 2-D frames from pieces of stout wire. Plant ivies on each side of the pot and then push the frame into the potting mix. Start to weave the ivies around the frame.

2 Continue to weave the trailing ivy stems up and around the wire frame, tucking in the strands as you go. Tie in with small pieces of string if this is necessary.

3 Once the two stems are in place, cut off all other trailing parts of the plant. The foliage will gradually thicken out to cover the wire frame completely.

legs or feet which are pushed into the ground, but some are much taller and include shapes on top of tripods or obelisks, the entire structure being covered with ivy. There is no reason why you should not create your own. Simple shapes are easy to make out of chicken wire and if you are good with your hands there is no reason why you should not attempt to create more complex shapes such as birds or animals. There is also no need to restrict yourself to static animals. A fox can be running or a bird can be in flight. You can be witty and combine several animals in a group on a lawn, for example.

Choosing ivy

Normally only one ivy plant is required, though to create larger shapes it will be quicker if two or more are used. You can use any type of ivy, either green or variegated, although the smaller-leaved varieties are best as the overall shape is smoother. There is no reason why two different ivies, say a green and a gold form, cannot be used to create

an even more effective sculpture, a sheep with a green body and yellow head for example.

Planting and shaping

Plant the ivy and then place the framework over it. As the stems

grow, tie them in so that they eventually cover the whole shape. Once an area is covered, trim off any stray shoots and continue until the whole frame is covered. Regularly trim off any shoots that stick out, so that a recognizable shape is maintained.

Suggestions for formers and shapes

balls	ducks	teapots
cubes	herons	windmills
pyramids	dogs	boats
cones	sheep	aeroplanes
obelisks	cows	cars
moons	camels	pigs
birds	foxes	peacocks
swans	ponies	stars
geese	cats	horses

Hedges

Hedges are a good alternative to walls and fences as a method of sealing off your boundaries or creating individual areas or screening within a garden. A hedge is relatively cheap, but like all plants in a garden it is a living thing and will need a certain amount of time spent on it to keep it in shape.

As well as their use as physical barriers, hedges also make visual ones, creating backdrops against which to grow other plants. Internal hedges can also be used to create an air of mystery, as a visitor is never quite certain what lies just beyond and always has the urge to move further into the garden, just to see what is there.

Unlike walls and fences, of course, hedges grow and so need trimming from time to time. Generally, this is a relatively easy procedure and there is a wide variety of equipment available to help you carry it out. Some hedging plants are slow-growing and it can take several years to achieve a mature hedge. However, they only need one or possibly two trims a year. Fast-growing shrubs, on the other hand, produce a hedge quickly but need more frequent pruning to look neat.

LEFT Neat hedges and archways can make a garden, providing not only screens but also a background for other plantings. They can be all kind of sizes, as here, to cater for different needs.

Creating a hedge

Many hedges are inherited, but you may be lucky enough to have the chance to create a hedge from scratch. There is a range of texture and colour as well as styles of hedge that might influence your decision.

Types of hedge

There are two basic types of hedge (with a few minor variations). The majority of hedges can be called formal. They are composed of tight-growing shrubs that are kept neatly clipped. Informal hedges are allowed to grow in their natural way, usually with long stems arching over. These look very casual and have the advantage that their flowering stems are not removed. Not only will they flower at some point during the year, but they may also provide colourful fruit. They are usually pruned only once a year, or even once every two years. They do take up more space, however, so are best restricted to internal hedges, otherwise relations with neighbours might become somewhat strained.

Sub-categories are really only variations of these. Country hedges often contain a number of different types of shrub. The variation of textures and colours looks attractive

ABOVE Hedging plants come in several ages. Biggest is not always best as the smaller ones often establish more quickly and catch up.

but the growth rate of the different types varies, so the hedge can look rather ragged unless it is clipped frequently. Another type is the tapestry hedge, which is composed of different varieties of the same type

ABOVE When buying, it is much cheaper to obtain hedging material bare-rooted, direct from the ground, rather than in containers.

of shrub. This provides a patchwork of colour when, for example, green and golden yews are used.

Consider whether you want an evergreen hedge or a deciduous one that is transparent in winter. Finally, hedges can be categorized by use. Hawthorn (*Crataegus*), holly (*Ilex*) and berberis all provide thick prickly hedges that are good for keeping livestock and other intruders out. Yew, on the other hand, produces a hedge that provides a superb backdrop for other plants.

Planting a hedge

Hedges are usually grown from bare-root plants bought from specialist nurseries, as the quantity required makes container-grown shrubs prohibitively expensive. They are usually available for planting from late autumn to early spring.

Informal hedging plants

Berberis	Rosa (rose)
Escallonia*	Tamarix
Forsythia	(tamarisk)
Fuchsia	Viburnum*
Garrya*	
Ribes sanguineum	
(flowering currant)	* Evergreen

DIFFERENT TYPES OF HEDGE

ABOVE Yew makes a tight hedge that is particularly suitable for neat formal hedging. It only needs cutting once a year.

ABOVE Garrya makes an attractive informal hedge, with its dangling cream tassels. Too much pruning would spoil the shape.

ABOVE Most conifer hedges need to be clipped regularly to stop them becoming too large, when they will be difficult to renovate.

HOW TO CREATE A NEW HEDGE

The more thorough the preparation before planting and pruning the hedge, the better the hedge will eventually be. First of all, dig the ground well and add plenty of well-rotted organic material. Hawthorn, also known as quickthorn, is, as its name implies, one of the quickest as well as one of the most impenetrable plants with which to create a hedge.

YEAR ONE Hawthorn plants should be cut back soon after planting to encourage them to branch at the base and produce a thicker hedge.

YEAR TWO Cut back the resulting shoots so that these also branch. Keep repeating this until a thick hedge has been formed.

For a narrow hedge, set plants at 30cm (12in) intervals (use a wider spacing for more vigorous shrubs). For a wider and more substantial hedge they can be planted in two staggered rows, about 30cm (12in) apart, at 45cm (18in) intervals. The ground should be well prepared in advance. Remove any perennial weeds and dig in plenty of organic material. When planting a hedge, leave a gap between the hedge and any border that is to lie in front of it. This will allow you access to the hedge for cutting.

ABOVE A holly hedge takes a long time to get going, but eventually forms a good-looking, impenetrable screen or barrier.

Initial pruning and training

Advice for this tends to vary with fashion, but most deciduous hedging, such as beech and hornbeam, should only be lightly cut back on planting, no more than a third. Faster-growing shrubs, such as hawthorn and privet (*Ligustrum*), should be cut back low down, to 30cm (12in) or even less above the ground to make them bush out. Evergreens generally only need to have any overlong shoots cut back, leaving the leaders to achieve their finished height before they are stopped. As the hedge nears its final shape, keep trimming back any shoots that extend beyond the desired profile.

Formal hedging plants	
Hornbeam (*Carpinus*)	Portuguese laurel (*Prunus lusitanica*)*
Elaeagnus*	Yew (*Taxus*)*
Euonymus*	Hemlock (*Tsuga*)*
Beech (*Fagus*)	
Holly (*Ilex*)*	
Privet (*Ligustrum*)*	*Evergreen

ABOVE An interesting pattern can be created by using shrubs with differing foliage colours. They are known as tapestry hedges.

ABOVE Mixed hedges produce an interesting texture but the shrubs often grow at different rates and need frequent pruning.

ABOVE Informal hedges, such as pyracantha, need less clipping and have the added advantage of flowers, but can look untidy.

Maintaining hedges

Hedges have to be cut regularly in order not only to keep them neat and tidy to look at, but also to prevent wayward stems whipping against people as they walk past.

Tools

There is now an extraordinary range of tools for cutting hedges. Hand shears are still the favourite of many gardeners who only have small areas of hedging to cut, as well as of those who like a more controlled method of trimming. Mechanical hedge trimmers, powered by either electricity or petrol engines, are widely available and relatively cheap. It is much quicker to cut a hedge using these, but, equally, any mistake is usually much more noticeable than one made with hand shears. Electric trimmers are lighter and cheaper than petrol ones, but you are restricted by the length of cable (unless you have a small, movable generator to produce the power). Cordless machines are available, but their power supply, and hence cutting time, is limited. Petrol ones are much

ABOVE This formal yew hedge has been immaculately maintained. Achieving a hedge as straight and neat as this needs a good eye as well as regular practice.

heavier, but these are more versatile in that they can be used anywhere without a power lead. They are also more powerful, cutting through most, even overgrown, hedging material. Gardeners with a lot of hedging would do well to invest in professional-standard machines, which cost a little more but are much better machines. New on the market are petrol cutters on extended poles. These can be very heavy to use, but allow the gardener to reach high hedges without the need for ladders

or scaffolds. Since it is possible to alter the angle of the head, they can also be used to reach hedges over ditches or narrow flower beds.

Another technical development that is especially useful to gardeners with tall hedges to maintain is the availability of scaffolds and specially designed stepladders that enable safe access to the tops of high hedges. These are expensive and sometimes cumbersome, but are easier and far safer to use than conventional ladders.

PRUNING FORMAL HEDGES

Formal hedges, whether they are flat-topped or have curved tops, need regular clipping in order to keep them compact and under control. If they are at the front of the house, you will also want to keep them looking neat and tidy. Remember always to try to clip back to the previous contour of the hedge or it will gradually get larger.

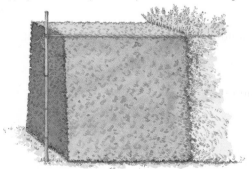

FLAT-TOPPED FORMAL HEDGES A flat-sided and flat-topped hedge has very distinct, clear-cut lines. The base should be a little wider than the top.

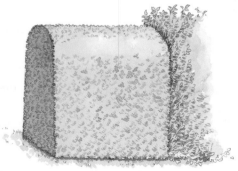

FORMAL HEDGES WITH CURVED TOPS An alternative to the flat top is to use a curved one, which is less formal. One advantage of this shape is that it is better at shedding snow.

PRUNING A FORMAL HEDGE

1 Quick-growing formal hedges will need trimming several times a year, but many evergreen hedges remain respectable with just one or two cuts during the year.

2 The clippings are easier to deal with if you lay a plastic sheet along the base of the hedge. You will be able to pick up most of them easily by gathering up the sheet.

3 If you are using hand shears, try to keep the blades flat against the side of the hedge. If you cut with a stabbing motion, then the finish is likely to be uneven.

4 Achieving a level top can be difficult. String stretched taut between two canes can make all the difference. Remember to have the guide low enough to allow for growth.

5 Try to hold the blades of the shears flat and horizontal when you are cutting the top. This may mean standing on steps or even a raised plank resting on two sets of steps.

6 Power tools can make the job easier, but you should use protective goggles and gloves. Use the hedge trimmer with a wide, sweeping motion, keeping the blade parallel to the hedge.

Templates

A final piece of useful equipment is a template, something you will have to make yourself, as every hedge is unique in terms of size and shape. If you have a good eye or are not too bothered about precision, then it is possible to cut a hedge without a guide, but if you are not careful the hedge can get bigger and bigger as you cut just outside the previous line each time. A simple folding guide can be made from lengths of batten, joined with string. Use long pieces to mark the sides of the hedge. Attach a shorter piece to the end of each to mark the top of the hedge. Stretch strings between points on each of the guides to allow you to cut to the same profile each time. If you only cut one side of the

7 Some conifers produce stray vigorous side shoots, and simply nipping these off with secateurs (pruners) may be enough to improve the appearance between proper trims.

8 This carefully clipped yew hedge displays all the graceful formality and strength of a well-maintained hedge.

hedge, two uprights with strings attached will suffice. Alternatively, make one guide and move it along the hedge as you cut. For low box hedges or to shape a hedge top, cut the templates from sheets of plywood.

You can cut a hedge to whatever shape you like, but it is usual to have straight sides that narrow towards the top to allow maximum light to reach the leaves at the bottom. However, there is no reason why the top should not be wavy or irregular.

ABOVE Beech hedges only need cutting once or twice a year and have the advantage of holding on to their dead leaves all winter.

Formal hedges

These are usually cut tight to produce a dense, solid face. Depending on the type of hedging material, they will require from one to four cuts a year. For an even more sheer appearance, they can be cut more often. In general, they are best cut with hand shears or power tools. Regular trimming is easier if the hedge is no higher than can be comfortably cut from the ground. This saves a lot of time and effort and is, of course, much safer as no ladders or scaffolds are needed. However, if taller hedges are required as screens, windbreaks or simply as backdrops, then some means of elevation will be necessary. Use a template to ensure that the hedge is cut to a regular shape.

Semi-formal hedges

There are some hedges that, although regularly trimmed to a tight shape, are a little more ragged. This is because they are composed of plants that have larger leaves, such as laurel (*Prunus*), which cannot present the tight, cropped appearance of yew or box. These are cut in the same way as formal hedges, although you should really cut them with a pair of secateurs (pruners). Shears or trimmers will cut many of the leaves in half, which looks ugly and leads to a brown line along the cut edge.

ABOVE Tightly cut formal hedges always contrast well with informal backgrounds and are perfect as a backdrop to borders.

PRUNING AN INFORMAL FLOWERING HEDGE These hedges need little clipping other than to take off the flowered stems and any overlong shoots. A loose shape is what to aim for.

PRUNING AN INFORMAL HEDGE

1 Most flowering hedges are best trimmed when the flowers have finished. Exceptions are where attractive fruits or berries will follow, such as *Rosa rugosa*.

2 The simplest way to prune a large, informal hedge is with hand shears or a powered hedge trimmer. Only do this with small-leaved plants, such as berberis, though.

3 Although taking longer, secateurs will do a better job, especially with large-leaved plants. To restrict size, cut back overlong shoots to a suitable replacement shoot or cut out entirely.

Informal hedges

These are not trimmed or cut in the normal manner. Instead, the stems are allowed to arch gently as they would on a single shrub. Some pruning is required or they will soon become overgrown. In order to ensure flowering, they are treated in exactly the same way as single shrubs: those that flower on new wood are cut back in spring and those that flower on the previous year's wood are pruned after flowering.

4 (*above*) Shortening long shoots each year will keep most informal hedges looking good.

5 (*right*) The shrub roses usually used for hedges do not require heavy pruning. If they become congested, cut out the oldest and thickest stems close to the base.

General maintenance

It is important for the health and shape of a hedge that weeds, especially woody ones such as brambles, are not allowed to grow up through it. You should regularly strim underneath the hedge, cutting off weeds and grass, and dig out any brambles or alien shrubs or trees that have seeded themselves. Ivy seed can be dispersed by birds and then the ivy climbs through and over the hedge, possibly even killing it. It may then collapse itself, leaving a large hole. Remove it as soon as you see it, even if you think it looks rather attractive.

Heavy falls of snow should be knocked from hedgetops, as the weight can pull the stems out of shape.

ABOVE Two lavender hedges bordering a path give the garden a wonderfully informal quality and provide a useful feature in cottage gardens.

Shaped hedges and arches

The conventional hedge has straight sides and a level top. The crispness and evenness appeals to many gardeners and a well-cut hedge is often taken as a sign of a skilled gardener. There is, however, no holy writ that says that hedges should be so geometrically shaped.

Uneven hedges

Without necessarily setting out to, some gardeners often end up with a hedge that is full of bulges and graceful curves, a bit like rolling surf. Initially, these may simply be hedges that have grown out of line, with some individual plants perhaps growing quicker than others, but as time passes the irregularities become more exaggerated and the rounded contour is a feature of the garden. Often, with age, the top becomes broader than the base and suddenly, perhaps because of snow or wind, branches are pushed apart and a split opens up in the hedge.

Shaped hedges

While an uneven hedge often just seems to occur spontaneously, it is possible to create a non-conventional hedge by design. A typical example would be one that has a crenellated or castellated top, like the battlements of a castle. To achieve this, allow alternate blocks of the hedge to grow taller. To create a wave effect, cut the top into a series of graceful mounds. The sides can also be shaped.

One popular feature is a seat cut into a thick hedge. If the hedge is really large, an arbour can even be created within it. A moon window, a round hole in the hedge through which you can see into the distance or into the next area of the garden, can bring a certain dynamism to a design. It is made simply by cutting

ABOVE Hedges do not have to be straight. All kinds of exciting shapes can be used. However, make certain that you cut tight to the shape each time or it will eventually be lost.

a hole in the hedge. This will look bare around the edges at first but with regularly trimming the inner surface eventually fills out to match the rest of the hedge. To keep the hole regular in shape, some gardeners insert a couple of metal hoops to act as formers.

ABOVE Arches are important as they frame glimpses of what lies ahead. They can easily be formed in an existing hedge.

Arches

One of the most popular ways of articulating the top of a hedge is to create an arch. If the hedge is tall enough, this can be achieved simply by cutting through the hedge and creating an internal archway. On a lower hedge the arch must be created above the top line of the hedge. Essentially the arches are created in the same way. Cut a hole in the hedge to the required width. Leave the tops of the shrubs on either side of the proposed arch uncut and allow them to grow upwards. Gradually pull over the inner growth and tie together to form a rudimentary arch. As the main stems produce side shoots, trim these until eventually a solid top to the arch matching the hedge is formed. The "doorway" can be a sudden eruption in the line of the hedge, if the top is cut as a square or a semi-circle, or it can start some way down the hedge so that the line forms a gentle swell, more like a wave.

CREATING AN ARCH IN A HEDGE

Archways are not difficult to form in an existing hedge, although it will take several years for the arch to grow into its finished form. The main problem is to avoid accidentally cutting off the unkempt growth in the initial stages. Do not leave the shaping too long because it is easier to pull the shoots into shape while they are still young.

INITIAL PRUNING Any existing gap can be turned into an arch. Alternatively, a gap can be cut into the hedge but the inside faces will take several years to green over with leaves.

EARLY YEARS Leave up to three strong stems on each side of the hedge to grow vertically. Prune the rest of the hedge normally. At first the new growth will look a bit ragged.

SUBSEQUENT YEARS After one or two years, the shoots will be long enough to bend over to form the framework of the arch. If necessary, insert a wooden or metal framework to get the best shape.

ESTABLISHED PRUNING As the bent shoots fill out, trim them back so that they bush out, eventually creating the shape that you want. Once established, it can be trimmed as normal along with the hedge.

ABOVE An archway that has been gradually developed by allowing branches to grow tall and then training over a metal former.

ABOVE A beech archway has the advantage that it holds on to its dead leaves throughout the winter, so its shape is still defined.

ABOVE An archway in progress. When tall enough the branches will be pulled over the gap and tied together to form the basis of the arch.

Renovating hedges

Over a period of time, or through lack of attention, many hedges become overgrown, and there comes a point when you have to bite the bullet and reduce it to near its original size. Such renovation is a rather daunting task but it can usually be successfully achieved.

Types of hedging

Not all hedging plants respond well to hard pruning. Yew (*Taxus*), holly (*Ilex*), hawthorn (*Crataegus*), beech (*Fagus*) and hornbeam (*Carpinus*) can all be cut back hard and they will soon regrow. Nearly all conifers object to such treatment. They will not reshoot and can even die. An overgrown conifer hedge is usually best replaced.

Techniques

Tackle an overgrown hedge by treating one surface at a time. This leaves plenty of foliage on the uncut surfaces to provide food and energy to allow the cut branches to regenerate. You should be aware that cutting a hedge

ABOVE Yew is one of the few conifers that can be really heavily cut back if it gets overgrown, without dying in the process.

RENOVATING AN OVERGROWN HEDGE

1 It is possible to reduce the width and height of an old hedge by drastic pruning over a couple of seasons. Tackle one side the first year and the other side the following year.

2 Use a pruning saw for the thick shoots at the centre of the hedge. However, you can use secateurs (pruners) or long-handled pruners on shoots that are thin enough.

3 New growth should appear from the stumps. Trim this growth back when it is about 15cm (6in) long to encourage bushy growth, then gradually allow it to reach the desired width.

HOW TO RENOVATE A HEDGE

An overgrown hedge can look a daunting task, but with the exception of some conifers it is not a difficult one. However, the process does take several years to complete and the hedge can look scruffy until it has filled out once again. Do not try to avoid this by cutting all the sides at once, as this may kill the hedge and will certainly slow it down.

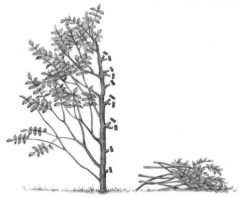

YEAR ONE Start by dealing with one side of the hedge only. Cut it back to just inside the line that will form the new surface.

YEAR TWO OR THREE Once the hedge starts to grow back, cut the other side in a similar way. Cut the top of the hedge the following year.

hard back will result in an ugly appearance for at least the first year, but after that it will gradually fill out and will eventually look better for the harsh treatment.

First year

Cut back one face of the hedge. Reduce it to approximately 15cm (6in) shorter than the desired finished surface so that there is space for it to thicken out sufficiently. Try to make the face as flat as possible. If any of the branches are too thick to cut with shears or hedge trimmers, substitute secateurs and/or long-handled pruners. For really thick branches, a saw may be necessary. The other faces of the hedge should be trimmed only lightly, as normal.

Second and subsequent years

Leave a whole year before tackling the next face and then repeat the process, cutting back the second side heavily to up to 15cm (6in) below the final surface. Cut the top as normal and trim over the face you cut hard the previous year to ensure that the growth is even. This will also help to thicken the growth. Allow another year to pass, then tackle the top. Cut back to just below the required height. In subsequent years, you may trim the hedge as normally recommended for the type of plant.

Laying a hedge

Hedge-laying is a specialist task, but some gardeners tackle it successfully

ABOVE Laying a hedge is an art, but everyone has to start somewhere and it is possible for the gardener to create a very acceptable one.

themselves. The technique is best suited to country hedges composed of hawthorn, blackthorn or a mixture. The crudest form involves simply cutting partway through the thick stems of an overgrown hedge and bending them over, laying them on top of one another and hammering stakes in to keep them in line. This produces a bushy, rather ragged hedge. A more attractive, stronger and better-grown hedge can be achieved by first driving in hazel or chestnut stakes at about 1m (3ft) intervals along the hedge. The more flexible stems are then partially cut through, bent over and woven between the stakes to make a neat, relatively narrow hedge. Any pieces sticking out that cannot be woven in are cut off. Further lengths of hazel are then woven along the top to prevent the laid growth springing back. The now near-horizontal stems will throw up new upright growth, which, when trimmed, will make a dense, impenetrable hedge.

Ornamental Climbers and Wall Shrubs

Climbers and wall shrubs are important plants in gardens, providing height and structure, both around the margins of the garden on walls and fences, and also within the garden on poles, tripods or trellis. Not only do they provide colour and texture, they also create dappled shade when grown over pergolas or arbours. Climbers are also useful as screens both within the garden and around its margins.

Climbers and wall shrubs are generally very easy to grow. Some can be allowed to grow wild through trees, but the majority benefit from some pruning and training. They are no more difficult to prune that any other shrub. Nature is very forgiving and if you do make a few mistakes while you are learning, new growth will soon hide them. Use your common sense, knowledge of the plants and the information in this chapter.

LEFT Climbers add a vertical dimension to the design of the garden and there are plenty of attractive climbing plants, such as clematis, which fulfil this function.

How climbers grow

How climbers grow is not something that many gardeners think about until they come to prune them, and then they begin to notice the differences. There are basically four types of climber, all with different methods of attaching themselves.

Twining plants

These attach themselves to host plants by means of their twining stems. Unpruned, they become a tangled mass of stems. A prime example of this group is honeysuckle (*Lonicera*). This embraces its host so tightly as to dig into it, leaving a distinct groove when removed. It can be difficult to remove dead or unwanted material on such climbers as it is often in the tight grip of newer wood.

Clinging plants

Some plants are equipped with modified roots that cling to surfaces like suckers. These, such as ivy (*Hedera*), are adapted to climb up tree trunks, cliff faces and rocks. In the garden, they provide useful cover on walls. However, they are often vigorous and can climb on to (even into) roofs, so have to be cut back regularly. When removed, they can leave dead roots stuck to the wall. If you need to paint a wall behind such a climber, it will have to be cut to the ground and allowed to start again.

Scrambling plants

The third category of climbing plants that needs to be mentioned is those that scramble up through other plants. They have no method of gripping the plant but rely on surrounding branches and twigs to support and hold them. Climbing roses and some clematis are in this category. Since they have no natural

ABOVE Some climbers are twiners. Hops and honeysuckle, for example, twine their way round their host.

ABOVE Climbers such as the climbing hydrangea have tiny aerial roots with which they attach themselves to walls.

ABOVE Some plants, such as rambling roses, scramble through or over other plants to reach the light.

DIFFERENT CLIMBING METHODS

The plants that we use as climbers in the ornamental garden are that which have adapted themselves to clamber up through other plants as well as up cliffs and over rocks in the wild so that they can expose their flowers to the light. In the garden, we create artificial hosts over which they can climb and scramble.

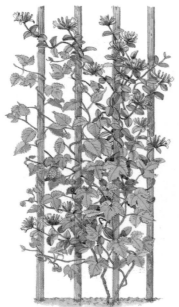

TWINING PLANTS (here hops and fuchsia) Twining plants are best grown up vertical supports, such as poles, wires or trellising. They will also twine round other plants, although they may strangle them in doing so.

SCRAMBLING PLANTS (here clematis and roses) Scramblers are best grown through other plants, such as roses through a large tree. They can also be grown up various types of framework but will need tying in.

ABOVE Many clematis have tendrils (modified leaves) which they use to attach themselves to their host and their own stems.

way of holding on, they need to be tied into their support unless they are being allowed to climb through a shrub or tree. Even then, odd wayward shoots may need to be tied in. These types of climber need rather more attention, but if grown

against walls they can easily be removed for painting or other maintenance tasks, and then replaced. Most of the other categories of climber will also scramble up through shrubs and trees.

Plants with tendrils

This group of climbers, typified by many of the clematis, climbs through other plants by clinging on to them with tendrils. These are thin modified stems or leaves that twist into coils, gripping their host. Such plants can be self-supporting if given the right support, such as another plant or section of chicken netting. Odd stems can stray from the main plant and may need tying in.

Climbers that twine

Aconitum hemsleyanum
Actinidia (some)
Akebia
Ampelopsis
Fallopia
Humulus
Ipomoea
Jasminum (some)
Lonicera
Mandevilla
Phaseolus
Schizandra
Tropaeolum (some)
Wisteria

Climbers that cling

Decumaria barbara
Decumaria sinensis
Hedera canariensis
Hedera colchica
Hedera helix
Hydrangea anomala subsp. petiolaris
Parthenocissus henryana
Parthenocissus quinquefolia
Parthenocissus tricuspidata

Climbers that scramble

Akebia
Bignonia
Billardiera
Clematis (some)
Eccremocarpus
Euonymus (some)
Jasminum
Lapageria
Lathyrus (some)
Plumbago
Rhodochiton
Rosa (some)
Solanum (some)
Tropaeolum (some)
Vinca

Climbers with tendrils

Campsis radicans
Clematis (some)
Cobaea scandens
Lathyrus
Mutisia
Passiflora
Vitis

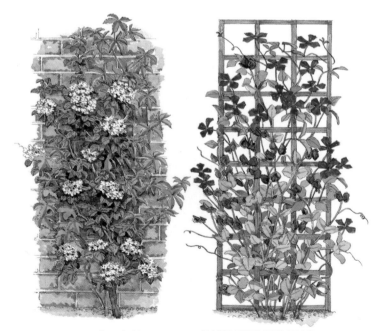

CLINGING PLANTS (here climbing hydrangea and boston ivy) Climbers that have their own aerial roots are best grown against a wall or fence. They can also be grown through trees, but can smother them.

PLANTS WITH TENDRILS (here sweet peas and clematis) Plants with tendrils wrap them round both the support and themselves. They are suitable for growing up trellises, wires, structures such as tripods, and other plants.

Support techniques

Climbers need some means of
support. In the wild, this is provided
by trees and shrubs or cliffs and
rocks, but in the garden it is possible
to choose a variety of supports to
show off the plants to advantage.

Walls

Plants look good growing up walls.
The walls show off the plants and
the plants soften the shape of the
walls. Self-clinging climbers will
grow up walls without any further
support, but all other types will need
something to be tied in to. This can
be wires, netting, trellis or special
nails with lead heads that can be
twisted around the branches.

Fences

Wire or netting fences look better
clothed in climbers. Their structure is
ideal for most climbers. Close-board
fences and more solid structures need
wires, netting or trellis fitted to them
for the climbers to grip or be attached
to. Check that all fences are strong
enough to take the weight of the
climber. Bear in mind that in wind the
climber will add stress to the fence.

GROWING CLIMBERS ON WIRES

1 Wires should be firmly
fixed to walls. One method
uses screw eyes and involves
drilling holes and using a
plug of some sort.

2 Put the appropriate size
plug in the hole and screw
the eye well into the wall,
leaving it sticking out by
3–5cm (1–2in).

3 Alternatively, a vine eye
can be hammered into the
wall. With hard walls, a pilot
hole should be drilled first.

4 Use a strong wire and run
it through the eyes of the
support. Tension it as tightly
as you can, then turn it back
on itself and twist it.

5 Tie the climber or wall
shrub in to the wire using a
proprietary tie or some
garden string.

6 As the climber or wall
shrub continues to grow, tie
in the shoots until the whole
space is evenly covered.

Trellis

This is a framework of wood, or
sometimes plastic, which can be used
as a support for climbers on another
feature, such as walls or fences, or in
its own right, supported between

poles. Trellis can be used on the
boundaries of the garden as a fence
or can be used internally to screen
one part of the garden from another.
The shape and design of the
framework is irrelevant to the plants

GROWING CLIMBERS ON NETTING

1 Proprietary netting designed
to be attached to walls and fences
can be used to support climbers.
Special clips are provided that
screw or are nailed into the wall.

2 Carefully align the top two
clips, using a spirit level, so that
the netting will be straight.

3 Attach the netting to the top
two clips.

4 With the netting held in place,
align the other clips so that the
netting is tight and straight, and
then fasten them in place.

5 Train the climber up through
the netting. Scramblers without
any means of self support will
need to be tied into position.

but can have a visual impact in the garden. A wide range of patterns is now available from garden centres and other sources. Many climbers will attach themselves to trellis, but some will need tying in.

Poles, tripods and obelisks

These methods of support all create a single climbing space for a climber, rather than a long line. Supports for climbers such as these make very pleasing decorative features in the garden. They can either be functional (for instance, three uprights inserted in the ground and tied at the top) or decorative in their own right (a carefully constructed and painted obelisk, for example). Poles should have netting attached to them in order to give the climbers something to grip on to. Tripods and obelisks may also need this, depending on how they are constructed.

GROWING CLIMBERS ON TRELLIS

1 An attractive support for a climber can be provided by using trellis. The trellis must be firmly fixed to a wall. Start by drilling a hole in the wall.

2 Screw a batten to the wall, rather than fixing the trellis directly to it. This will provide a gap behind the trellis.

3 Attach the trellis to the battens. It is a good idea to use hinges on the bottom batten and catches on the top one, so that it can be eased away from the wall for maintenance.

4 The firmly attached trellis is ready to support a climber or wall shrub. Most plants benefit from being tied in, even if they are self-clingers.

USING TRELLIS AS A SCREEN

1 Dig a hole in the position of the first post. It should be at least 45cm (18in) deep.

2 Place the post in the hole and make certain that it is vertical.

3 Fill the newly dug hole with a dry mix of concrete.

4 Dig the second hole one panel length away from the first post.

5 Attach the panel to the first post, using a hammer and nails, and then place the second post in its hole and attach the panel to that.

6 Make certain that the second post is upright and then fill in with a dry mix of concrete, ramming it down firmly.

7 Continue to add panels and posts until the trellis is finished. Until the concrete is set, the posts may need a brace to keep them upright.

ABOVE Honeysuckle in full bloom, covering trellis that has been used as a screen.

Arches, pergolas and arbours

Although their function is different, the construction of arches, pergolas and arbours is basically the same in that they all have sides and a top. Each may be made from wood or metal or can be constructed from panels of trellis. Many climbers will readily attach themselves to these structures and completely cover them (including the top), in the case of an arbour forming a green room. Wayward shoots should always be tied in, particularly thorny ones, as

GROWING CLIMBERS UP TRIPODS

1 Place three poles into holes in the ground and refill the holes with earth, or concrete if it is an exposed site.

3 Saw off the ends flush with the uprights, and add the rest of the horizontal bars, making as many levels as you want.

5 Water the plant well and then mulch around it in order to preserve moisture and keep weeds down.

6 The finished tripod. A smaller one can be made by sloping three poles towards each other and tying or nailing them at the top.

2 Nail a cross bar between two of the poles using galvanized nails. Use overlong lengths to avoid splitting the wood.

4 Put the plant either in the centre or on one of the sides. Avoid the corners if these have been concreted.

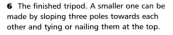

ABOVE An archway with wisteria trained over it. Eventually, as it ages, it will be the wisteria holding up the arch.

they may catch on people walking through. When making these structures, always take into account the extent of the plants when fully grown. It is all too easy to make arches that will be too narrow when they are clothed with flourishing climbers.

Trees and shrubs

In the wild most climbers clamber up through trees and shrubs, and to a much lesser extent up cliffs and over rocks. In the garden, the latter is relatively rare but the former has all kinds of possibilities. One of the great advantages is that you can use climbers that flower at different times to the tree or shrub; thus the support might flower in spring and the climber in summer or late summer, making effective use of the space. There are some climbers, *Clematis viticella* and all its cultivars, for example, that are pruned back to the ground each spring, so that the shrubby support is uncluttered when it flowers but by the end of summer the climber has grown again and fills the shrub with flowers. It is important that any tree or shrub that is used as a support is in good health, as the extra weight of the climber, plus the windage its bulk

ABOVE Climbers can be trained over archways. Some, like this ivy, will soon find their own way over and need little tying in.

creates, can put a tremendous strain on the plant. It is dangerous to grow climbers through dead trees. It is not such a good idea to grow ivy through a tree because it will eventually smother it and is likely to kill it. Having said that, it is perfect for adding a decaying, gothic look to a garden.

BUILDING AN ARCH

1 Make sure that the arch is wide enough to include the width of the plants and still leave enough room to walk through it.

2 Dig the holes for the uprights in the appropriate places, preferably at least 45cm (18in) deep, but more if possible.

3 Make certain that the uprights are vertical and then concrete the arch in position. Cover the concrete with soil to disguise it.

4 Assemble the top of the archway on the ground, choosing a pitch that will look right. Experiment with temporary fixing if necessary.

5 Using galvanized nails, secure the top to the uprights, being careful not to knock the uprights out of the vertical.

GROWING CLIMBERS THROUGH SHRUBS

1 The shrub does not have to be large. Small shrubs can accommodate small climbers, such as *Clematis alpina*.

2 Prepare the ground beside, not under, the shrub, otherwise the climber might be starved of water.

3 Plant the climber in the prepared soil and tie its shoots to one or more canes, leading them into the shrub.

4 Finally, water the ground around the shrub thoroughly and apply a mulch to prevent the evaporation of moisture.

Initial training

Most climbing plants have a natural tendency to grow straight up. Some kind of training is essential if you want them to provide good coverage on a wall or trellis.

On receipt of the plant

Most plants that you buy from garden centres and nurseries need little initial pruning after planting. Remove or cut back any damaged shoots or any that are dead or diseased. (This applies mainly to plants dug up by friends. You would normally reject plants in this state for sale in nurseries.) Any weak shoots should also be cut off. Most climbers are sold in pots, but occasionally they may be bare-rooted. If you have not got the time to plant these immediately, they should be heeled in in some spare ground.

After planting

The plant should be set close to its support. However, if planting against a wall or fence, site it at least 25cm (10in) away, preferably more. Check the stems again and cut out any that have been damaged during

ABOVE The rose 'Albertine' trained on wires on the tiled side of a garage. It is important to tie in all the shoots. You will also need to ensure that the rose does not grow into the eaves.

transportation or planting. Train the shoots towards the support. If this is a wall or fence, place several canes at an angle between it and the plant. Tie the shoots to these. If they are long enough, start training them up the wall by tying into the support. When planting against trellis or poles, the plants are usually close enough to train the shoots directly on to the supports. In both cases, even twining plants are best tied in

to start with, although they will soon start finding their own way of clinging to the support.

With most forms of support, it is important to ensure that the initial training separates the various shoots, so that the climber is well spread across the wall or trellis rather than concentrated in a tangled column up its centre. With some of the more woody climbers, such as roses, it is a good idea to arch the stems so that

TRAINING A CLIMBER AGAINST A FENCE

1 Prepare a planting hole and check that it is the correct depth. Most plants need to be at the same depth as they were in the pot.

2 Put the plant in the hole and then train the shoots to their support, spreading them as widely as possible to give a good coverage.

3 Once planted, water thoroughly and then apply a mulch to prevent evaporation and help keep weeds down.

ABOVE Climbers, particularly annuals, are suitable for growing in containers. Various supports are available.

the tips are almost as low as their origin. This will encourage them to produce more shoots along their length, ensuring good coverage of the wall or whatever support you are using. You should also separate out the stems of plants climbing up a single pole, for even coverage.

As the plant grows, tie in any shoots that are beginning to wave free from the support. Even self-twining plants need tying in from time to time. If possible, direct some of the shoots to fill spaces so that eventually the whole wall or support is covered.

ABOVE A collection of different types of proprietary plastic plant ties and string. Ties are quick but string is cheaper.

DIFFERENT TRAINING METHODS

The basic principle of training climbers is to ensure that the plant covers as much as possible of its allotted space. The simpler the system of training that you use, the easier it is to prune the climber. Tangled shoots can take a lot of time to sort out. Below is a selection of methods for training ornamental climbers.

TRAINING AGAINST TRELLIS When planting against a piece of trellis, spread out the bottom shoots as widely as possible, the outside ones preferably horizontally so that a curtain of foliage is created.

A BADLY TRAINED CLIMBER ON TRELLIS When training up a trellis, make sure that the stems are well spread out at the base, so that they cover the whole of the allotted space rather than, as here, forming a tight column.

TRAINING AGAINST A WALL The same principle applies to a wall as to a trellis. Spread out the shoots as widely as possible so that the space is clothed all the way from the ground.

TRAINING OVER AN ARCH Plant on the outside of archways so that the passageway is not constricted by the growing plant. Train the shoots right over the top of the arch, keeping an even spread.

Established pruning

In many ways the principles involved in pruning climbers are the same as for other forms of ornamental shrub. The only basic difference is that you are dealing with long, vertical stems and pruning may involve using ladders or platforms.

ABOVE It is essential to cut back wall climbers when they reach the line of the gutter to stop them getting under the tiles and eaves.

Routine pruning

Pruning established climbers can appear daunting. Start by cutting out any dead, damaged or diseased wood. In the case of a tangled climber, such as a mature *Clematis montana*, there may be a mass of dead material within it. Next remove any weak or unproductive growth. Also cut back any crossing stems or stems that are causing congestion. Finally, look for

some of the older stems and cut these back hard, either to strong new growth or completely to the ground. This will stimulate new growth, which will keep the climber healthy and productive. The best time to do this

varies but winter is often a good time on a deciduous climber as it is easy to gain access to the base of the plant.

Summer pruning

Some climbers flower on the previous year's wood. These should be pruned in summer, as soon as the plant has finished flowering. This promotes new growth, which will ripen in time to produce the following year's flowers.

Arched stems

All new wood should be trained as it grows. With climbers such as honeysuckle, tie in the new growth to fill gaps and provide an even spread. With woodier subjects such

PRUNING AN ESTABLISHED CLIMBER

1 A honeysuckle growing over a pergola. This climber is becoming overgrown and is in need of pruning.

2 The first task when pruning is to remove all the dead and damaged wood. Honeysuckle often has a lot of the former.

3 Cut the dead wood back to the next healthy shoot or, if congested, take it back even further, but always to a shoot.

4 The next task is to cut out some of the congested wood, preferably taking out the weakest and oldest growth.

5 Select some of the strongest and most healthy growths to be retained. These are likely to be the youngest wood.

6 Tie these healthy shoots in to the post or pillar or the cross members of the pergola, using garden string.

PRUNING ESTABLISHED CLIMBERS

The pruning of established climbers is often ignored, mainly because it involves working with a ladder. It can also be difficult, but it is essential that ornamental climbers are just as well maintained as any other shrubs in the garden. Some climbers need quite a lot of work in order to keep them at their best, while others just need trimming round the edges.

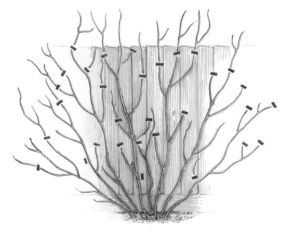

AN ESTABLISHED CLIMBER Take out any dead or damaged wood. Remove any congested wood and then take out a few of the oldest stems back to a good shoot. This will promote rejuvenation.

EAVES AND GUTTERS You will need to stop many self-clinging wall climbers getting into gutters and obscuring windows.

as roses, the new wood should be trained, as far as possible, in a horizontal curve. This not only promotes flowering along the whole branch, but also stimulates new shoots, which can also be trained in a curve, so that the wall is covered when the climber is in full bloom. Tie the stems vertically and they will flower only at the top. To achieve this, there are some climbers, such as roses, where you will have to take the climber off the wall, spread it on the ground, prune it and then put it back, tying the stems into nice curving arcs. Fortunately, it is not necessary to do this every year.

Gutters and roofs

While the aim is to cover as much of a wall with a climber as possible, it is not advisable to let them extend above the gutter level. Many climbers, and in particular self-clinging ones, will find any gap and penetrate the roof-space of the building. They can even go up under the eaves and squeeze in between tiles. They can also clog up gutters, not only with their stems but also with their fallen leaves. Make certain, therefore, that they do not reach this height. Every autumn, cut back any shoots that have ventured above the top of the wall. It is a good idea to cut them back by at least 30cm (12in), so that they will not immediately grow back the following spring. Do the job in autumn rather than spring, as you will then be able to clear the stems and leaves from the gutters before the winter rains.

On houses and other buildings, it is also important to ensure that the climbers are kept back from windows, and, in the case of self-clingers such as ivy, from any woodwork that is regularly painted.

ABOVE To rejuvenate a climber, cut back some of the older wood to a strong shoot.

ABOVE Wood that is dead or contains die-back, as here, should be cut back to a good shoot.

Clematis group 1

Clematis are normally divided into three groups as far as pruning is concerned. The grouping reflects their time of flowering and the best way to prune them to achieve the maximum number of flowers. Group 1 consists of those that flower on the previous season's wood and so require little or no pruning (or the flowering wood will be removed). The typical clematis in this group is *Clematis montana* and its cultivars. Several other species also fall into this category.

Initial pruning and training

Plant the clematis deeper in the soil than it was in the pot. The pot soil line should be about 5cm (2in) or more below the level of the ground. This is to ensure that if the plant suffers from clematis wilt, there will be some adventitious buds that will throw up new shoots and so ensure the plant's survival. Little initial pruning is then required other than to remove any damaged wood. You also need to make sure that the shoots are well spread out

ABOVE A white form of *Clematis montana*. This needs little in the way of pruning, but if it is left unattended it can become rather congested.

PRUNING CLEMATIS GROUP 1

1 Clematis in this group can largely be left to their own devices in terms of pruning, but some, especially *C. montana*, can get very congested and over-heavy.

2 Little new growth on this clematis needs to be removed, except for a few straggly growths or where the climber is starting to outgrow its position.

3 The surface of the climber looks almost the same, but beneath it is likely to be a tangle of dead wood, which will need removing.

ABOVE When pruning clematis, find a pair of strong shoots and cut across the stem just above, being careful not to damage them.

HOW TO PRUNE CLEMATIS GROUP 1 In this group the flowers are formed on the previous year's wood, so a harsh pruning will remove these and hence its ability to flower in the current year. This group needs very little pruning other than that required to keep the plant under control and to remove any dead wood that may accumulate. The latter will tend to build up, making the plant very congested.

and tie any new ones in to a fan shape so that the whole of the support will be covered.

Established pruning

This is the easiest clematis group in that theoretically no pruning is required, as the flowers are formed on the previous year's wood. However, it is prudent to cut out any dead wood, as this can quickly build up, especially on *C. montana*. This accumulation of dead wood will not only stifle the clematis, making it look like a vast bird's nest, but it will also create a tremendous weight that may well bring down the support. So, at least every couple of years, go through the climber and take out any dead wood you can find – a tedious job but worth doing. If the clematis grows beyond its bounds, there is no harm in

Group 1 clematis

All the cultivars of the various species below also belong to Group 1.
C. alpina
C. armandii
C. cirrhosa
C. macropetala
C. montana

cutting off the offending shoots at any time of the year as long as you cut back to a strong bud.

Renovation

C. montana, in particular, can become very overgrown and full of dead wood if it is not regularly maintained. At some point, you will inevitably have to prune it severely to bring it back

under control, which is a satisfying task. Fortunately, *C. montana* can be cut back very hard and will still rejuvenate, so after taking out all the dead wood, cut back into the older wood, leaving some of the younger shoots. If extreme action is called for you can cut it back almost to the ground. All this should take place immediately after flowering.

Clematis group 2

The second group of clematis includes most of the large-flowered varieties, including 'Lasurstern' and 'Nelly Moser'. These tend to have two flowerings, the main crop in the early summer on the previous year's wood and then a second crop on the new wood in late summer or autumn.

Initial training

Ensure that the young clematis is planted deeper in the soil than it was in the pot. Make sure that the pot soil line is about 5cm (2in) or more below ground level. This is to ensure that there will be some adventitious buds that will throw up new shoots and so ensure the plant's survival if the plant suffers from clematis wilt. You should find that little initial pruning is required other than to remove any damaged wood, although many gardeners like to cut back all stems to a pair of strong buds about 30cm (12in) or so above the ground. Also ensure that the shoots are well spread out and tie any new ones in to a fan shape so that the whole of the support will be covered.

ABOVE *Clematis* 'Barbara Dibley' is typical of the large-flowered varieties that belong to this group of clematis.

Established pruning

This is the most complicated of the clematis groups, although once you have done it a few times, it presents no problems. It is also reassuring to know that even if you cut something off that you didn't mean to, it doesn't really matter as the plant will tolerate being cut hard back. Pruning takes place in late winter, before the

ABOVE The double *Clematis* 'Royalty'. Group 2 clematis need a little more attention than those in the other two groups.

growth really gets under way (some growth may even have started by mid-winter, but do not worry about this, even if it gets cut off).

Firstly, remove any dead, dying or diseased wood. Next, cut back all the remaining shoots to the first pair of strong buds, which can be at varying points on the stems. In some cases, you will remove only a short length

PRUNING CLEMATIS GROUP 2

1 The clematis in early spring looks very difficult to prune, but it is not quite as bad as it appears.

2 Start by removing a few of the older shoots back to a pair of buds at the base, so that the plant is constantly rejuvenated.

3 Next cut back all the remaining stems to the topmost pair of strong buds. If necessary, retie all the shoots, spreading them out if possible.

HOW TO PRUNE CLEMATIS GROUP 2 This group can be left unpruned but the flowering wood would get higher and higher, as well as more congested, so it is better to prune lightly to keep them under control. Take the opportunity to retie shoots to fill gaps and relieve congestion. Take back the shoots to the topmost pair of strong buds. Any dead or damaged wood should also be removed and one or two of the oldest stems can be removed almost to the base to rejuvenate the clematis.

ABOVE 'Lasurstern' is a Group 2 clematis. The large purple flowers make a wonderful feature in the garden.

but in others you may cut back half the stem. Look carefully at the remaining structure and retie any shoots that may be better used to fill gaps, so that you achieve as even a spread as possible.

Renovation

If the clematis becomes neglected or simply overgrown, you can cut it back quite severely and it will generally recover. If you are a little uncertain, reduce the plant by a third every year until it has all been renewed.

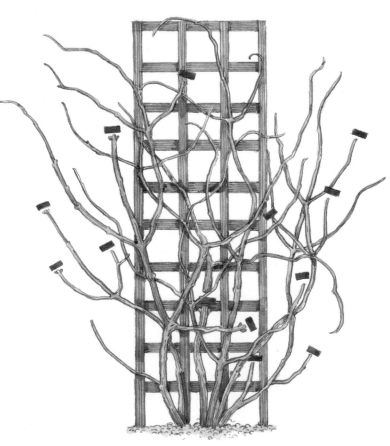

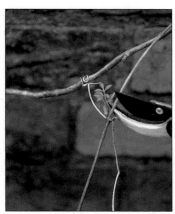

ABOVE The best time to prune is late winter before growth starts, but this may have started by then so do not damage new shoots.

Group 2 clematis

C. 'Barbara Dibley'	C. 'Elsa Späth'	C. 'Moonlight'
C. 'Barbara Jackman'	C. 'Fireworks'	C. 'Nelly Moser'
C. 'Belle of Woking'	C. 'H.F. Young'	C. 'Proteus'
C. 'Countess of Lovelace'	C. 'Lasurstern'	C. 'Star of India'
C. 'Daniel Deronda'	C. 'Marie Boisselot'	C. 'The President'
C. 'Dr Ruppel'	C. 'Miss Bateman'	C. 'Vyvyan Pennell'

Clematis group 3

The third group is another easy group to deal with. It is typified by *C. viticella* and its host of cultivars. These are mainly the smaller-flowered varieties, which tend to produce their blooms in late summer and into autumn, on the current year's wood. If they are left unpruned, the climbers get taller and taller and the flowers appear right at the top, leaving an unsightly mass of tangled brown stems at eye-level. They are ideal for growing through other shrubs such as roses. At the beginning of the summer, the clematis is not far into the bush so the roses can be clearly seen, but by late summer, when the roses have finished, the clematis is in full flower, giving the shrub a second flush of life.

Initial training

When planting the young clematis, check that it is planted deeper in the soil that it was in the pot. You will

ABOVE Group 3 are good for growing through other shrubs as, being cut to the ground each year, they do not swamp their host.

ABOVE All the *viticella* group of clematis belong to Group 3, and are pruned in the same way. These include 'Pagoda', seen here.

need to have the pot soil line about 5cm (2in) or more below the level of the ground. The reason for this is to ensure that if the plant suffers from clematis wilt, there will be some adventitious buds that will throw up new shoots and so ensure

the plant's survival. On planting, cut back all stems to a pair of strong buds about 30cm (12in) or so above the ground. As the new shoots develop, ensure that they are well spread out and tie them in so that the whole of the support will be covered.

ABOVE The tangled wood resulting from one year's growth. Fortunately, there is no need to sort it all out – it can all be cut off.

PRUNING CLEMATIS GROUP 3

1 The main pruning technique with this group is to cut all the stems back to a bud or new shoot close to the base of the plant.

2 Any remaining dead or damaged wood should be cut right back to the base. There will always be a few such shoots.

Group 3 clematis

C. 'Abundance'	C. 'Fair Rosamund'	C. 'Star of India'
C. 'Ascotiensis'	C. 'Lady Betty Balfour'	C. *tangutica*
C. 'Bill Mackenzie'	C. 'Little Nell'	C. *tibetana (orientalis)*
C. 'Comtesse de Bouchard'	C. 'Madame Julia Correvon'	C. *viticella* and cvs
C. 'Duchess of Albany'	C. 'Perle d'Azur'	
C. 'Etoile Violette'	C. 'Royal Velours'	

ABOVE An impressive amount of growth is put on during one season and the plant gathers strength each year; it will soon cover this tripod.

Established pruning

In late winter, cut back all stems to the first strong pair of buds above the point where you cut them last year. Pull all the old growth from the supports. There will probably be some growth starting towards the tips of the old growth, but do not be afraid to cut this off. The plant will soon burst into life from the base.

ABOVE Do not cut the shoots too high, especially when they are young, or they will gradually get taller as the years go by, leaving the base bare.

HOW TO PRUNE CLEMATIS GROUP 3 The group 3 clematis are very easy to deal with, which can be a relief because the previous year's growth always looks a tangled mess. Pruning is best done in late winter and regrowth will start almost immediately. Cut all the stems back to the first pair of strong buds above where you cut the previous year. Cut out any dead stems completely. As the new stems grow, weave or tie them in as necessary.

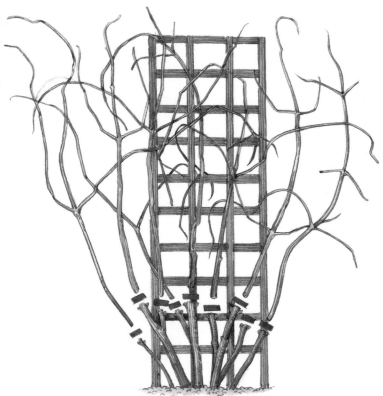

Unusual clematis

There is a small group of clematis that can be pruned either as Group 2 or Group 3. Treated as Group 2, they will flower earlier with larger flowers. As Group 3 they will flower later (which can be an advantage), but with smaller flowers.

C. 'Duchess of Sutherland'
C. 'Ernest Markham'

C. 'Gipsy Queen'
C. 'Hagley Hybrid'
C. 'Jackmanii'
C. 'Jackmanii Superba'
C. 'Maureen'
C. 'Mrs Cholmondeley'
C. 'Niobe'
C. 'Rouge Cardinal'
C. 'Ville de Lyon'
C. 'W.E. Gladstone'

Wisteria

Pruning wisteria causes most gardeners more anguish than any other climber. In fact, it is a simple matter and all you need to remember is that wisteria needs pruning twice a year, instead of once a year as with most other climbers.

Supports

Although wisteria can be trained as a standard tree, it is most commonly seen as a wall climber. It cannot cling to the wall by itself like ivy, so needs a support. Its sheer size means that wooden trellis is usually out of the question. It is best supported on a series of parallel wires fixed securely to the wall with vine eyes. The wires should be about 30cm (12in) apart, with the bottom one about 60cm (2ft) from the ground, or higher if you wish. Put a stake into the ground to support the main stem for the first couple of years.

Initial training

Plant in winter or early spring. Cut back the leader to about 1m (3ft) above the ground and remove all side shoots. During the summer, choose two well-placed laterals and tie them into the wires at an angle of 45 degrees. Cut back any side shoots on these to three or four buds. Remove all other laterals. Tie the leader in a

ABOVE Wisteria can create a wonderful walkway when trained over a pergola. The main stems twine their way up and across the poles.

ABOVE Summer pruning consists of cutting back the shoots to within five or six leaves of the new growth. Shorten this again in winter.

vertical position. During its second winter, remove about one-third of the length of the laterals and gently pull them down to the horizontal. Cut the leader off at about 75–90cm (30–36in) above the top lateral. The following summer repeat the process of the first summer and tie in two good new laterals at an angle of 45 degrees. Remove all other new laterals. Tie down to the horizontal in winter and cut back the top third of each lateral, including the two trained the previous year. Cut back all side shoots to three or four buds. Continue in the same vein until the wisteria covers the whole wall.

Established pruning

Once established, continue to prune wisteria in both summer and winter. In late summer, prune each lateral and side shoot to within about five or six leaves from the main lateral. Allow the main lateral to develop until it has filled its space. Once this has happened, cut back annually to five or six leaves of the new growth. In winter, return to the same shoots and reduce them further to two or three buds. If you do this every year, the wisteria should not become overgrown. If it does, remove one main branch each year over several years, allowing a suitable replacement to develop.

ABOVE Wisterias are ideal for training on to walls, which help to protect the young buds from late frosts.

ABOVE The shoots that are not required for extending the wisteria's coverage should be cut back to two or three buds in winter.

TRAINING A WISTERIA

Wisteria is often thought by many gardeners to be a difficult plant to train and prune. This is mainly because the task needs to be done twice a year, once in the summer and then again in the winter. However, the actual pruning process is not at all difficult and should soon become a matter of routine, although it might involve some ladder work.

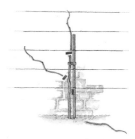

YEAR ONE, WINTER Plant the wisteria in winter or early spring. Cut back all the side shoots and cut back the leader to about 1m (36in).

YEAR ONE, SUMMER In the following summer, select two strong shoots and tie these into the wires. Also tie in the vertical leader. Remove all other laterals.

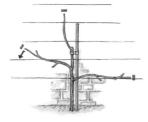

YEAR TWO, WINTER In the second winter, gently pull the two laterals down to the horizontal. Cut off the leader about 75–90cm (30–36in) above the laterals.

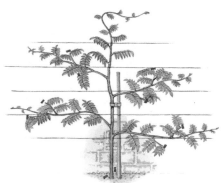

YEAR TWO, SUMMER The following summer, repeat the process that you completed in the previous year, this time adding a second tier of new laterals.

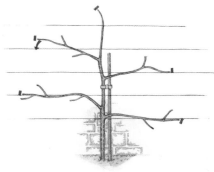

YEAR THREE, WINTER Again, repeat what you did in the previous winter and continue until the space is covered with horizontal branches, which will form the framework.

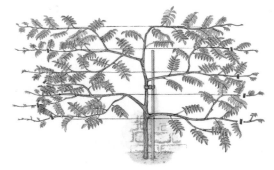

ESTABLISHED PRUNING, SUMMER Once the wisteria is established, prune any new shoots that are not required to fill a space back to five or six leaves of the new growth.

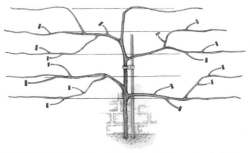

ESTABLISHED PRUNING, WINTER Each winter cut back all the shoots pruned in the summer to two or three buds. Cut out completely any shoots that cross or cause congestion.

Renovation pruning

With controlled pruning every year, plants should never become overgrown and need a complete overhaul. However, sometimes pruning is forgotten or put off until such time as it is too late. And you often inherit shrubs and climbers that have been allowed to run riot.

Making a start

There are some cases where you can literally chop the plants off close to the ground and start again, but generally a more controlled approach is required. Furthermore, in some cases it may be possible to carry out the renovation in one year, but in other cases it may take several years to renovate the plant completely. So before you start, it is important establish what kind of plant you have. An ancient wisteria may be permanently fixed to a wall, but there are some climbers, roses for example, that can gradually be untied and lowered to the ground for pruning before being returned to the support. This is a good opportunity to check all the supports to make sure they are in good condition, with none of the wires corroded or likely to snap. If the wall or support is painted, this may also be the time to give it a couple of fresh coats.

Pruning

First, cut out all the dead wood along with anything that is damaged or diseased. This allows you to see

RENOVATING A CLIMBER

1 Once climbers become a tangled mess, they will need a complete overhaul. It is often easier to untie the climber from its support in order to carry out the work.

2 The best place to start is to take out all the dead or damaged wood. This clears out quite a lot of unwanted material, making it easier to see where to go next.

3 Next, cut out some of the thin and congested wood to open up the structure. Quite a lot of wood can be removed at this stage of the renovation process.

4 Take out some of the older wood right back to a bud just above the soil, so that the plant rejuvenates from the base.

5 Start to tie back some of the remaining shoots, spreading them evenly across the space and trying to fill in any gaps.

6 The renovation is almost completed. There are still a number of weak shoots that remain and these should be taken out as well.

HOW TO RENOVATE CLIMBERS

If at all possible, you should attempt to keep the climbers in your garden under control. However, you will inevitably find that occasionally they get unruly, or you may be taking over a garden that has an array of congested, overgrown plants.

Some climbers do not like being pruned too hard, so spread the hard pruning over two or more years for these.

CUTTING HARD BACK There are some climbers, such as honeysuckle, that can be pruned back very hard, taking them almost to the base.

BASIC RENOVATION Cut out any dead or damaged wood and then turn your attention to taking out weak growth along with any branches or stems that cross or cause congestion. Finally take out some of the older wood completely.

Aftercare

Prune all new wood every year in the normal way, so that the climber does not need renovating again. Tie in all new growths as they appear. To encourage new growth, top-dress the area around the base of the climber with a general fertilizer, then water and mulch.

the framework of the living climber. After this, remove any weak, spindly growth, cutting back either to a main branch or to a good strong shoot. Any crossing or rubbing wood can now be removed. At this point, look at what you have got left and, if you feel that to remove any more may damage the plant, leave it until next winter. However, if possible, remove at least one main stem of older wood. Usually this can be cut back right to the base. It may be possible to take out two. By the following year, new growth should have replaced these. Gradually, over the next two or three years, take out all the old growth, so that you are left with a vigorous new plant.

ABOVE Summer reveals the recovered plant. Here, the right-hand side needs some stems trained horizontally, as on the left.

Wall shrubs

There are certain shrubs that, while not strictly climbers, look good when trained against walls. Chaenomeles, for example, will grow perfectly happily as a free-standing shrub, but has a loose and sparsely flowering habit. When trained tight against a wall, it comes into its own and will often flower profusely for many weeks.

Supports

Although most of the wall shrubs can be grown as free-standing plants, they still require support when grown against a wall. This is not only to give them strength in their unnatural position, but also to prevent the wind bouncing off the wall behind and blowing them forward. They also tend to reach forwards towards the light. It is possible to attach some form of trellis or heavy netting, either wood, metal or plastic, to the wall. This can be very effective in small quantities, and if hinged at the bottom, the plant can be eased away from the wall for painting and maintenance, as required. However, to cover larger areas of wall and for a more discreet look, parallel wires anchored to the wall with vine eyes are better. The wires should not be tight against the wall but should be held at least 5cm (2in) away from it.

Initial training

Plant the shrub at least 30cm (12in) away from the wall, preferably more. The soil is often poorer close to a wall and is usually too dry. When the shrub is fully grown the fact that it is not planted tight to the wall will not be apparent. On planting, some method may be needed to attach the shrub to the wall. If the main shoot or shoots are long enough, they can be tied directly to the lower wires,

PRUNING FREMONTODENDRON

1 Fremontodendron is coated with a dust that can cause problems if it is inhaled, so wear a mask and goggles when pruning.

2 As with most pruning jobs, the first routine task is to cut out all the dead, diseased or damaged wood.

3 Not much else is required, except to remove any misplaced shoots. Tie the remaining shoots into the framework.

4 Use string or a proprietary plant tie for tying in. Fremontodrendons are best trained as a fan or an espalier.

but in many cases it will be necessary first to tie the shoots to a cane or canes that are angled towards the wall.

The main way of training depends on the shrub and its natural habit. Some can be trained with a central "trunk", with branches spreading to

either side of it, while others are best as fans. For a less formal look, simply tie in main branches as they develop and cut out any shoots that project from or grow towards the wall. This usually works well as long as you also cut out any crossing or congested wood, and tie in odd shoots into gaps to produce even coverage over the wall.

A more formal way is to train a shrub as a fan or even as an espalier in the same way as you would a fruit tree. For a fan, start with two strong laterals at the bottom and tie these in at an angle of 35 degrees. Allow other sub-laterals to develop on these and tie them in at an angle until the whole wall space is covered. Chaenomeles responds well to this training. For an espalier, allow two laterals to develop and tie them in to horizontal wires. Allow the main leaders to grow and produce two more laterals the following year. Train these sideways and so on until all the wires have horizontal arms on them. A suitable subject for this training is *Fremontodendron*.

Established training

Apply the same principles as you would to a free-standing shrub. Also, remove all shoots that grow towards the wall or away from it, and make certain that there are no crossing or rubbing shoots. If areas become bare (perhaps because of the need to cut out dead or damaged wood), train new shoots to cover the spot.

WALL-TRAINING AN ESPALIERED PYRACANTHA Pyracantha is a classic wall shrub. It can be trained flat against a wall, rather than letting it bush out into a more shrub-like shape in the open garden. Pyracantha has rather vicious spines, so it is advisable to wear gloves when pruning it. For a more formal-looking pyracantha, the initial training could shape the plant into an espalier with decorative tiers of horizontal branches. Cut out all of the wood that points away from the wall, and so spoils the effect.

PRUNING A WALL-TRAINED PYRACANTHA

1 Most of the pruning is carried out in the summer. Cut back shoots to just a couple of buds to prevent the bush from becoming too dense, and to expose the fruit.

2 Cut back shoots that are growing away from the wall to one bud or, if the area is already well supplied with shoots, take them out completely.

3 A young pyracantha still in the process of filling out. This has been trained into an espalier shape, but it could also be trained as a fan.

Pruning ceanothus

Evergreen ceanothus not only look good against walls but, especially in cooler areas, also appreciate the protection a wall provides. They do not respond well to hard pruning.

Supports

Either use wires or a section of trellis attached to a wall as a support. Trellis provides more points at which to anchor the stems. Once the shrub has grown, it will hardly be seen.

Initial training

Allow the shrub to develop in its natural way, but remove all shoots that grow either towards or away from the wall. Also take out any shoots that cross over others or cause congestion. Aim for even coverage across the allotted space. Do not cut back into old wood to try to stimulate growth.

Established pruning

Evergreen ceanothus flower either on the previous year's wood or on the current year's wood. They are very reluctant to break again from old wood, so all that is required, beyond removing any dead, damaged or diseased wood, is to tip-prune the previous year's shoots back to one bud in early spring. This will produce flowering shoots and maintain the shrub's shape and size. Old overgrown ceanothus should be dug out.

WALL-TRAINING A CEANOTHUS There are two distinct types of ceanothus: the evergreen and the deciduous. It is important to keep control of the shape if you use a ceanothus as a wall shrub, because it is difficult to cut back if it becomes overgrown. Train the shrub to be relatively flat against the wall, cutting back any shoots that stick too far out from the wall. Then, lightly tip-prune the previous year's growth if the shrub is likely to get too large.

ABOVE The flowers of evergreen ceanothus appear on the previous year's wood, so do not cut it back unless you need to.

ABOVE If ceanothus is grown as a free-standing bush, there is little pruning required. It can be allowed to grow naturally, the only pruning being the removal of dead wood.

ABOVE This clearly shows the new shoots developing, which will carry next year's flowers. If it is necessary to control the plant, they must be pruned only lightly.

Pruning chaenomeles

Chaenomeles makes a superb wall shrub. The aim is to keep it cut back tight to the wall. Some varieties will flower throughout the year, often profusely.

Support

This is best supported on a system of parallel wires, at about 30cm (12in) intervals.

Initial training

There are two ways to train a chaenomeles against a wall. The more professional way is to create a fan, much in the same way as for a fruit fan. Plant a young specimen and cut off the leader immediately above the top one of two strong laterals. Tie these in at an angle of about 30 degrees and remove all other laterals. Cut out their tips to about 45cm (18in) from the main trunk. Allow these to develop two side shoots each and tie these in. Remove the tips of the side shoots in a similar fashion and reduce all other side shoots to one bud. Continue doing this each year until the whole space is covered with an evenly spaced framework of stems. Alternatively, allow the shrub to

FAN-TRAINING A CHAENOMELES Chaenomeles can be grown as a free-standing shrub in the garden, but is most commonly seen grown as a wall shrub, where it should be kept tightly pruned. The best way in which to train a chaenomeles is as a fan against a wall or fence, allowing the stems to branch until the whole space is evenly covered.

develop naturally, tying in the main six or seven side shoots as they appear, so that the area is well covered. Allow these to produce side shoots in order to fill in the gaps. Cut off any shoots pointing towards or away from the wall. You also need to cut out any shoots that are not needed for the main framework to one bud. This method produces a more informal but still very attractive specimen.

Established pruning

Once the main framework is complete, cut back all side shoots to one bud to create flowering spurs. Chaenomeles is vigorous and will produce another long shoot in a matter of weeks, so cut these back to one bud when you see them. If the spurs become congested, remove a few of the older ones in winter. If the shrub gets unruly, it can be pruned hard back, but it is best to spread this over several years.

PRUNING CHAENOMELES

1 Cut out any crossing stems or any that form a congested area. The shoots should cover the wall or fence in an even spread.

2 Once established, cut back all side shoots to one or two buds or leaves. They grow rapidly and will need pruning several times a year.

3 Tie in all the shoots to wires stretched across the wall or fence. Failure to do this will result in the plant growing away from the wall.

ABOVE A free-standing chaenomeles, showing its sprawling natural habit, which is quite different from tightly wall-trained plants.

Roses

These are some of the most popular garden plants. Every year, there are hundreds of new varieties to add to the thousands that are already in existence. Fortunately, these all fall into distinct pruning categories so that gardeners who already grow roses have no difficulty in coping with the new arrivals. However, to anyone new to gardening, pruning roses can seem a bewildering topic. There seem to be so many varieties and different types, each requiring a different method.

In spite of the number of different types of rose and the differences in pruning each, common sense applies to them all. It is quite comforting to know how difficult it is to kill a rose by mis-pruning. It has been shown that you can simply hack off stems with a chainsaw and the rose will remain healthy and produce masses of blooms. But proper pruning is more satisfying and produces a neater result.

The key to successful rose pruning is to take your time and to wear stout gloves. Just learn about the types you have in the garden and add to your knowledge and experience as you include new roses to your collection. After a couple of attempts, you will find that rose pruning becomes second nature and your roses will bloom more beautifully each year.

LEFT Who can resist a wonderful and abundant display of roses? This is achieved through careful training and pruning, neither of which is very difficult.

Pruning roses

There are a number of different types of rose, each group being distinguished by the way it grows. The habit of growth dictates how the rose should be pruned. Fortunately, roses are very resilient plants, and it is quite difficult to kill one through mis-pruning. The worst you can do is inhibit flowering for one season.

Timing

Pruning generally takes place in three stages. The first is to cut off the flowers as they fade. The second is usually considered optional and is undertaken mainly in windy areas: in late autumn, taller shoots on bush roses can be cut back by up to half to prevent the bushes being damaged by the wind. The main pruning then takes place in late winter to early spring.

ABOVE Roses need attention throughout the year, including deadheading in summer if your display is to continue in perfect condition.

ABOVE Most roses are grafted on to a rootstock, which can produce suckers. Remove these when you see them.

Basic cuts

Cut shoots of roses back to either a bud or a shoot, preferably a strong one in both cases. Thinner wood can be cut with secateurs (pruners) while thick stems can be cut with either long-handled pruners or a pruning saw. It is important that your tools are well maintained and sharp, so that you make a clean cut with no tears or bruising. The cut should be just above a bud or shoot and should gently slope away from it so that any rain runs away and does not lie in the junction with the stem. Never cut through a stem between buds, as this will cause die-back from the point of the cut downwards to the bud. This may introduce infection into the plant or cause the stem to die back beyond the bud. This also applies to deadheading.

Training

There are several methods of training roses besides growing them as simple bushes. Long stems are usually best tied in or they will thrash about and tear other shoots

ABOVE A well-pruned floribunda rose showing the well-balanced shape and size of bush that should be aimed for.

with their thorns. If allowed to grow upright, they will tend to produce flowers only at the tops of their shoots. If they are pulled down into an arc, flower buds form all along the upper surface, resulting in more prolific flowering. Tie in rose stems either with special garden ties or soft garden string. For more permanent training, use tarred string.

ABOVE Deadheading is important to maintain continuous flowering. Cut back to the first leaf, bud or shoot.

Deadheading

This is a routine job needed by most roses. If allowed to remain on the bush, fading flowers can look unsightly and will detract from the beauty of those that remain. At this stage, the flower's life is over and seed formation begins, which is very costly in terms of the plant's energy. By cutting off the flower heads, energy is diverted into producing more flowers. On the other hand, there are some roses that have beautiful hips, so these should not be deadheaded. As a general principle when deadheading, cut back to the first healthy bud below the faded flower. Do not just cut the flower head off at random.

Suckers

Most roses are grafted on to a rootstock, often a wild rose. From time to time this rootstock can throw up a sucker from below the graft, often from below ground. This is usually readily identifiable, as it is usually very straight and looks completely different from the main rose. It should be removed as soon as it is seen or it can take over the bush. Dig back the soil around the plant to find its point of origin. Pull it away from where it joins the rootstock. Suckers cut off at ground level will regrow.

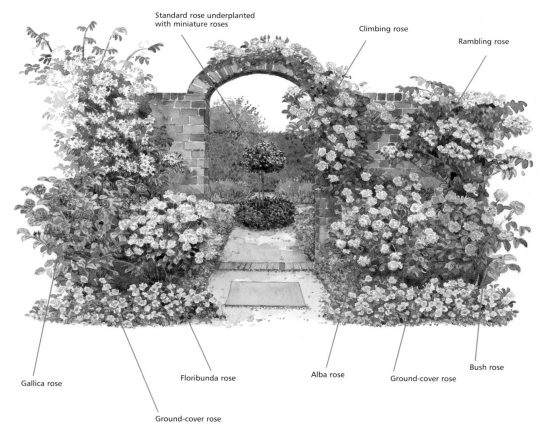

Standard rose underplanted with miniature roses

Climbing rose

Rambling rose

Gallica rose

Floribunda rose

Ground-cover rose

Alba rose

Ground-cover rose

Bush rose

A ROSE GARDEN There are a wide variety of roses. They all vary slightly in their initial training and established pruning, but within this variation the principles remain the same. The basic aim with all these different types of rose is to create a healthy plant, with no congestion or crossing wood that can rub against and damage other stems. The bushes and climbers should not be crowded, so that light can enter and air circulate. Deadheads should be removed to promote further flowering.

Bush roses

Bush roses are usually divided into two distinct types: hybrid teas, which produce single, large flowers, and floribundas, with clusters of flowers. These are some of the most popular of all roses, with a very wide range of colours available. Since they are relatively heavily pruned each year, they tend to take up little space. There is a certain upright formality about them, so they are mainly used in rose beds rather than in less formal, mixed beds with herbaceous plants.

Supports

Bush roses are usually grown as bushes and normally require no support at all, even when they are first planted.

Initial training

Plants are bought either as container or as bare-root plants. If you cannot plant bare-root roses straight away, heel them into a spare bit of ground, so that their roots do not dry out. Plant container roses at the same depth as they were in the pot. The best time for planting is between late autumn and early spring. Prune all

Some hybrid tea roses			
'Admiral Rodney'	Christopher	'Etoile de Hollande'	Pot o' Gold
Alec's Red	Columbus	Fragrant Cloud	'Prima Ballerina'
'Apricot Silk'	Congratulations	'Grandpa Dickson'	Remember Me
'Blessings'	Dawn Chorus	'Harry Wheatcroft'	Royal William
Blue Moon	'Deep Secret'	'Lovers Meeting'	Silver Anniversary
Buxom Beauty	'Doris Tysterman'	'National Trust'	Tequila Sunrise
Cherry Brandy	Elina	Peace	Whisky Mac

the shoots back to about 10–15cm (4–6in) above the soil level to a strong, outward-facing bud. If there are any weak, damaged or badly placed (i.e. crossing or rubbing) shoots, either cut these low down to a good bud or remove them completely if necessary. If a container rose is planted at any time other than winter, leave the initial pruning until its first winter.

Established pruning

Bush roses establish very quickly and a year after planting the pruning regime will become established. Deadhead the roses once the flowers begin to fade. In windy areas, in late autumn after flowering and before the winter winds set in, reduce all the shoots by about half to prevent

wind-rock and thrashing stems. The main pruning can start at any point between mid-winter and early spring, while the bushes are still dormant. If you cut back too early, growth is stimulated and you may have to prune again after a mild winter. Start by cutting out any dead, damaged or diseased wood, as well as any thin, weak growth, then deal with what is left. In the case of hybrid teas, cut back all stems to a strong outward-facing bud about 15–25cm (6–10in) above the ground. Shorten any laterals or side shoots to two or three buds. As the plants begin to age, cut out one or two of the older stems completely at the base to encourage new growth and rejuvenate the plant. With floribundas, the pruning is very

PRUNING A HYBRID TEA ROSE

1 As with most pruning, the first task is to remove any dead, diseased or damaged wood, cutting back to a bud in sound wood.

2 Next remove some of the older wood, especially if, as here, it has die-back, caused by bad pruning in the past in which the cut was made too high above a bud.

3 Cut back the remaining growth to an outward-facing bud, 15–25cm (6–10in) above the ground, or just above the previous year's pruning.

4 Any suckers, such as the one in front of this rose, should be removed from their point of origin below ground.

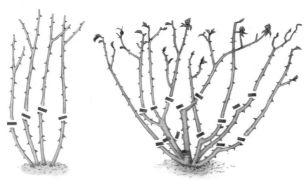

PRUNING A NEWLY PLANTED BUSH ROSE Plant new bush roses between autumn and early spring. All the stems will be too long when the rose arrives from the nursery. As soon as you have planted the rose, cut all stems back to an outward-facing bud, about 10–15cm (4–6in) above the ground.

PRUNING AN ESTABLISHED HYBRID TEA Hybrid teas are a very popular type of rose for the garden, and generally these are given the severest of pruning. In spring, after removing any dead or diseased wood, cut back all the remaining shoots to within 15–25cm (6–10in) of the ground, at an outward-facing bud.

PRUNING AN ESTABLISHED FLORIBUNDA The floribundas are pruned in a similar manner to the hybrid teas, but are not treated quite so harshly. After removing all the dead, damaged or diseased wood, cut back all the remaining shoots to about 25–30cm (10–12in) above the ground and any laterals to two or three buds.

similar but need not be so drastic. After removing dead, damaged or diseased wood as well as any weak growth, shorten each stem to about 25–30cm (10–12in) from the ground. Again, any laterals can be reduced to two or three buds.

As with most roses, any suckers that appear from below the graft should be removed at their point of origin, which in many cases is below ground. If left, they will produce different growth and flowers.

PRUNING A FLORIBUNDA ROSE

1 Floribundas can get tall, so it may be necessary to cut them back by about half in the autumn in order to prevent wind-damage.

2 In the spring remove any dead, diseased or damaged wood, cutting right back to a bud or shoot in sound wood.

3 Remove any shoots or branches that are crossing others, especially if they rub against them.

Some floribunda roses

Amber Queen	Iceberg
'Anne Harkness'	Irish Eyes
'Arthur Bell'	'Korresia'
Beautiful Britain	L'Aimant
Betty Harkness	Lilli Marlene
'Bonfire Night'	'Masquerade'
Centenary	Princess of Wales
'City of Leeds'	Remembrance
'English Miss'	Sexy Rexy
Fellowship	Sunset Boulevard
'Glenfiddich'	Trumpeter

4 Cut back the remaining shoots to a basic framework, about 25–30cm (10–12in) above the ground.

5 Weak shoots such as this should be cut right back to a stronger main stem or to the main framework.

ABOVE Here, more attention is required to even out the heights of the stems to produce a more rounded bush as well as removing weaker stems and cutting back stems to a bud.

Repeat-flowering shrub roses

Shrub roses have become increasingly popular and there have been several new introductions. They tend to make larger plants than hybrid teas and floribundas and are good as specimens or in large mixed plantings. They all need minium pruning or training when they are first planted.

Modern shrub roses

Start by removing any wood that is dead, damaged or diseased. Beyond that, there is not a great deal to do other than prune back the tips of a number of the side shoots. After a few years, remove a couple of the oldest main shoots every year or two to encourage new growth and prevent congestion. Some of the modern varieties with flowers in clusters should have their shoots cut back by up to one-third.

Ground-cover roses

Most are similar to the modern shrub roses but spread sideways rather than growing upwards. Apart from taking out any dead wood, you can usually leave these to fill their allotted space. Cut them back if they

ABOVE A favourite modern shrub rose, 'Constance Spry'. This rose is not repeat-flowering but is pruned in the same way.

stray too far. After a few years, remove some of the oldest wood to rejuvenate them.

Rugosa roses

These are similar to the modern shrub roses. Remove all the dead, damaged or diseased wood and then tip-prune the longer stems. When the plants are several years old, remove one or two of the oldest stems completely to the ground to keep the shrub vigorous by promoting fresh growth from the base.

ABOVE A Bourbon rose, 'Boule de Neige', which is not pruned too severely: just reduce stems by about one-third.

Hybrid musk roses

Take out all the dead, damaged and diseased wood, then cut back all the main stems by about one-third and shorten side shoots by about half. Once the bush has matured, cut one or two of the oldest main stems to the ground each year or so to rejuvenate the plant.

Bourbons, Portlands and China roses

These are old-fashioned roses, many of some antiquity. Although

ABOVE 'Old Blush China' is, as the name implies, an old China rose. The pale pink, double flowers, produced from summer to autumn, are lightly scented.

ABOVE 'Blanche Double de Coubert' is a Rugosa rose. The sweetly scented, white flowers open from pointed, pinkish buds from summer to autumn.

ABOVE 'Souvenir de la Malmaison' is a Bourbon rose with very fragrant, pale pink flowers. The flowers may be spoilt by wet weather.

ABOVE 'Madame Isaac Pereire', a Bourbon, makes a tall, loose bush and is better trained as a climber. The cerise-pink flowers are richly fragrant.

ABOVE A Rugosa rose that requires very little pruning other than removal of dead wood and tip-pruning of long stems.

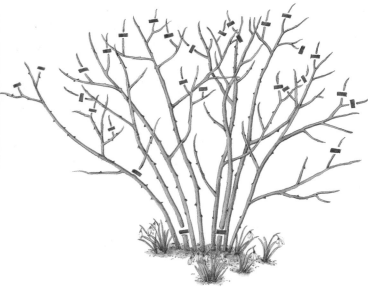

PRUNING AN ESTABLISHED MODERN SHRUB ROSE Most modern shrub roses are repeat-flowering, but there are some that are single-flowering and are treated in the same way. What little pruning there is should take place in the spring. Deadheading should be carried out throughout summer. After taking out any dead, diseased or damaged wood, cut back the tips of some of the longer shoots and remove one or two of the oldest stems completely. Other than that there is little to do.

the main flush of flowers is in early summer, they are repeat-flowering. The main pruning is in late winter to early spring before growth begins. (In windy gardens, it may also be necessary to reduce very long shoots by about a quarter in autumn.) In winter, as well as cutting out any dead, damaged or diseased wood, cut all shoots back by about one-third. Once the bush has reached maturity, remove one or two of the oldest stems every year or so as a programme of continuing rejuvenation. In windier gardens, more vigorous varieties with longer shoots can be tied down to a series of arched, pliable hazel sticks which are placed just inside the perimeter of the plant. The tops of the arches should be about 1m (3ft) above ground-level. This technique keeps the shoots steady in the wind and promotes increased flowering. The whole structure should be untied when you want to prune the rose, and then rebuilt with new sticks.

Some modern shrub roses	Some ground-cover roses	Some rugosa roses	Some hybrid musk roses	Some Bourbons, Portlands and China roses
'Abraham Darby'	'Cardinal Hume'	'Agnes'	'Buff Beauty'	'Boule de Neige'
'Charity'	'Fairyland'	'Belle Poitevine'	'Callisto'	'Bourbon Queen'
'Chaucer'	'Ferdy'	'Blanche Double de Coubert'	'Cornelia'	'Commandant Beaurepaire'
'Constance Spry'	'Flower Carpet'	'Fimbriata'	'Erfurt'	'Comte de Chambord'
'Gertrude Jekyl'	'Ice Fairy'	'F.J. Grootendorst'	'Francesca'	'Louise Odier'
'Graham Thomas'	'Jacquenetta'	'Fru Dagmar Hastrup'	'Golden Wings'	'Madame Isaac Pereire'
'Jacqueline Du Pré'	'John Cabot'	'Max Graf'	'Kathleen Ferrier'	'Old Blush China'
'Mary Rose'	'Nozomi'	'Pink Grootendorst'	'Penelope'	'Perle d'Or'
'Perdita'	'Snow Carpet'	'Roseraie de l'Ha'	'Prosperity'	'Souvenir de la Malmaison'
'Prospero'	'White Bells'	'Sarah van Fleet'	'Thisbe'	
'Warwick Castle'			'Will Scarlet'	
'Windrush'				

Single-flowering shrub roses

A second category of shrub roses comprises the older ones that flower only once, in the early summer. These are quintessential "English garden" plants. The soft shapes of the shrubs and subtle colours of the flowers allow them to fit in well in mixed borders, surrounded by perennials. There are a number of different groups.

Alba, Damask, Centifolia (Provence) and Moss roses

This is a large group of old-fashioned varieties, once the mainstay of many rose gardens. In spite of their single flowering, there are some gems among them. They are best pruned in summer, after they have finished flowering. First, remove any dead, damaged and diseased wood, then cut back all shoots by up to one-third of their length. After a few years, once the shrub becomes established, cut out completely one or two of the oldest main stems every year or so to promote ongoing rejuvenation. In windier gardens, tie more vigorous varieties with longer shoots down to a series of arched, pliable hazel sticks placed just inside the perimeter of the plant. The tops of the arches

ABOVE Moss roses, such as 'William Lobb', are usually pruned in summer after flowering when shoots are cut back by about one-third.

should be about 1m (3ft) above ground-level. This procedure keeps the shoots steady in the wind and promotes increased flowering. The whole structure should be untied for pruning and then rebuilt with new sticks.

Gallica roses

The main pruning of a Gallica rose is after it has finished flowering. Take out all dead, diseased and damaged wood. Cut back the side shoots to a good shoot or to the main stem itself. As these roses tend towards dense growth, in winter remove any dead material from the

ABOVE 'Köningen von Danemark', an Alba rose, is pruned in summer after flowering, cutting back the shoots by about one-third.

centre of the plant. It also helps to remove one or two of the oldest stems each year to help keep the shrub vigorous.

Species roses

Most species flower only once during the year. They need very little pruning beyond the removal of dead, damaged and diseased wood. You can also cut back any particularly long shoots that stray beyond their accepted bounds. Once the shrub is well established, cut out completely one or two of the oldest stems every year or so to promote replacement growth. Pruning should take place in winter.

Some Alba, Damask, Centifolia (Provence) and Moss roses

'Alba Maxima'
'Belle Amour'
'Chapeau de Napoléon'
'De Meaux'
'Fantin-Latour'
'Félicité Parmentier'
'Isphahan'
'Jeanne de Montefort'
'Königen von Danemark'
'Madame Hardy'

'Maiden's Blush'
'Robert le Diable'
'Spong'
'Unique Blanche'
'William Lobb'

Some Gallica roses

'Alain Blanchard'
'Anaïs Ségalas'
'Belle de Crécy'
'Cardinal de Richelieu'
'Charles de Mills'
'Duc de Guiche'
'Président de Sèze'

'Tuscany Superb'
'Versicolor'

Some species roses

Rosa ekae
R. glauca
R. moyesii
R. nitida
R. pimpinellifolia
R. rubiginosa
R. sericea
R. septipoda
R. willmottiae
R. xanthina

ABOVE 'Madame Hardy', one of the Damasks which are summer-pruned after flowering by cutting back the shoots by about one-third.

ABOVE *Rosa* × *centifolia* 'Cristata' ('Chapeau de Napoléon'), which, like all the Centifolias, is lightly pruned in summer after flowering.

ABOVE Deadheading is vital as it ensures that the rose flowers for the maximum length of time, as well as keeping the bush neat.

ABOVE 'Charles de Mills', one of the Gallicas. Prune in summer after flowering by cutting back the side shoots to a strong shoot.

PRUNING AN ESTABLISHED GALLICA ROSE Gallicas are pruned in summer by removing some of the side shoots back to a strong shoot or to a main stem. In winter some of the older wood is completely removed.

PRUNING AN ESTABLISHED ALBA ROSE Albas and the related roses are pruned after flowering, by cutting back most of the stems by about one-third. Some of the longer side shoots should be cut back to a main stem.

Miniature, patio and polyantha roses

Miniatures are essentially small bushes that are suitable for growing in containers or for growing anywhere where a small bush as opposed to a larger rose is required. There are three basic types: miniature roses, usually around 30cm (12in) high; patio roses, which are in effect small versions of floribunda roses; and polyantha roses, which are small bushes with clusters of small flowers.

Miniature roses

Plant the bush in the same way as a larger rose. Cut back the most sound shoots to about 8cm (3in) and discard any weak or damaged ones. During the winter of the following and subsequent years, again cut out any dead, diseased or damaged wood along with any weak shoots, or crossing or congested wood. This leaves you with next year's framework. Trim this slightly by tip-pruning all the shoots. After a few years, when the plant is well established, cut out one or two of the old stems completely so that the bush is rejuvenated. Some miniature roses respond better to harder pruning. If the above regime gives poor results, cut back the remaining shoots to about half or less of their length.

ABOVE Many gardeners are reluctant to remove weak growth, but it can congest a plant without adding to its effectiveness.

ABOVE The miniature rose Angela Rippon. Once a framework has been established, only a light tip-pruning is required.

ABOVE The softly coloured 'Ballerina', which is one of those hybrid musk or polyantha roses, that can be used in either a border or a pot.

Patio and polyantha roses

A patio rose forms a compact little bush that is usually covered in wide clusters of flowers throughout the summer, until stopped by the first hard frosts of autumn. Polyantha roses are small bushes, often with a graceful habit. The airy sprays of bloom associate particularly well with herbaceous perennials and other shrubs in a mixed border.

Pruning patio and polyantha roses is relatively easy, as it is the same as for the floribundas. On planting, cut back the stems to 8–10cm (3–4in)

ABOVE A patio rose, Top Marks. Patio roses when first planted have all their stems cut back to 8–10cm (3–4in) above the ground.

ABOVE Sweet Dream, a patio rose. These are pruned in spring, cutting back all the stems by up to two-thirds to outward-facing buds.

ABOVE Sweet Magic, a patio rose, which, once established, has one or two of the oldest stems removed each year to rejuvenate it.

PRUNING AN ESTABLISHED MINIATURE ROSE Miniature roses are pruned in the spring. In spite of their miniature size, they are treated no differently from a full-size rose. Initially, prune back all the shoots to about 8cm (3in). When established, remove all dead and damaged wood along with any weak growth, and then tip-prune the remaining shoots.

PRUNING AN ESTABLISHED PATIO OR POLYANTHA ROSE Patio roses are initially pruned in the same way as miniature roses. Once established, they are generally pruned in the spring. Pruning involves removing any dead or weak wood and cutting back any remaining stems by up to two-thirds. Deadhead throughout the summer.

above ground to a strong bud. Established pruning consists of removing dead, damaged or diseased wood and cutting back all stems to about half to two-thirds of their length to an outward-facing bud or a strong shoot. Every few years, take out one or two of the oldest stems to promote new growth.

ABOVE Polyantha roses, like 'Gloria Mundi', are pruned in spring in the same way as patio roses and are best deadheaded as the flowers fade.

Some miniature roses

Amber Sunset
Angela Rippon
Apricot Sunblaze
'Baby Bio'
Baby Masquerade
Blue Peter
Bush Baby
'Easter Morning'
Gentle Touch
Golden Penny
'Lavender Jewel'
'Little Flirt'
Mandarin
New Penny
Peach Sunblaze
Peek-a-boo
Peter Pan
Red Bells
Robin Redbreast
'Stars 'n' Stripes'
'Sweet Magic'
White Cloud

Some patio roses

Amber Hit
Anna Ford
Bonbon Hit
Boys' Brigade
Bright Smile
Carefree Days
Conservation
Danny Boy
Festival
Flower Power
Fond Memories
House Beautiful
Innocence
Make a Wish
Our George
Pearl Anniversary
Rainbow Magic
Shine On
Sweet Dream
Sweet Magic
Thank You
Top Marks
Wee Cracker

Some polyantha roses

'Ballerina'
'Bashful'
'Cameo'
'Coral Cluster'
Doc
'Eblouissant'
'Fairy Damsel'
Fairyland
'Gloria Mundi'
'Jean Mermoz'
'Katharina Zeimet'
Lovely Fairy
'Margo Koster'
Marjorie Fair
'Paul Crampel'
'Perle d'Or'
'White Cécile Brunner'
'White Pet'

Standard roses

Standard roses have always been popular. They make excellent centre-pieces for a formal bed and also work well in containers, especially when used in pairs, perhaps placed on either side of a path, entrance or flight of steps. Standards are roses that have been grafted on the top of a tall stem, traditionally either 1.1m (40in) (full standards) or 75cm (30in) (half-standards). Within this group, there are two other categories: bush varieties, which have a hybrid tea, floribunda, miniature or patio rose grafted on to the stem, and weeping varieties, which have a spreading ground-cover or rambler grafted on to a tall rootstock.

Supports

All standards need supporting, preferably to the point just above the graft, which is the weakest point on the stem. A stout stake is needed for most, held with a proper tree or rose tie, but smaller ones in a container can be supported by a cane. If the stake rots through, breaks or weakens, replace it. Special umbrella-like frames can be purchased for training weeping varieties.

Bush standards

Most standards are purchased ready grafted and with the initial shape

ABOVE Standard roses guarding the entrance to a lawn. They are an excellent sight and are easy to prune.

already in place. However, it is possible to create your own from scratch, by grafting the desired bush on to a stem of *Rosa rugosa*, for example. As these are no more than bushes on a stalk, they are pruned in the same way as the typical plant. So, standard patio roses are pruned as for ordinary patio roses, while miniature standards are pruned as for ordinary miniatures. The only difference is that any side shoots that develop on the main stem (the rootstock) should be removed as soon as they appear.

Weeping standards

These take a bit more effort, but are still not difficult. The stems have a tendency to rise into the air rather than weep and to get a good shape it is best to tie the stems in position on an umbrella-like frame that can be purchased from most garden centres. This not only allows you to train the stems downwards but also creates an even spread of stems around the crown of the plant. Little pruning is required until the standard has fully developed. In early autumn, remove all dead, damaged or diseased wood.

Ramblers can be very vigorous, so it is a good idea to remove wood that has flowered back to one or two buds above the graft. This will prevent the standard from becoming too crowded. At the same time, reduce all side shoots to just two or three buds. On less vigorous ramblers, simply remove one or two of the oldest stems each year, so that a balance is kept and the number of stems neither increases nor decreases. Standards created from ground-cover plants are not so vigorous, but they have a tendency to become more congested, so thin out stems as necessary and tie in or cut off any shoots that persistently grow upwards.

HOW TO PRUNE A STANDARD ROSE

1 Start, as always, by removing any dead, damaged or diseased growth. At the same time, take out any weak stems.

2 Cut out any stems that cross over others, especially if they are rubbing and causing wounds. This will also reduce congestion.

3 For standard polyanthas, reduce the remaining shoots by half to two-thirds of their length. Patios should just be tip-pruned.

4 The basic framework of a standard polyantha rose. Aim for an open tulip shape that is not too crowded with stems.

PRUNING A STANDARD ROSE

Most standards already have the initial shape formed when they are purchased from the nursery or garden centre. The intention is to keep this basic framework intact without it becoming too over-crowded, especially in the centre of the bush. Weeping standards will need a slightly different treatment, especially the vigorous types.

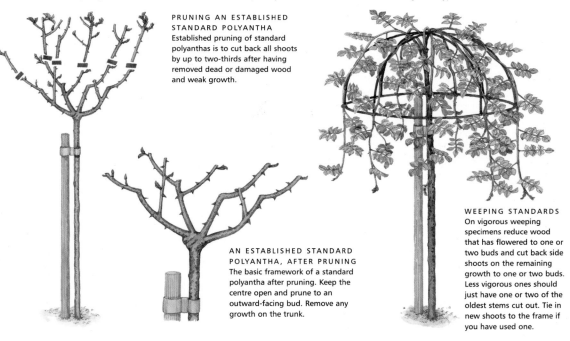

PRUNING AN ESTABLISHED STANDARD POLYANTHA
Established pruning of standard polyanthas is to cut back all shoots by up to two-thirds after having removed dead or damaged wood and weak growth.

AN ESTABLISHED STANDARD POLYANTHA, AFTER PRUNING
The basic framework of a standard polyantha after pruning. Keep the centre open and prune to an outward-facing bud. Remove any growth on the trunk.

WEEPING STANDARDS
On vigorous weeping specimens reduce wood that has flowered to one or two buds and cut back side shoots on the remaining growth to one or two buds. Less vigorous ones should just have one or two of the oldest stems cut out. Tie in new shoots to the frame if you have used one.

ABOVE As usual, it is important to remove any dead, damaged or diseased growth from weeping standard roses.

RIGHT These weeping standard roses, with their pale pink flowers, look striking planted on either side of a pathway, leading to an entrance in the hedge.

Climbers

Many people think of climbing roses as a single group, but in fact there are two: climbers and ramblers. The distinction is more than just a whim on some ancient rose-grower's part, and it affects the way they are pruned. Climbers are to all intents and purposes the same as bush roses except that they are much taller and need some form of support. Indeed, many varieties of rose may be grown as a large bush or trained as a climber.

Supports

Climbers can be trained in a number of ways. They can be tied in to wires stretched horizontally across walls or fences, or trained up vertical structures such as posts, obelisks and tripods. They can also be trained to cover pergolas, arbours and arches. They can be allowed to scramble into trees but this is mainly the province of the ramblers. If grown in trees, they are not very easy to prune and can lose their vitality.

Some climbing roses

'Aloha'	Handel
Altissimo	'Madame Alfred
Bantry Bay	Carrière'
'Climbing	'Maigold'
Iceberg'	'New Dawn'
'Climbing Mme	'Pink Perpetué'
Caroline Testout'	'Schoolgirl'
'Danse du Feu'	Summer Wine
Dublin Bay	'White Cockade'
'Gloire de Dijon'	'Zéphirine
Golden Showers	Drouhin'

PRUNING A CLIMBING ROSE

1 A climbing rose trained around a pillar. It can be pruned *in situ* or untied, pruned and then tied back into place.

2 After cutting out dead and damaged wood and reducing flowered stems by up to two-thirds, cut out a few of the older stems.

3 After pruning tie in the remaining shoots using proprietary rose ties or soft garden string. Do not strangle the plant.

4 When the rose is in flower, remove all the faded ones by cutting out their stem back to a leaf, shoot or bud.

RENOVATING AN OLD CLIMBING ROSE

1 Sometimes it is necessary to take drastic action in order to renovate an old climbing rose. A better support also needs to be provided.

2 The thickest of the stems should be cut through with a saw. Be careful when you reach the end of the cut that the stem does not split.

3 Thinner material can be cut out using secateurs (pruners) or long-handled pruners, again taking care not to split the remaining stubs.

4 The resulting stool. In most cases, it would be better to spread the removal of the old wood over two or more seasons.

Initial training

No pruning is required after planting climbing roses, beyond cutting back any damaged growth. As the new stems develop, spread them out so that they cover the whole of the area and tie them in. To stimulate side shoots, lightly cut back longer shoots. Continue to tie them in as they grow.

Established pruning

Prune between late autumn and early spring. Firstly, take out completely any dead, damaged or diseased wood. Also remove any weak growth. Prune back all flowered shoots by between half and two-thirds to a strong bud or shoot. After a few years, cut out one or two of the oldest, least productive stems,

ABOVE Deadhead as often as possible, cutting back the longer shoots that stick out over a path or into the middle of an archway.

either right back to the base or to a strong shoot low down. Tie in all the new growth to fill gaps and extend the framework. Avoid cutting back too vigorously, especially in the initial stages, as many climbing versions of bush varieties may revert to the bush habit.

ABOVE A mixture of climbers provides interest throughout summer. Careful pruning will ensure that no one plant dominates.

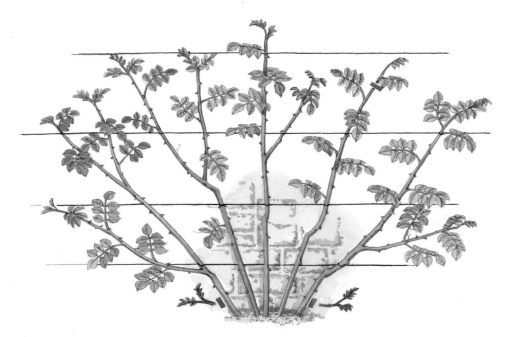

PRUNING A CLIMBING ROSE Climbing roses can be trained up a variety of supports. They tend not to be too vigorous and so are suitable for arches and the like, where more restrained growth is required. Train the rose so that it covers as much as possible of its allotted space. After flowering cut the flowered shoots up to two-thirds back to a shoot or strong bud. Also, remove any suckers that appear at the base of the rose.

Ramblers

Ramblers differ in many ways from climbers. They generally produce longer stems, which makes them suitable for scrambling through trees. Most flower best on the previous year's wood and produce a single flush. The best time to prune them is in summer after flowering.

Supports

Ramblers are very versatile. They can be trained against parallel wires on a wall or fence, or over frames such as obelisks, pergolas, arches or arbours. Many are excellent for growing up through old trees. Whatever the supports, they should be strongly mounted.

Initial training

Plant in the winter months and cut back any damaged wood. If the stems are long, prune them back to 45cm (18in) to stimulate new growth. As the new shoots appear, tie them in, spreading them out to get maximum coverage of the available space.

Established pruning

Many gardeners find the task of pruning ramblers so daunting that

ABOVE 'Bobbie James' is a very vigorous rambler that is suitable for growing through trees. Be careful when pruning because it has very vicious thorns.

Some rambling roses

'Aimée Vibert'	'Dorothy Perkins'	'Sander's White'
'Albéric Barbier'	'Félicité Perpétue'	'The Garland'
'American Pillar'	'Goldfinch'	'Veilchenblau'
'Bobbie James'	'Paul's Himalayan Musk'	'Violette'
'Debutante'	'Rambling Rector'	'Wedding Day'

they just ignore them and let them get on with it. While this approach is successful for a while, you will soon find a tangled mass of stems, with a diminution of flowering capability. When growing vigorous ramblers through tall trees, however, pruning may not be practical. In most other cases, pruning is not really difficult. Firstly, cut out any

ABOVE 'Veilchenblau', unlike 'Bobbie James', is almost thornless and a good rambler for places near which people will pass.

ABOVE 'American Pillar' is a very old, small-flowered rambler that remains popular in spite of its tendency to get mildew.

PRUNING A RAMBLER

1 A sad-looking rambler that has just finished flowering. Now is the right time to prune it, starting as always by removing any dead wood.

2 Remove any stems that are rubbing against others, and any others that are causing too much congestion; an open framework is required.

3 To rejuvenate the plant, cut out some of the old stems to the base each year. Cut back other stems that have flowered to a good shoot.

4 Tie in all the shoots, spreading them widely over the support so that the whole area is evenly covered. Tie in new shoots as they develop.

dead, damaged or diseased wood. The next task is to encourage new wood. Most rambling roses produce new shoots directly from ground-level, so take out up to one-third of the oldest shoots, which will be replaced with new ones. Do this immediately after flowering, and the new growth will have matured enough to flower the following year. Some gardeners like to take the whole framework of stems off the wall and sort it out on the ground, while others prefer to attack the plant *in situ*, following each stem as it winds through the rest. If a vigorous rambler becomes overgrown from neglect, it will normally tolerate being cut back very hard to the base, but the best policy is to do a little every year.

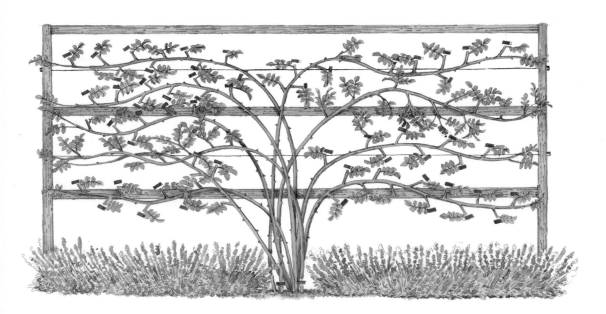

PRUNING A RAMBLING ROSE Ramblers can become very large and cover a wide area. Some gardeners find it easier to remove the whole plant from its support and prune it on the ground, replacing the shoots when they have finished. Remove some of the old shoots from the base to encourage new flowering growth. Try to spread the shoots as widely as possible across the support.

Training over structures

Both climbers and ramblers look sensational trained over a structure of some kind, preferably over a walkway or seating area so that you are able to enjoy their beauty and scent to the full.

Choice of rose

Virtually any of the ramblers or climbers can be used. If you will be in close proximity to the rose, avoid varieties with vicious thorns, such as 'Bobbie James', and choose a thornless one, such as 'Zéphirine Drouhin'. This is less critical for larger structures where the roses are kept well away from passers-by. Another factor, especially for arbours over sitting areas, is to choose one with a good fragrance. Scented, long-flowering roses, such as 'Mme Alfred Carrière', will give much pleasure and this one has the advantage of being almost thornless. You will often find

ABOVE A rose climbing up the pillar of a pergola. Short climbers are ideal for this, with other plants providing the cover for the top.

ABOVE This arbour will be much more attractive once it is covered with roses, making it a pleasant place to sit and relax.

that the roses will flower on the top of the arch or pergola, but leave the sides devoid of blooms. The best way of coping with this is to plant another, shorter-growing variety to provide flower-power for this area. For roses that flower only once, in early summer, a viticella clematis can be grown over the structure for later attraction. Clematis in this group are cut to the ground each spring, so they do not interfere with the early flowering of the rose.

Supports

Whatever the structure you create, it must be solidly constructed. A climber or rambler in full leaf, spread over a large structure, is like a large sail in a wind and will put great pressure on the construction. Check regularly that it is still in sound condition. There must be ample points at which to tie in the rose. It can be a good idea to cover the top of the structure with a wide-mesh wire netting. This is almost invisible when covered by the rose, and prevents stray stems hanging down

as well as providing plenty of tying-in points. When building an arch or any other structure, remember that the rose will project from the uprights and hang down a little way from the top, so allow extra space between posts and in the height.

Training

Plant the climber or rambler on the outside of the structure so as not to restrict the space inside. Spread the stems out so that they cover the whole width of the upright, and wrap them around if it is solid, such as a brick pier. Tie the shoots down well at the top and spread them out so that the whole area is covered. Check regularly that there are no stems, especially thorny ones, projecting outwards. Once established, prune as described on the previous pages, depending on whether the rose is a climber or a rambler.

ABOVE A rose trained round a tripod. Wrapping it round a support in this manner ensures a good coverage and plenty of flowers.

Training over hoops

In smaller gardens there may not be room to accommodate large structures that can support roses. However, as long as you do not choose too vigorous a rose, it is still possible to grow many of the larger shrubs and some of the climbers and ramblers by creating a domed structure of sticks, to which the stems can be tied.

Choice of roses

Most of the larger shrub roses, as well as the climbers and ramblers, respond well if their stems are arched over. Many roses flower only at the tips of their stems, but if the stem is bent over in a low arch, it will produce flowering buds along the length of the stem. This method is suitable for shrub roses and the less vigorous climbers and ramblers.

ABOVE 'Isaphan' completely covers its support, creating a dome of flowers. New shoots are beginning to appear at the top.

Supports

You can commission a blacksmith to make a set of metal hoops, but this may be expensive. An alternative is to use thin flexible sticks, such as from a hazel or pollarded sweet chestnut. Insert one end into the ground, bend it over and drive the other end into the soil. The top of the arc should be about 1m (3ft) from the ground and the ends should be about 1–1.2m (3–4ft) apart. Arrange these in a circle around the rose, with each hoop overlapping the next.

Training and pruning

Essentially the pruning is as it would be for the type of rose you are using. You should also tie in the stems of the rose in an arch around the hoops, as well as in a dome across the circle formed by the hoops.

HOW TO TRAIN A ROSE OVER A HOOP

1 Choose some pliable rods – hazel is very good – that are straight and can be easily bent into a hoop without breaking.

2 Push these into the ground around the plant, forming a series of hoops to which the stems of the plant can be tied.

3 Carefully pull down the shoots and tie them to the hoops, arching them slightly. Some can be tied across the centre of the circle that you have created.

4 The finished plant does not look very engaging at first, but the curved stems will soon produce a mass of young flowering shoots that will look spectacular.

5 The rose bush in the spring, just before flowering. It is now an attractive dome of foliage and will soon be covered with a mass of flowers.

Training over pillars, tripods and obelisks

Sometimes it is necessary to create a vertical accent somewhere in a border, or even in the garden as a whole, but there may be insufficient room for a large structure. One of the simplest solutions is a column, either a wooden pole or a brick or stone pillar. Increasingly common are tripods and obelisks, either bought or home-made, which serve the same function.

Choice of roses

As long as they are not too vigorous, there is a wide choice of climbers and ramblers that are suitable for growing up a simple column. The ramblers are possibly best, as their stems are reasonably flexible and they respond well to training. There are a number that are relatively short, reaching only 2–3m (6–10ft), and these are the best ones from which to choose.

Supports

These should be well bedded into the ground so they will not blow over in the wind. Stems can be tied directly to the pole, but for a wider range of anchor points, wrap some wire-netting around the pole. Tripods and obelisks should have horizontal bars or wires. These prevent stems from slipping down the pole.

Training and pruning

The aim is to make certain that the stems do not run straight up the pole, otherwise you are likely just to get a few flowers at the top. Wrap the stems round in a spiral, twisting them both clockwise and anti-clockwise. This is best done when the shoots are young as they are more pliable. Once established, prune as for a climber or rambler.

TRAINING A ROSE UP A TRIPOD

1 Most tripods are in the open ground, but it is also possible to create one for smaller plants in a large container.

2 Erect a strong structure of three to five poles or canes. Make certain that they are well bedded and will not blow over.

3 Secure the canes well at the top. Use nails or wire in the case of poles and string if you are using canes.

4 Cross bars should be nailed to the uprights, or string or wire wound round to offer support for the climbing rose.

TRAINING A ROSE UP A PILLAR

1 Dig a hole at least 60cm (2ft) deep. Put in the post and check that it is upright. Backfill with earth, ramming it firmly down as it is filled.

2 Roses can be tied directly to the post, but a more natural support is created if wire netting is secured to the post.

3 Plant the rose a little way out from the pole to avoid the compacted area. Lead the stems to the wire netting and tie them in. Roses, unlike some other climbers, will need to be tied in as they climb.

4 Single-post pillars add interest to flower borders. This 'American Pillar' rose has clothed the thin post, creating a well-filled-out, irregular shape.

Training through trees

There are few more glorious sights than a large tree filled to overflowing with a rose in full bloom. To achieve this you need a suitable tree in the right place.

ABOVE 'Paul's Himalyan Musk' wound round a tree. Usually the flowers appear well up into the tree, so these lower ones are a bonus.

ABOVE The stems of a rambler reaching up into the top of a tree. Note how the rose has been planted away from the base of the tree.

Choice of roses

The more vigorous ramblers, such as 'Félicité Perpétue', 'Rambling Rector' or 'Bobbie James', are ideal for this purpose. Choose one that will continue to flower well on old wood, as it is not always practical to prune a vast rambler in a tree.

Supports

Many people think an old tree is needed for this, but while the tree should be large, it must not be aged and weak. A large rose scrambling through a tree will add considerably to its weight and a weak tree will be doubly vulnerable in a gale. Choose a healthy tree such as an old apple tree that may be past its best fruiting, but is still strong.

Training and pruning

Plant the rose around 1.5m (5ft) away from the trunk of the tree (any closer and it will be deprived of light and moisture). Plant on the windy side of the tree, which will blow the rain towards its roots and blow the stems into rather than away from the crown. Ideally, this should also be the sunny side, where there is most light. Train the stems to a rope or poles that run from the base of the rose into the lower branches of the tree where they meet the trunk. Make certain that this structure does not chafe the tree, cushioning it if necessary. Once the rose has grown into the tree, spread out the stems and tie them in so that they clamber up through as wide an area as possible in the crown. To prune, take out any dead, damaged or diseased wood and every few years remove some of the older wood. No further pruning is usually required.

TRAINING A ROSE THROUGH A TREE

1 Plant the rose well away from the base of the tree where it can receive rain and sun. Remove any ivy in the tree or it may swamp the rose.

2 Make certain that there is plenty of well-rotted organic material dug into the soil in order to provide a good start for the rambler.

3 Plant the rose to the same depth as it was in its container or nursery bed. Spread out the roots and water well before mulching.

4 To get the rose to start to climb into the tree, tie the stems to canes that slope from the base of the rose into the tree.

Training over trellis

Trellis panels are ideal for roses. They can be seen from both sides and create a very effective screen between two areas in a garden. Trellis can also be used as breaks across a long garden or to surround a garden within a garden, or even on the garden's boundaries. You might, for example, wish to separate a kitchen garden from an ornamental garden. Lengths of trellis can incorporate an archway that is also covered with roses. Generally, trellis panels are not very high and roses grown against them are easy to train and prune.

Choice of roses

Virtually any climbing or rambling rose can be used. As long as you are prepared to control them, even the more vigorous ones can be used. Trellis is, however, ideal for shorter, less vigorous roses that stay within 2–3m (6–10ft).

Supports

Trellis can be bought as panels or can be home-made. The beauty of trellis is that it has plenty of horizontal and vertical bars to which the stems can be tied, making it easy to create an even coverage. The upright poles that support the panels must be well anchored as they will take a lot of stress, particularly in a wind.

Training and pruning

Allow plenty of space between the roses so that the overlap between adjacent plants when fully grown is minimized. Train the shoots horizontally or in a fan shape to produce as wide a coverage as possible. Tie in any loose shoots as they grow. Pruning is as for climbers or ramblers, as previously described.

TRAINING A ROSE AGAINST WALL-MOUNTED TRELLIS

1 Plant the rose at least 30cm (12in) away from the base of the wall. Ensure that the soil has been well provided with organic material.

2 After planting, remove any dead or damaged growth and cut out any weak shoots that will not develop properly.

3 Train the shoots towards the trellis with canes and tie in the stems to the trellis as soon as they reach it.

4 Spread the shoots of the rose out as widely as possible so that the rose will eventually cover as much of its allotted space as possible.

Rope swags

Roses trained on rope swags (a "calenary") can be used as a very decorative boundary or along the side of a path. A swag is a very effective way of growing climbing or rambler roses in a small garden.

Choice of roses

The roses chosen should be vigorous and have flexible stems. Ramblers are the best bet. Since they will flower mainly along the ropes, it can be a good idea to plant one of the less vigorous climbers that will only climb as far as the top of the post to cover the upright with flowers.

Supports

Solid posts at distances of about 2.5m (8ft) are required to support a thick rope that will dip slightly in the middle. Do not let it dip too low as the rope will stretch with time and can sag. The rope should ideally be 5cm (2in) in diameter, the type sold by ship's chandlers.

LEFT A prolific swag of roses that covers the supporting rope very well. Some gardeners prefer a narrower band of roses so that the swag-shape is more in evidence.

Training and pruning

Plant the rose at the base of the upright, preferably at least 30cm (12in) away from it. Train the stems upwards in a spiral, then wrap them along the ropes. Spread the rose out to both sides of the upright. Alternatively, you might wish to plant a different rose on either side of the upright and then train the roses in different directions at the top. The pruning that is required depends on whether you use climbers or ramblers. Cut out any vigorous sideways shoots so that the line of the swag is maintained. After a few years, cut out some of the older stems in order to rejuvenate the plants. This will entail either unravelling all the stems and tying in the ones that remain or, if it is simpler, following the old stem through the swag and cutting it out in sections.

TRAINING ROSES ALONG ROPE SWAGS

Rope swags of roses are not difficult to achieve, as long as the posts are firmly embedded in the ground and the ropes are strong and well attached to their support. Choose a thick rope because thin ones can look silly. Make certain that the ropes are well secured to their poles, using galvanized or stainless-steel fittings, which will not rust.

INITIAL TRAINING Train the roses up the post, preferably winding them around to create a better coverage and then along the ropes. The stems can be wound around the ropes, but should still be tied in.

ESTABLISHED PRUNING Keep the rose pruned so that it does not become too top heavy, or the wind may destroy it. Tie in the new stems throughout the summer as well as deadheading.

Perennials and Annuals

When thinking of pruning, most gardeners will think first of woody plants, such as trees, shrubs and climbers, but, if they are to perform to their best, perennials and annuals also need some attention. The main reason why they are not included in most pruning books is that they die back each year and start afresh the following year, so they can be left to their own devices. But one of the reasons we grow them is to add to the appeal of our gardens, and they are undoubtedly improved with a bit of care.

Trees and shrubs form the backbone of our gardens, while perennials and annuals provide the filling, giving colour and excitement that changes as the months go by. Some perennials have more than one season of interest, and the garden can look quite different from one month to another. Annuals, however, flower mainly throughout the summer. The advantage with annuals is that you can change your colour scheme from one year to the next, giving quite a different feel to the garden each time.

Pruning perennials and annuals is not a difficult task, and there is not such a strict regime as with woody subjects.

LEFT A garden of softly coloured flowers. In order to maintain this level of attraction, the plants will have to be regularly deadheaded.

Pruning perennials and annuals

Perennials and annuals are the colourful mainstay of the flower garden, providing colour throughout the year in both beds and containers. While they can be left to their own devices, a little attention to pruning will extend their flowering period and enhance their attractiveness.

ABOVE Sweet Williams (*Dianthus barbatus*) are usually grown as a biannual, but if they are cut back to new buds after flowering they will flower again the following year as a perennial.

Perennials

Although the term "perennial" can refer to any plant that continues for more than one year, it is usually used in the garden to refer to herbaceous plants that disappear below ground at some point during the year, and reappear the following year. They are deservedly popular, both as flowering and foliage plants. On the whole, their flowering period is relatively short, but their season can be extended with appropriate pruning, and this may even result in a second flowering. Even if there is no repeat flowering, pruning will often result in a new flush of leaves, which will turn the plant into a foliage feature. The pruning of perennials is a continual process throughout the year, not, as with most shrubs, a once-a-year effort.

Annuals

What we refer to as annuals in gardening are not always annuals. Many are short-lived perennials that are better treated as annuals and thrown away at the end of the year, while others are biennials, which flower in their second year. None of this affects the pruning, except that some, such as sweet Williams (*Dianthus barbatus*) and antirrhinums, can be pruned back at the end of the year to provide another display the following year. Generally, annuals are pruned to keep them flowering for as long as possible and to ensure that they stay neat and compact over their long growing season.

ABOVE Perennials need to be provided with some form of support. A range of different types, such as a tripod, canes and pea-sticks, can be seen in this spring picture.

ABOVE Most perennial climbers need no pruning other than cutting down once they have finished. They are helped by having a little initial training to make certain that the shoots find their support.

ABOVE Reduce the flowering height of Michaelmas daisies (*Aster*) by cutting them down at an early stage, causing them to regrow.

ABOVE Petunias will perform over the whole summer and well into the autumn if they are regularly deadheaded to conserve energy.

ABOVE Repeatedly cutting sweet peas for flower arrangements as well as deadheading will produce a constant supply of flowers.

Tools

The tools required are likely to be those that any gardener already has to hand. The main requirement is for secateurs (pruners), although for the softer stems of annuals, scissors will do just as well. Shears are useful for quickly clipping whole plants, and some gardeners even use the lawn mower to shear over large quantities of pulmonarias, for example, in order to promote a fresh crop of leaves.

Timing

Perennials can be pruned at almost any time. In some cases, pruning starts as soon as growth emerges, when the tips of shoots are removed to promote bushiness. At the end of the season, dead stems can be cut back. In between, there is a constant removal of dead flowers and damaged stems, and adjustments of every kind. The pruning of perennials and annuals is an ongoing process, so you should wander round your borders (and containers) with secateurs in hand at least once a week, if possible. This also gives you the chance to look at and appreciate your plants.

Some gardeners like to remove the final dead stems in the autumn, while others prefer to wait until late winter so that the birds can feed on the remaining seeds.

ABOVE Hanging baskets, window boxes and other containers filled with annual flowers benefit from being deadheaded on a regular basis, as well as having any overlong stems cut back to rejuvenate and prolong the display.

Pruning and training perennials

Most gardens include some perennials in the borders, sometimes whole swathes of them creating drifts of colour. In order to maintain the appearance of such beds, as well as of the many perennials grown in containers, regular pruning is essential.

Bushing out plants

Quite a number of the more bushy perennials, such as *Dianthus*, make better plants if they are encouraged to bush out. Pinching out the growing tips stimulates side shoots to develop. This can be done with scissors or with your fingers, preferably at an early stage in the plant's development.

Dwarfing plants

In small gardens, some plants can grow too large for their allotted position. Michaelmas daisies (*Aster*), for example, may grow to 1.2m (4ft) in situations where it would be preferable to have them at 60cm (2ft). Allow the plants to develop normally. When they are about 45–60cm (18–24in) tall, you can cut them back to the ground. They will start to grow again, but should flower when they have reached only around 60cm (2ft). This works best with plants that

ABOVE Dianthus will bush out if the tips are removed from the young plants. This helps to create a much more floriferous shape.

are clump- or mat-forming with many individual stems, such as *Aster* and *Sanguisorba*.

Deadheading

Throughout the season, deadheading will help in two ways. Firstly, flowers tend to get lost among masses of dead and dying flowers. Secondly, seed formation uses up a lot of the plant's energy, and if the flower-heads are removed before this gets under way, all this energy is diverted into providing more flowers. The flowered stems of some perennials should be cut right to the base

(single-flowered stems), while others should be cut back to the first bud or shoot, which will then branch out and produce further flowers.

Cutting back for foliage

Some plants, such as many of the geraniums, *Alchemilla* and *Pulmonaria*, will produce a second flush of leaves if the plant is cut back completely after flowering. In most cases, the foliage will be vigorous enough to turn the plant into an effective foliage plant. If the old leaves are left on, they can look lacklustre and be a host to mildew and other fungal diseases.

MAKING A CAT'S CRADLE

1 Push some canes into the ground in a random pattern around and through the plant. Cut off the tops of the canes so that they will be hidden when the plant grows.

2 Tie strings around the canes, forming an interlaced pattern of individual cells through which the plant stems will grow.

3 The finished support. The network of strings will prevent the stems, once they have grown, from falling over, and yet it will remain hidden.

DIFFERENT METHODS OF SUPPORT

1 A proprietary plant support. The uprights are pushed into the ground and then the stems grow through the mesh, providing a strong support.

2 Proprietary interlinked stakes can be used to support plants by placing them around and, if necessary, through the middle of the plant.

3 For larger areas or drifts of plants sheep netting or other large-mesh netting can be supported between strong stakes.

Autumn clear-up

As the year progresses, more and more plants will have finished flowering and the borders will gradually fill up with dead or dying stems, leaves and flowers. If the borders still have plenty of late-flowering plants, the old material should be removed to show up the remaining ones to their best advantage. Once the majority have finished, there are two differing opinions as to what should be done. Some gardeners leave the remaining stems over winter so that birds can gather seed and insects during the winter months. Then everything is cut down in spring. Others like to cut down everything as soon as

4 For more upright plants such as delphiniums, a cylinder of large-mesh wire-netting can be used. Support this with a strong stake.

5 For single-stemmed plants a cane can be inserted behind the plant, where it is less likely to be seen, and the stem fastened with string or ties.

possible to keep the garden neat and save time the following spring. If you do leave them till spring, be certain to cut the dead material away before the new shoots appear at the base, as it can be difficult to cut this

out without damaging the new growth. Often a compromise is the best solution, cutting back some plants to reduce the workload later, but leaving enough for the birds to enjoy in the autumn.

USING PEA STICKS

1 If available, a cheap method of support is to use hazel branches pushed into the ground around the growing plant.

2 The tips of the branches are bent over and intertwined – and tied if necessary – to form a network of twigs through which the plant stems grow.

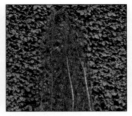

3 Support climbers and taller clumps of plants with bunches of sticks, pushed firmly in the ground and tied together.

4 When cutting back plants, do not leave it too late or the spring growth will make it difficult to remove the old stems without damaging the new ones.

Pruning annuals

Annuals are regaining some of their former popularity, not so much as bedding plants in beds and borders, but as interesting subjects for containers. To make sure they perform at their best, they need constant pruning. Just checking them over once a week will improve them considerably.

Shaping the plants

Many annuals benefit from being pinched out to make them more bushy. Taking out the tips of the main shoots as soon as the plant starts to develop, either with scissors or with your fingers, will make the plant produce more shoots. Constant pinching out will produce a very dense, bushy plant, and this technique can also be used to shape plants. For example, by pinching out side shoots at a certain distance from the main stem, you can make some plants grow taller to form dense columns or pyramids. Others, cascade chrysanthemums being a good example, can be shaped to form dense cascades of flowers. The upright shoots of many trailing plants that are used in hanging baskets and other containers can be removed to encourage the plant to trail.

ABOVE Straggly plants can be cut back toward late summer so that they are more compact and neater with new foliage and flowers.

TIDYING UP

1 Once annuals have started to produce seed they should either be removed or cut back to prevent too much self-sowing.

2 The trimmings or the removed plants can be put on the compost heap, the heat from which should kill any remaining seed.

DEADHEADING ANNUALS

1 Dead flowers running to seed in an annual display not only spoil its appearance but also slow down the production of new flowers.

2 Cut off the dead flowers with secateurs (pruners) or scissors if it is easier. Some flowers can just be pulled off by hand.

3 The same window box after the dead flowers have been removed. It looks more attractive and will produce more flowers.

PINCHING OUT

1 Many annuals have a tendency to grow tall and straggly, but these can be improved by pinching out the tops to make them bush out.

2 (*right*) This *Senecio cineraria* has bushed out into an attractively shaped plant after the tip of the central shoot was removed.

Annual climbers

A number of the annual climbers, sweet peas (*Lathyrus odoratus*) being a good example, benefit from the removal of the tips of the main shoots. This encourages the plant to produce plenty of side shoots, which can be spread widely to cover a large area. Allowing the leading shoot to develop by itself will often result in a tall, spindly plant that does not flower freely.

ABOVE A number of annuals benefit from a support, such as this *Thunbergia alata*. The support is well hidden under the foliage.

Deadheading

As soon as the flower of an annual is pollinated, it will start setting seed. This is very expensive in terms of the plant's energy. If the flower is removed before the seed develops, all this energy is channelled into new flowers as the plant continues to try to reproduce itself. Far more flowers, and a longer flowering season, will be achieved by deadheading. Besides, the plant will look much more attractive without the dead flowers.

Rejuvenating

As the season progresses, so the stems of annuals grow longer and longer. They can look particularly straggly in containers. In most instances, these can be cut back not only to make the plant look neater, but also to rejuvenate it so that it produces new stems. These new stems will often produce larger flowers than the ones produced at the tips of straggling stems. The superb baskets you see in the autumn are not just the result of good feeding and watering, but also constant pruning.

In some cases, flowers may take a while to reappear, but usually the new foliage that is produced will add a fresh note to the display. Foliage, in many cases, is just as important as flowers in an arrangement.

CUTTING SWEET PEAS

1 Most annuals will produce a lot more flowers if the developing seed pods are cut off, as setting seed uses a great deal of energy.

2 Cutting flowers for indoor decoration will help to encourage the formation of even more flowers. They run to seed if left uncut.

Directory of Ornamental Plants

The preceding pages give detailed information on strategies for pruning most ornamental trees, shrubs and climbers. The following is an alphabetical directory of plants, giving times and methods of pruning each plant. The plants listed are those that are among the most commonly grown in gardens.

Some pruning techniques are more involved than others, but none is beyond the capabilities of most gardeners. Pruning, like anything else, takes practice, but you will soon be able to prune the range of plants growing in your garden with confidence. If you are in any doubt, simply err on the safe side and do not take off too much. It is mainly when pruning evergreens (including many conifers) where caution has to be exercised, as some are not quite so willing to reshoot from old wood. Generally, trimming back into the current year's growth is safe.

In all cases, remove dead, damaged or diseased wood as well as any weak wood as a matter of routine. Also follow the general principles of pruning. For example, when cutting back, do so to a strong bud or to a strong shoot. If you follow these simple rules, then the plants in your garden will perform well year after year.

LEFT Regular attention to pruning helps to create a healthy and well-balanced garden. Different plants need different types of attention, none of which is complicated, although all are important.

Abelia × grandiflora

ABELIA
Abelia
An evergreen shrub that flowers in summer on the previous year's wood. The main pruning is in the summer after flowering when some of the oldest wood is removed to encourage new growth from the base, which generally breaks readily. A second pruning is required in early spring to remove any dead wood and any stems that have been damaged during the winter. Some of the more tender varieties are grown as wall shrubs and new shoots should be tied into wires as they appear.

ABUTILON
Flowering maple
Tender evergreen and deciduous shrubs that are mainly grown in pots and put out in summer or given a warm, sheltered place in cooler areas. Wall-trained specimens (*A. vitifolium*) should be allowed to develop with a leader, a replacement being encouraged if the original one is broken. The main pruning is deadheading (important on this plant).

Abutilon megapotamicum

No other pruning is usually required. *A. megapotamicum* can also be wall-trained as well as planted as a free-standing shrub. Older wood can be cut out in mid-spring and the previous year's wood cut back by about one-third. Any wood that has died should be cut back to a good shoot.

ACER
Maples
Deciduous trees that can be grown with clear trunks (especially those with attractive bark) or as multi-stemmed trees. Pruning should only be carried out when the trees are dormant, in winter, otherwise they bleed badly. Large varieties can be trained as central leader trees and little subsequent pruning is required. Multi-stemmed species and varieties should be pruned as a bush tree on a short leg or trunk. Once developed, little further pruning is necessary. Some variegated varieties revert and any such shoots should be removed when they are seen, even in summer (if caught at this stage the cuts are too small for bleeding to be a problem).

ACTINIDIA
Actinidia
Twining, mainly deciduous climbers that are grown for their foliage. Best suited to training on walls or fences. Pruning should take place in the latter half of winter or early spring. On planting, cut back stems to a few strong buds on each. Train five or six of the strongest resulting shoots on to the support, spreading them widely. Remove the rest of the shoots. In the next winter, cut back all shoots by half to two-thirds and tie in the new shoots during the summer. From now prune only to contain its

Actinidia kolomikta

size, cutting back shoots to the desired length. Remove some of the old wood in late winter to promote new growth.

AKEBIA
Chocolate vine
A vigorous deciduous climber that twines for support. It can be grown on any support used for climbers. Allow five or six shoots to develop and tie these in, spreading them out. Cut back by about two-thirds to promote new shoots and tie these in as necessary, as they develop. Once established, the plant can become very vigorous and need cutting back to contain it. Remove some of the old shoots from time to time. It is an early flowerer, and any pruning should take place after this, in mid- to late spring.

ALNUS
Alder
Deciduous trees. They can be grown as either single- or multi-stemmed trees. Initial training is needed if a single stem is required but the plant will usually develop into a multi-stemmed tree of its own accord. No pruning is required once fully grown although many, if they grow too large, can be pollarded, and will readily regenerate from the stump. Any pruning that is required can be done in winter.

AMELANCHIER
Deciduous trees or large shrubs. With care these can be grown as a single-stemmed tree, but they are more inclined to grow with multiple stems. The best time to tackle any pruning is during the winter. During initial training and subsequent pruning, the main aim should be to ensure that the branches stay open and do not

Amelanchier lamarckii

become crossed and congested. *A. stolonifera* produces suckers around the base and these need to be controlled to prevent it becoming vastly overgrown.

AMPELOPSIS
Vigorous, deciduous climbers, grown mainly for their foliage, that cling with the aid of tendrils. They will grow on most types of support, including trees. Little initial training is required other than tying in to its support. In positions where it can ramp about, it can be left to its own devices, but elsewhere, especially on walls, it should be controlled by pruning back long shoots in spring if necessary to near the main branches. In summer, cut back any excessive growth to a strong bud. Make certain that it does not find its way into gutters and under the eaves.

ARBUTUS
Strawberry tree
Evergreen trees with interesting bark. They are generally open, shrubby trees. They need good staking until they are established. Little initial training is required unless you want to train them as a standard tree, in which case the early removal of the lower branches is necessary. Thereafter little pruning is required beyond the removal of damaged wood. Any pruning should take place in late spring.

AUCUBA
Aucuba
Large evergreen shrubs that are used either as free-standing shrubs or as hedging. After planting, cut back the shoots by roughly one-third to make them bush out. Repeat the following spring. Once established, cut

Acer palmatum

back any overlong stems, reaching well into the bush. Otherwise, no pruning is required. If it outgrows its space or becomes bare at the base, cut hard back and it will reshoot. If used as a hedge, trim with secateurs (pruners), as shears or hedge cutters will cut the large leaves in half, spoiling the appearance.

AZARA
Azara
Evergreen shrubs that are marginally tender. They can be grown in the open in warmer areas, but elsewhere are best trained as fans against a wall. They are usually grown as multi-stemmed shrubs and need minimal training or pruning. They can be grown as hedging and will take well to clipping, but this usually means that the fragrant spring flowers are lost. They can be cut hard back if necessary. Prune in spring, after flowering.

BERBERIS
Barberry
A very popular genus of evergreen and deciduous shrubs with small leaves, clusters of yellow or orange flowers and colourful berries. Many have very spiny stems, so it is advisable to wear gloves when pruning. They can be grown as multi-stemmed shrubs or used in a formal or informal hedge and will need little or no formative training. They can easily be kept to size as they take pruning well, but it is better to choose carefully from the many varieties so that the plant can be allowed to develop its natural shape. There is usually no need to prune except to keep the plant in bounds, or to take out some of

the older wood to rejuvenate it, although this seems to be rarely necessary. Larger specimens can become bare at the base. In this case cut back the longer stems to a suitable new shoot to re-clothe the lower part of the shrub. Generally, pruning is done in the winter.

1 Berberis can become overgrown, with the flowers and leaves well above head height, while the base is just a mass of bare stems.

2 As always, the first task should be the removal of any dead, damaged or diseased wood. This will then give you a clear idea of what is left.

3 Take out some of the wood that is causing congestion. A number of these stems can be thinned out to the plant's advantage.

4 While thinning, look out for any shoots that cross and rub against other branches. These should ideally be removed.

5 Continue through the plant, leaving young material to develop but cutting out older wood, so that the plant is rejuvenated.

6 Finally, shape the outside of the shrub. Always prune back to a strong shoot or to a healthy-looking bud.

BETULA
Birch
Deciduous trees, generally with attractive bark. There are several weeping forms. Little training and pruning are required, although it is desirable that they are kept as a central-leader tree and any pruning should be done with this in mind. Generally they are pruned with a bare trunk, but one or two species are more shrublike and will produce more than one leader, or branch from ground level to develop as multi-stemmed bushes. Weeping forms sometimes develop a drooping trunk. Tie this firmly to a strong stake to keep it upright until the wood has developed sufficiently for it to stand upright. Remove any shoots that appear below the graft of a weeping variety, as these

will tend to grow upright and will be out of character with the rest of the tree. Birches tend to weep sap when cut, so the best time to prune is autumn or early winter.

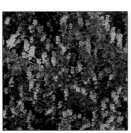

Berberis aristata

Berberis 'Georgeii'

Betula pendula

BOUGAINVILLEA

Vigorous deciduous or evergreen climbers with insignificant flowers that are surrounded by very brightly coloured bracts. They are tender plants and must be grown in warm positions, which means they are most frequently grown against the walls of buildings. In cooler climates they must be grown in containers and overwintered inside. Strong trellis or wire supports are required to get an even spread. Initial training is important. Tie in five or six of the strongest shoots, removing the rest. Spread them out so that they cover the widest possible area. Cut these shoots back to about 15cm (6in) to a strong shoot and then treat as a fan until the whole of the space is covered. To prevent overcrowding, any congested shoots should be removed in spring. Also in spring, cut back all side shoots to two or three buds to form a spur system, as with *Chaenomeles*. After flowering, cut all the flowered stems back to a non-flowering shoot. If they become overgrown, they can be cut back hard, though it is best to do this selectively, taking out a few older shoots each year.

BRACHYGLOTTIS
Brachyglottis

In the garden, these are mainly evergreen shrubs, although the genus also includes trees and perennials. It is still often referred to by its previous name, *Senecio*. Little initial training is required and pruning is restricted mainly to keeping the rather straggly shrub in shape. The foliage is mainly silver and the flowers yellow. Regular hard pruning in spring will improve the quality of the foliage but will prevent flowering (in any case, many gardeners grow it just for the foliage and cut off the flowers before they open). If flowers are required, prune after flowering to ensure flowers the following year. Overgrown shrubs can be cut back hard, but it is better to take out a few of the older stems each year. Old shrubs are best replaced.

Buddleja davidii 'Dartmoor'

BRUGMANSIA
Angels' trumpets

A small genus of tender evergreen shrubs and trees, grown for their large flowers and still often referred to as *Datura*. In cool climates, they are best grown in containers and overwintered inside. Wear gloves when pruning as some parts contain toxic substances. Prune hard in spring before growth starts, cutting back to strong buds close to the ground or to one or two buds on low side shoots. Gradually extend the framework. If the plant gets too large, cut it back hard. Deadhead after flowering.

BUDDLEJA
Butterfly bush

Deciduous shrubs grown for their flowers and foliage. There are basically three types of buddleja from the point of view of pruning. Only one group is cut back hard, but all will take hard pruning, so if you make a mistake there is no lasting damage (though flowers for that season are

Callistemon citrinus

likely to be lost). *B. davidii* and its cultivars are pruned back hard to within 30cm (12in) of the ground, early each spring. *B. crispa* and *B. fallowiana* are pruned in the same way. *B. alternifolia* flowers on the previous year's wood and can be pruned after flowering. Cut back the old flowered shoots to a non-flowering shoot or strong bud. Occasionally take out some of the oldest wood completely. *B. globosa* flowers on new wood produced from the previous season's growth. It requires very little pruning. Take out a little old wood in spring to rejuvenate the plant. If the plant becomes too large with age, it can be pruned back hard to renovate it.

BUXUS
Box

Evergreen shrubs grown mainly for hedging and topiary. As a free-standing shrub, little

Camellia 'Cornish Spring'

formative or subsequent pruning is required. For hedging or topiary, cut the young plant back hard to promote bushy growth, then trim to shape as it grows. Once developed, trim as often as necessary to keep its shape. Box can be cut back hard if necessary, but be warned: the old wood is very hard.

CALLISTEMON
Bottlebrush

Tender evergreen shrubs. In cooler areas, grow in containers and move inside for winter or plant against a warm wall. Generally, no pruning is required, although stopping the plant, by removing the tips of the new shoots, can be done initially to produce bushy growth. Wall specimens can be tied in to wires or trellis.

CAMELLIA
Camellia

Evergreen shrubs and trees. Little pruning is needed apart from removing any damaged wood or any shoots that produce flowers

PRUNING BUDDLEJA

1 Buddlejas put on a lot of growth during the year and most will need to be pruned back drastically in the spring.

2 Cut back all the stems to one or two buds of the previous year's wood. This should be just above ground-level.

3 The finished stool. Remove one or two of the oldest stems right back to the base, in order to stimulate new growth.

that are not typical of that variety. A bushy shape can be encouraged on young plants by carefully pruning young shoots back in spring. Overgrown plants can be cut back hard in spring.

CAMPSIS
Trumpet vine
Deciduous climbers grown for their foliage and flowers. They are best grown against tall walls using wires as supports. When planted, cut back shoots to about 15–20cm (6–8in) from the ground to promote strong growth, which should be trained as widely over the space as possible. It flowers on new growth, so cut back new shoots in the spring to one or two buds of the main stem. To renovate, the whole plant can be cut back to within 30cm (12in) of the ground, but it is better to remove a few of the oldest stems each year and tie in replacements.

CARPINUS
Hornbeam
Deciduous trees, grown mainly as hedging, but also as trees. For trees, train as a feathered or central-leader tree. Thereafter, little pruning is required. For hedging, trim as required, usually once or twice a year.

CARYOPTERIS
Caryopteris
Deciduous shrubs grown for their foliage and flowers. Initial training consists of pruning each stem back to just a few buds to create a good framework. Established

Ceanothus griseus

pruning consists of cutting back the previous year's growth in spring to within a bud or two of the old wood. Do not cut back into old wood as this is reluctant to produce new growth.

CASTANEA
Sweet chestnut
These are mainly grown to produce fruit or wood and are suitable only as specimen trees in big gardens, where they should be trained as central-leader trees. Little pruning is required once established.

CATALPA
Bean tree
Deciduous trees. Initially train as a leader tree with a bare trunk, after which it will naturally branch out to create a large, open-crown tree. Once established little pruning is needed. Once trees become old, they may become unsafe. Branches can be cut back, and will rejuvenate. By this stage, however, professional help may be advisable. Catalpas can also be coppiced or pollarded and, if so, will produce larger leaves.

CEANOTHUS
California lilac
Deciduous or evergreen shrubs. Evergreens are dealt with in *Ornamental shrubs.* Deciduous varieties are more frequently grown as free-standing specimens than the evergreens. Initial training should aim to produce a strong framework. Cut back all stems by half to two-thirds to an outward-facing bud. The following year, in spring, cut back the previous year's growth, again by half to two-thirds. Once established, cut back all flowered stems by about half and other shoots to just one or two buds. Cut out completely any congested or unproductive wood. As with evergreen ceanothus, deciduous varieties do not break easily from old wood, so do not cut back into it. Renovation is seldom successful.

CERATOSTIGMA
Ceratostigma
Mainly evergreen and deciduous shrubs. In most colder climates they are cut back each winter by frost. In spring, cut all stems back to about 5cm (2in) above the ground. In milder areas, where the stems are retained, build up a framework and then cut back the previous year's growth each spring to within a bud or two of the old wood.

CERCIDIPHYLLUM
Katsura tree
A deciduous tree. This normally grows naturally as a multi-

Cestrum parqui

stemmed tree, despite its upright growth. Generally, no initial or subsequent training is required. Allow the tree to develop to its natural shape.

CERCIS
Judas tree
Deciduous trees and shrubs. *C. japonicum,* the Judas tree, is grown mainly for its early flowers. It normally forms a multi-stemmed tree which should be allowed to develop naturally. Cut out any damaged and dead wood, as it can be affected by coral spot.

CESTRUM
Deciduous or evergreen shrubs. *C. parqui* is possibly the hardiest and the one most commonly grown in cooler areas. No initial training is required. If cut to the ground by severe frosts, cut back the dead material at the base. Even in a mild winter, the tips die back after flowering and should be cut back to a bud in sound wood. Remove some of the older wood each year. It tends to sucker, so it may also be necessary to remove some of the new suckers to contain its growth. Prune in early spring.

CHAENOMELES
Flowering quince
Deciduous or evergreen shrubs. They are usually trained as wall shrubs but they can also be grown as free-standing garden shrubs. These can become large and straggly, so are really suitable only for large gardens. They need little pruning beyond cutting back the longer stems if they outgrow their allotted space. Take out one or two of the oldest stems each year to rejuvenate the plant.

PRUNING CERATOSTIGMA

1 Ceratostigmas put on a lot of growth each year, and become rather bushy. In colder climates, it is usual to cut back all of this growth.

2 There is no need to cut the shrub stem by stem: just take a pair of shears and cut it to 5cm (2in) above the ground.

3 The stubby remains will all grow back. In warmer areas, cut back the previous year's growth to one or two buds of the old wood.

Cistus × cyprius

CHOISYA
Mexican orange blossom
Evergreen shrubs. Little if any initial pruning is required as they naturally form a fine bush. Established pruning consists mainly of cutting back flowered stems to keep the bush compact and to promote further flowering. They are hardy, but frost can cut back some shoots. Remove these in spring. If necessary renovate by cutting back hard in spring.

CISTUS
Rock rose
Evergreen shrubs. Little initial pruning is required although some may need tip-pruning to encourage them to bush out. Once established, little pruning is needed beyond the removal of any dead wood. Plants can become straggly, but they resent being cut hard back as they will not break from old wood.

CLEMATIS
Clematis
Evergreen and deciduous climbers grown for their flowers. Pruning is dealt with in a separate section.

PRUNING CISTUS

1 Cistus form dense, compact evergreen shrubs. They need very little pruning, either at the initial or established stages.

2 Take out any dead wood and trim back lightly to the previous year's growth if you need to keep the plant within its space.

CLERODENDRUM
Clerodendrum
Mainly deciduous or evergreen shrubs. Of the two commonly grown in gardens, *C. bungei* is a suckering shrub that is usually cut back by winter frosts in cool areas. In spring, cut out all frosted stems to the ground. Remove any suckers as necessary to restrict the plant's spread. *C. trichotomum* is more shrubby and should be trained on a short leg. Once formed, cut back the previous year's growth to one or two buds in spring. Any suckers that arise should be taken off below ground-level at source.

CLIANTHUS
Parrot's bill
Evergreen shrubs. They are best grown against a wall, tied in to wires or trellis. Initial pruning consists of cutting back the stems on planting to produce strong shoots, which should be trained in to the wall. In spring stop these shoots to produce more, until the

wall is covered. Once covered, pruning is restricted to removing a few of the oldest stems each year in spring back to a new shoot, and tying in the new growth to fill the gaps as it appears.

COBAEA
Cup-and-saucer vine
Evergreen and herbaceous climbers of which only one, *C. scandens*, is in general cultivation. This is a perennial but is often treated as an annual and discarded each autumn. Initial training consists of stopping the shoots to make it bush out and tying it into supports, aiming for as wide a spread as possible, for maximum interest. Where grown as a perennial, it should be cut back in spring, reducing the previous year's growth by half to three-quarters.

COLUTEA
Bladder senna
Deciduous shrubs. The simplest pruning method is to let the

shrub develop naturally and restrict pruning to cutting out just a few of the oldest stems each spring. However, for a tighter shrub and a longer flowering period, it can be cut back hard almost to ground-level each spring. Shrubs that have not been pruned can be renovated by cutting them hard back in spring.

CORNUS
Dogwood
Deciduous trees and shrubs. Trees should be allowed to develop naturally as single-leader trees. If left to their own devices, however, many (*Cornus mas*, for example) develop as multi-stemmed trees or large shrubs. Once established, very little pruning is required. Removal of dead or damaged wood and any wayward branches should be carried out in winter. Shrubs vary, but those grown for their winter stems, mainly cultivars of *C. alba*, need to be cut back to just above soil level in early spring. If grown for their flowers, little pruning is required beyond taking out a few of the oldest stems each spring to rejuvenate the plant. Overgrown shrubs can be renovated by cutting back hard, almost to the ground.

CORYLOPSIS
Winter hazel
Deciduous shrubs grown for their winter catkins. Let the new plants develop naturally and prune only to remove dead wood. If it is necessary to cut back longer branches that have outgrown their space, do so after flowering (or

Clematis

Clematis 'Lasurstern'

Cornus alba sibirica

Cotoneaster conspicuus

Crataegus laevigata

Cytisus battandieri needs little pruning except for the removal in spring of any wayward or crossing shoots that may rub against others.

Davidia involucrata

cut them during flowering and use them in flower arrangements).

CORYLUS
Hazel
Deciduous trees and shrubs grown for their flowers, foliage and fruit. Those grown for flowers and foliage are usually grown as multi-stemmed plants. No initial training is required and little subsequent pruning, except to remove a few of the oldest stems each year once the shrub is established, to rejuvenate the plant. Overgrown shrubs can be cut back hard for renovation.

COTINUS
Smoke bush
Deciduous trees or shrubs. Little initial training is required, but subsequent pruning depends on what you want from the plant. Large, well-coloured leaves are best achieved by pruning hard back to one or two buds on a framework of branches 60cm (2ft) or so from the ground. Larger shrubs will have good, but not so spectacular, foliage plus the wonderful flower heads which

develop on older wood. To achieve this, restrict pruning to the removal of dead wood and any overlong or wayward stems. Renovation can be achieved by cutting back hard in early spring.

COTONEASTER
Cotoneaster
Evergreen and deciduous shrubs, grown for their foliage, flowers and fruit. The main garden species, *C. horizontalis*, can be grown either as a low-growing shrub or as a wall shrub. For the prostrate form no initial training is required and pruning should be kept to a minimum, as it is reluctant to break from old wood. To grow against a wall, provide support initially. Plants will soon grow flat against the wall. Remove any badly placed stems. Other species require minimal pruning.

CRATAEGUS
Hawthorn
Deciduous trees and shrubs. Some are grown as trees in gardens, but it is mainly used as country-style hedging, and is often known as quickthorn.

Flowering forms are usually trained as single-stemmed trees with a clear trunk, but if the leader is damaged they can become multi-stemmed. No pruning is generally required. If they become overgrown, they can be renovated by cutting back almost to ground-level. For hawthorn hedges, see *Hedges*.

CYTISUS
Broom
Semi-deciduous shrubs. Little pruning is required for the majority, but the most commonly seen broom, *C. scoparius* and its many cultivars, can become rather straggly. To prevent this, cut back the previous year's growth by about half to two-thirds after flowering. Do not cut back into old wood, as it does not break easily.

DAPHNE
Daphne
Evergreen or deciduous shrubs. These need little or no initial training or subsequent pruning – in fact, pruning is best avoided as it can promote die-back. Cut out any dead growth as soon as it is seen.

DAVIDIA
Handkerchief tree
A large deciduous tree grown for its decorative bracts, which look like handkerchiefs and surround the inconspicuous flowers. Initial training should be confined to ensuring that it develops as a single-leader tree. Keep the trunk clear of side shoots below the bottom branches.

DEUTZIA
Deciduous shrubs grown for their flowers. They produce a lot of basal growth which can grow tall and ungainly, so shorten stems initially to promote bushiness. Once established, cut back flowered shoots to a new shoot and cut out a few of the oldest stems each year to promote new growth from the base.

DEADHEADING HEATHERS

1 Heathers can get very straggly and it can then be difficult to get them back to a compact shape without replanting.

2 Lightly trim over the plant, removing the flowered wood back to one or two buds. This can be done with a pair of shears.

3 The finished plants. Do not cut back too hard as they will not recover if they are pruned back into the old wood.

Deutzia × elegantissima

Euonymus europaeus

ECCREMOCARPUS
Chilean glory flower
An evergreen climber. It is perennial but is often treated as an annual. In warmer areas, it will overwinter. In cooler ones, it can be cut to the ground by frosts, but will usually regenerate from the base. It can be trained up a trellis or up wires. It has tendrils and is self-clinging, but may need encouragement. On a young plant, pinch out the tips of the shoots so that it bushes out and provides a good coverage. Each spring, cut the previous year's growth almost back to old wood, to a strong bud.

ELAEAGNUS
Elaeagnus
Evergreen and deciduous shrubs and trees. These naturally form bushy shrubs and no initial training is required. Similarly, little established pruning is required, other than cutting back longer stems to maintain control, if necessary. This can be done in late summer. They will all take clipping well and although this may spoil the natural shape of the plant, it can be used to good effect in hedging. *E.* × *ebbingei*, in particular, makes a good hedge. For renovation they can all be cut back hard.

EMBOTHRIUM
Chilean fire bush
Evergreen trees. They can be trained as a single-leader or multi-stemmed tree. For the latter, no special initial training is required, but to create a single-stemmed tree, initial training and pruning should be directed towards creating a clear trunk up to 1.2–2m (4–6ft) high. Little established pruning is required. Both types are likely to sucker,

and unless they are needed as replacement growths, suckers should be removed at source.

ERICA
Heather
Evergreen shrubs and trees. The majority of heathers grown in gardens are the low-growing shrubs. These require no initial training, but it is important to clip them over once a year, after flowering, to stop them becoming straggly. They do not regenerate from old wood, so just shorten the previous season's growth to one or two buds. It is difficult to renovate old plants. Tree heathers, on the other hand, respond well to hard cutting and can be renovated. They are usually grown as multi-stemmed trees or large bushes and should be cut back in the first year or so to encourage bushiness. Once established, there is no need to prune other than to keep control of the size of the tree or bush. Do this after flowering. If necessary, it is possible to cut back into old wood.

ESCALLONIA
Escallonia
Evergreen shrubs. Escallonias need little initial training to form bushy shrubs. Once established, they still do not require a great deal of attention but benefit from the removal of some of the oldest wood to stimulate new growth. If they outgrow their position, longer stems, preferably flowered ones, can be cut back to a new shoot or strong bud. They can be

Embothrium coccineum

Eucalyptus gregsoniana

used as formal or informal hedging and can be clipped if necessary. They can be cut hard back for renovation.

EUCALYPTUS
Gum tree
Evergreen trees and shrubs. They are usually grown as single-leader trees. The trunk is kept clear of shoots up to 3m (10ft) for the taller growing specimens. Generally no pruning is required once established, other than to remove dead wood. If they outgrow their space, they can be cut back hard. Some, *E. gunnii* being a common example, can be cut right back, almost to the ground, and then grown as a shrub. The advantage of this is that it produces juvenile foliage, which is much in demand for indoor decorations. This juvenile stage of the foliage can be maintained by regular pollarding so that all the foliage is new.

Euonymus alatus

EUCRYPHIA
Eucryphia
Evergreen trees and shrubs. These are generally grown as single-leader or multi-stemmed trees, or large bushes. Little formative training is needed, as the trees tend to shape up naturally. Similarly, little is required once they are established, although dead wood caused by frost, and sometimes drought, will need to be removed.

EUONYMUS
Spindle
Evergreen and deciduous shrubs. Both require little initial training or established pruning, unless they have outgrown their position. The evergreen *E. fortunei* and its varieties can be trained against a wall, where they will usually grow without support. Tie in or cut out wayward shoots. Variegated forms may produce shoots that have reverted to green, and these should be cut out as soon as they are seen. Euonymus can be cut hard back if renovation is required.

EUPHORBIA
Spurge
A very large genus of trees, shrubs, perennials and annuals. They all exude an irritant sap when cut that can cause problems if it comes in contact with the skin and is very painful indeed if it gets into the eyes. Most of the perennials can be cut back to the ground as they begin to fade, but on shrubby ones, such as *E. characias* and forms, cut back flowered stems as low down as possible after flowering, leaving the new, unflowered shoots to develop. All will regenerate from hard pruning, but once plants get old it is best to replace them.

FAGUS
Beech
Deciduous trees. These large trees generally need no initial or subsequent pruning, other than to remove any dead wood, or to tidy them up if wind breaks one or more of the branches (if these are large a professional may be required to carry out the work).

Fagus sylvatica 'Pendula'

Ficus

Fraxinus ornus

Initial pruning can be used to keep the trunks bare up to about 3m (10ft). They can also be cut very hard and used as hedges. In this compact form, the dead leaves will usually remain on the twigs throughout the winter. Hedges should be trimmed once or twice a year and although slow to recover they can be cut back hard if they become overgrown.

× FATSHEDERA

Evergreen shrub grown for its large glossy leaves. It can be grown as a free-standing shrub, but is usually grown as a wall shrub. Although ivy is one of its parents, it is not self-clinging, so needs tying in to supports as it develops. It produces a number of upright shoots each year, which begin to bow over in the following year, extending the size of the shrub in an untidy way. Some of these can be tied in to fill gaps but the majority are best removed in the autumn of their first year while they are still upright, cutting them back to their origin. The whole plant can be cut hard back if necessary for renovation.

FICUS
Fig

Evergreen trees grown mainly for their fruit. In colder areas, they are often grown solely for their foliage, as the fruit does not ripen sufficiently. They are most frequently grown as wall shrubs, where they are trained as fans. To prevent them from becoming too rampant, it is best to restrict their roots by creating a bottomless box around them by inserting four paving slabs vertically into the ground. Initial and subsequent pruning is for a fan, although many lose this shape through neglect. Figs can be cut back hard if necessary for renovation.

FORSYTHIA
Forsythia

Deciduous shrubs grown for their spring flowers. Let the plants develop naturally with no initial training. They flower on older wood so any pruning should be after flowering. Cut back some of the oldest wood each year, either to strong new shoots or right to the base. Longer stems can be cut back if the shrub is becoming untidy or outgrowing its space. Forsythia can be grown as a hedge and even if kept cut tight back it produces a surprising number of flowers. It can be cut hard back if renovation is required. *F. suspensa*

can be grown as a wall shrub by tying its pendulous shoots in to wires. Cut out flowered stems to the base of the shoot, tying in replacement ones as they grow.

FRAXINUS
Ash

Deciduous trees grown mainly for their foliage. Little initial training is required. They develop naturally as single-leader trees, although it may be necessary to remove shoots to create a clear trunk up to the desired height. To grow for poles or firewood, develop as multi-stemmed trees and coppice them every few years. Once established, little pruning is required except for taking out dead wood as it appears. Die-back can progressively attack the tree, so it is important to take out any dead wood, cutting into sound wood. They can be cut back hard if necessary. Weeping forms should be trained and pruned as weeping standards.

FREMONTODENDRON
Flannel bush

Evergreen trees or shrubs grown for their foliage and flowers. The foliage and stems are covered with irritating hairs, which can cause damage to skin and, more dangerously, to lungs. They can be grown free-standing but are usually better as wall shrubs. Train with a central leader and tie all side shoots in to a wire framework. The side shoots can also be trained as an espalier so that the pairs of side branches are almost opposite each other and are parallel to the ground. Usually, however, the side branches are tied in to fill the

PRUNING FORSYTHIA

2 Cut out any congested wood, along with any that crosses other stems, especially if it rubs against or wounds them.

1 Forsythias flower on old wood so they should not be too drastically pruned or you will not get any flowers. Prune after flowering.

3 Cut out any dead wood, including any stubs left from previous poor pruning. One or two older stems can be taken out completely to rejuvenate the plant.

4 The completely pruned plant, now more open and far less crowded. If grown as a hedge, it is usually the inner, unpruned wood that flowers.

PRUNING HARDY FUCHSIAS

1 In cooler areas hardy fuchsias are usually killed back to the ground with frosts. They will quickly regenerate the following year.

2 Cut the shrub back almost to ground-level. In warmer areas, where they are not killed by frost, the pruning can be much lighter.

available space and the rest are removed. They flower on the current year's growth, so prune back flowered shoots to a new shoot. They do not respond well to renovation pruning.

FUCHSIA
Fuchsia

Small deciduous or evergreen shrubs, either grown in the open garden or in containers. Some are tender. They are usually grown as shrubs but many are also trained as standards. Initial training consists in pinching out the tips of shoots to promote bushiness. In cold winters they are cut back to the ground by frost, in which case remove the frosted wood back to a bud at the base of the stems in spring. If not frosted, cut back all side shoots to a strong bud. Tender fuchsias should be overwintered under glass to protect them from frost. The main structure is maintained but the shoots are tip-pruned to promote bushiness and to produce an even shape. On standards, keep the trunks clear of shoots.

GARRYA
Silk-tassel bush

Evergreen shrubs grown mainly for their silver winter catkins. No initial training is required, and the bush can be allowed to develop naturally. Once established little pruning is

required except to control it if it overgrows its space. Do this in spring, after flowers have faded. If space is restricted they can be grown as a wall shrub by training in some branches to the wall and removing those that stick out. A bit more pruning is required to keep these in shape, overlapping or congesting shoots should be removed in spring. If renovation is required cut hard back to the main framework.

GENISTA
Broom

Deciduous shrubs grown for their flowers. There is no need for any initial training and established pruning should be kept to a minimum as they dislike being cut back into old wood. After flowering the shrubs can be tidied or kept reasonably compact by cutting back some of the previous year's growth. Renovation is difficult because of the plants' dislike of being cut hard back so replace with new plants if necessary.

Genista lydia

HAMAMELIS
Witch hazel

Deciduous shrubs grown mainly for their winter flowers. No initial training is required. Pruning can be restricted to removing any dead or rubbing wood, or keeping within bounds. Although the flowers are very attractive in winter, avoid the temptation to cut stems for indoor decoration from all but mature plants as regrowth is usually slow. Although it is rarely necessary, it is possible to renovate with hard pruning but the plant is very slow to regenerate.

HEBE
Hebe

Evergreen shrubs grown for their foliage and flowers. Little initial training is required, and most can be allowed to develop naturally unless their shape becomes unbalanced, in which case remove the offending shoots. Larger varieties can, if left to their own devices, become overlarge and leggy, so regular pruning of flowered shoots after flowering, back to a new shoot, is recommended. Bushes can be kept

Hebe 'Great Orme'

to a rounded shape simply by shearing over every year, just cutting back the flowered wood. Dwarf hummock-forming varieties that are often used as groundcover can also be sheared over to keep them compact. Whipcord types can be left to their own devices. If these become leggy, shear them over to keep them in shape. Hebes can generally be cut back quite hard for renovation purposes.

PRUNING GENISTA

1 Broom is a rather untidy and straggly bush. It is difficult to renovate as it dislikes being cut hard back into old wood.

2 Do not cut back into old wood unless you have to. Dead wood, however, should be removed back to live growth.

3 The only pruning required is to trim back the previous year's growth to keep the plant neater or to control its size.

4 The finished shrub still looks fairly untidy. If it gets out of control, rather than pruning it, plant a new one.

Hedera helix 'Bruder Ingobert'

HEDERA
Ivy
Evergreen climbers used to cover walls and fences. The inconspicuous flowers in late autumn are a valuable food source for bees. Ivies climb by attaching themselves to buildings, trees, fences or anything else that lies in their path. They can also be used as ground cover. For training vertically, tie to canes or peg them down to the base of their supports to make certain that they become attached and climb. On buildings, walls and fences, new shoots should be spread out at the base to create a wide spread. For a wild, gothic look, ivy can be allowed to ramp unchecked over buildings and trees and hang down in curtains, but in other situations it benefits from more control. Little pruning is required other than to cut out shoots that venture above the eaves on buildings. Also cut off any strands that become detached or project forward and spoil the flat plane of the creeper. As ground cover, it needs to be sheared over to about 15cm (6in) every late winter to early spring. It is possible to train ivy over metal or wire frameworks to create a topiary effect. Keep it cut back, close to the former, so that the shape is well defined. Some gardeners dislike the smell of the flowers and the flies and wasps that congregate around them, so

PRUNING HELIANTHEMUM

1 Helianthemums are low-growing, hummocky shrubs. They dislike being cut back hard, but will get straggly if unattended.

2 Cut back the previous year's growth after flowering, being careful not to cut back into old wood, as this will not regrow.

frequently cut them off when they appear in autumn. The best time to prune ivy is in late winter to early spring, but little harm is done by doing it at other times.

HELIANTHEMUM
Rock rose
Low-growing evergreen shrubs grown for their flowers and foliage. Initial training is confined to tip-pruning the shoots to make the plants bush out. Once established, they have a tendency to become straggly and leggy unless they are pruned over once they have flowered. Cut only into the previous year's wood, not into old wood, as this is reluctant to break. Planted en masse, they can be cut with shears, but be careful not to cut into old wood or there will be bald patches. They are difficult to renovate, so start again with new plants.

Helianthemum 'Rhodanthe Carneum'

HELICHRYSUM
Helichrysum
Evergreen shrubs grown mainly for their foliage. The tender shrub *H. petiolare* is widely grown as a container and bedding plant. This should initially be tip-pruned to make it bush out and produce plenty of trailing shoots. If they are constantly pinched out it can be turned into a bushy foliage plant. After overwintering inside, cut out the old stems to new shoots, although it is often best to start again with a new plant. *H. italicum*, the curry plant, is widely grown in the open garden as a small, silver-leaved shrub. Little pruning is required other than to trim over the previous year's growth to keep the plants compact. Many gardeners do not like the yellow flowers and these can be removed before they open, restricting the shrub to a foliage plant. Cut back hard in order to renovate the plant.

HIBISCUS
Hibiscus
Deciduous and evergreen shrubs and perennials grown mainly for their flowers. Initial pruning is required to produce an even framework of branches. Take out weak, crossing and congested stems, and cut back remaining shoots to promote bushiness. Established pruning of hibiscus consists of cutting back the main shoots by about half and side shoots back to a couple of buds in spring. Also take out some of the oldest wood each year to promote new growth and remove any dead wood as soon as it is evident. Renovation can be achieved by cutting back reasonably hard, work that should preferably be spaced over two or more seasons.

HOYA
Hoya
Evergreen climbers grown for their flowers and foliage. They are tender and in cool climates can only be grown under glass. The sap can cause adverse reactions, so take appropriate precautions when pruning. No initial training is required other than tying the young shoots to their supports. Similarly, there is little established pruning, other than reducing the amount of growth occasionally to prevent congestion. Do this after flowering. Hoyas do not respond well to hard pruning.

HUMULUS
Hop
Perennial climbers grown mainly for their foliage. The bract-covered flowers are often used in interior decorations as well as for brewing beer. They are trained up wires, strings or a wooden framework. They twine but often need guiding initially or they go off sideways and grow up other plants. Twist the young stems clockwise (the opposite way to runner beans) round their supports. Cut to the ground in autumn.

Humulus lupulus 'Aureus'

Hydrangea arborescens

HYDRANGEA
Hydrangea
Deciduous shrubs and climbers grown mainly for their flowers. The main species grown is *H. macrophylla* and its cultivars. No initial pruning is required. Established plants should be pruned in spring by cutting back the previous year's flower heads to a strong bud. Also take out one or two of the oldest stems to regenerate the plant. Other species require minimum pruning. Exceptions are *H. paniculata*, *H. arborescens* and *H. cinerea*, which need to be cut back to a framework of branches by pruning the previous year's growth back to the lowest pair of strong buds in spring. Climbing hydrangeas support themselves by aerial roots but may need tying in initially if they are to cover a wall or fence. Once established they can be vigorous. Cut back all shoots that approach gutters and eaves, and keep clear of windows. They can be cut back hard to regenerate if required.

HYPERICUM
St John's wort
Deciduous and evergreen shrubs grown mainly for their flowers. Most plants require little initial training. Once established, in spring prune back all flowered stems to a new shoot and take out any dead or weak growth. Take out one or two of the oldest stems each year to promote new growth. They can be cut back hard if renovation is required. On ground-cover plants, such as *H. calycinum*, cut out all the previous year's growth. On larger areas this is best done with shears, hedge trimmers or even a strimmer.

Ilex aquifolium 'J.C. van Tol'

ILEX
Holly
Evergreen trees and shrubs grown for their foliage and for their colourful berries. Trees are usually grown as single-leader trees, but are also seen as multi-stemmed trees or large shrubs. Most trees and shrubs can be allowed to develop naturally and little subsequent pruning is necessary. Where grown as topiary or hedge plants, they need to be clipped over once or twice a year to maintain their shape. On trees and shrubs with variegated foliage, cut out any shoots that revert to plain green. Hollies can be cut hard back for renovation (on hedges it is best to spread this over three years).

Jasminum nudiflorum

INDIGOFERA
Indigofera
Deciduous shrubs grown for their flowers and ferny foliage. They require no initial training. Once established, they can be cut to a bud just above ground-level in spring. Left to their own devices, they can grow tall and straggly, in which case they can be cut hard back, again to just above ground-level.

JASMINUM
Jasmine
Evergreen and deciduous climbers and shrubs grown for their usually scented flowers. Initial training consists of tip-pruning the shoots back by half to develop plenty of shoots from the base, and tying these in over as wide an area as possible. Established pruning is restricted to ensuring that the plant does not become overcrowded and congested. Cut out dead wood, which can accumulate, and remove some of the older stems, so that new, rejuvenating growth

Kerria japonica 'Pleniflora'

is produced. If they become over-congested or over-burdened with old wood, it is possible to renovate them by cutting them back drastically to a basic framework. It will take several years to get back to full flowering if treated thus, and so it is best to renovate plants in stages.

KERRIA
Jew's mantle
A single species of deciduous shrub, which is mainly grown for its spring flowers (one cultivar also has variegated foliage). No initial training is required for kerrias. Once established, cut back the flowered wood immediately after flowering has finished, either to a new shoot or to ground-level. Also cut out any unwanted suckers because this shrub can spread. On variegated plants, cut out any shoots that revert to plain green. Kerrias can be renovated by cutting back hard almost to ground-level.

PRUNING JASMINUM

1 *Jasminum nudiflorum* naturally grows into a very tangled bush and if left will soon build up a lot of dead wood.

2 Cut out all the dead wood and thin out the shoots, trying to get an even coverage over the available wall or fence space.

3 A much reduced plant, but there is still some dead wood to be removed. Prune it yearly to keep this under control.

Laburnum × watereri 'Vossii'

KOLKWITZIA
Beauty bush
A single species of deciduous shrub grown for its flowers. No pruning or training is required on planting. When established, it is necessary only to remove some of the oldest stems each year after flowering to rejuvenate the plant constantly. If the plant suckers excessively, remove some or all of those that appear too far from the centre of the plant. Neglected plants can be renovated by cutting out most of the stems to ground-level, leaving just a few young stems.

LABURNUM
Golden rain
Poisonous deciduous trees grown for their flowers. They are often grown as specimens but can also be trained. They will normally develop naturally into single-leader trees, so no initial training is necessary other than the removal of any shoots that appear on the trunk. Once established, pruning should be kept to a minimum except for the removal of dead wood and any shoots that appear below the graft. Laburnums also make good candidates for training over arches, as tunnels or against a wall, where their long, hanging racemes of flowers can be seen to advantage. They can be grown as pleached trees, when established pruning will ensure that they do not become too congested and that shoots are cut back to produce flowering spurs. Against walls, they can be trained as fans, again with spur pruning. Pruning should take place in autumn or early winter, as at any other time the tree may bleed badly. They do not renovate well and so should be replaced if necessary.

LAPAGERIA
Chilean bell flower
One species consisting of an evergreen climber grown for its flowers. Little initial training is needed other than to ensure that it starts to twine up any vertical supports. Once established, very little pruning is required. It does not renovate well so start again, if necessary, with a new plant.

LAURUS
Bay
Evergreen trees or shrubs, either with single or multiple stems. Little initial training is required unless it starts to develop as a multi-stemmed tree in situations where a single-stemmed one is required. In this case, reduce the stems to one and grow on as a feathered tree. It is normal to leave on the lower shoots so that there is hardly any clear trunk. Once established, little pruning is required. If cutting branches for use in the kitchen, take care not to spoil the shape of the tree. Alternatively, just remove leaves from around the tree rather than whole shoots. They can also be developed as clipped forms and are commonly seen as "lollipops" in pots. Plants can be renovated by being cut back to a basic frame, but are slow to regenerate.

LAVANDULA
Lavender
Evergreen shrubs grown for their foliage, flowers and aroma. Once planted, initial training should aim to produce a bushy plant. On established plants, cut back the previous year's growth each spring to within a few buds of the old wood. This can be done with secateurs (pruners) or with shears. Do not cut back into old wood, as this is reluctant to break.

Lavandula angustifolia

Lavatera 'Kew Rose'

After flowering, cut back the long flower stalks. Renovation is difficult and so replace shrubs rather than cutting hard back.

LAVATERA
Tree mallow
Deciduous shrubs grown mainly for their flowers. Little needs to be done in the initial stages, other than to remove any weak growth. Once established, cut back each spring to a shoot or a few buds just above the ground, so that new growth is produced each year. In autumn, reduce the length of all shoots and in windy areas stake the plant, as it can suffer from wind rock. If a hole develops around the base of the trunk, any water that collects there can kill the plant over winter. Replace old plants, as they do not respond well to renovation.

LEYCESTERIA
Himalayan honeysuckle
Deciduous shrubs with hollow, cane-like stems. No initial training or pruning is required. Once established, remove a few of the old stems each year in spring. If the plant begins to sucker too widely, cut these back. If neglected and overgrown, it can be cut hard back almost to ground-level.

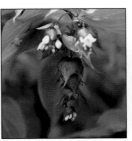

Leycesteria formosa

LIGUSTRUM
Privet
Evergreen and semi-deciduous shrubs and trees. They are grown for their foliage and occasionally their flowers but are most frequently seen as hedging. Grown as free-standing shrubs, they need no initial or established pruning, except when green shoots appear on variegated forms. These should be removed as seen. When used as hedging, it is important to promote thick growth right from the base, so cut back newly planted shrubs by half and continue to cut the new growth in a similar manner each year until the hedge is formed. Once formed, trim two or three times a year, ensuring that it is not allowed to grow away. If it does become overgrown, it can be cut back severely, as can free-standing shrubs.

LIQUIDAMBAR
Sweet gum
Deciduous trees grown for their foliage, especially the autumn colour. They are grown as a central-leader tree, which develops naturally, so there is little initial training or pruning apart from ensuring that a short trunk is kept clear. Once established, no pruning is necessary.

LIRIODENDRON
Tulip tree
Deciduous trees grown for their flowers and distinctively shaped foliage. This is a relatively easy tree to grow as far as the pruning is concerned, as there is very little to do. It is grown as a single-leader tree, the trunk cleared of shoots up to the desired height, usually about 2.5m (8ft). Once established, it is best to leave it alone, except for removing any dead or damaged wood.

Liquidambar styraciflua

Lonicera × brownii

Magnolia denudata 'Forrest's Pink'

Malus × schiedeckeri 'Hillieri'

LONICERA
Honeysuckle

Deciduous and evergreen climbers and shrubs. The climbers are the most frequently grown, but a lot of shrubby forms are available. Climbers should be trained to their supports so that they cover the maximum available space. If they are left unpruned, eventually the base will become bare and dead wood will accumulate in a top-heavy plant. It is best to prune a little each year after flowering, cutting back flowered stems to just a couple of buds. Take out any dead wood. They can be cut back hard to within 60–90cm (2–3ft) of the base, but will take a while to reach maximum flowering potential again. Bushes should be pruned after flowering, cutting out a few of the oldest stems and any weak growth to increase vigour. Any remaining longer shoots can be shortened to a new shoot to keep them in shape and within bounds, as some species can become rather leggy. Cut hard back to renovate. *L. nitida* is used as a hedging plant and should be treated in the same way as privet hedging. It can be cut back to near the ground to renovate.

MAGNOLIA
Magnolia

Deciduous and evergreen trees and shrubs. The trees are either single- or multi-stemmed. Initial pruning is usually aimed at creating the former. Do not remove lower side shoots to clear the trunk until after the leader is well developed. Multi-stemmed plants can be left to their own devices, but it may eventually be necessary to take off some of the lower laterals. Most can be left unpruned, once they are established. They can be renovated, but take it gently, a few branches at a time over a period of years. *M. grandiflora* is usually grown against a wall. Allow the leader to develop and tie in the side shoots to wires, maintaining as even a spread as possible. Once developed, cut back the shoots on the main branches to a couple of leaves after flowering. Shrubby forms should be allowed to develop unpruned according to their natural habitat. Once established, prune as little as possible.

MAHONIA
Oregon grape

Evergreen shrubs that are grown for their foliage and flowers. On the more vigorous species, cut out one or two of the oldest shoots from the base every few years. Otherwise, little pruning is required. If they get leggy or misshapen, cut back shoots after flowering to a strong shoot or bud. All can be cut hard back, but may take a while to get back to flowering size afterwards. *M. aquifolium* produces lots of suckers and tends to form a thicket. It can be kept in check by removing the perimeter ones or cutting them back every two or three years in order to produce fresh growth.

Mahonia aquifolium 'Apollo'

MALUS
Crab apple

Deciduous trees grown for their ornamental and edible fruit. Apple trees are dealt with under *Fruit Trees*. Ornamental crab apples are relatively easy to prune. They are grown as central-leader trees. They can generally be left to their own devices, except that the trunk should be cleared of shoots to the required height, usually around 1.2–2m (4–6ft). If the leader is lost, either grow the tree as a multi-stemmed bush or train in a new leader. Once established, little pruning is required. Some varieties produce many suckers or vertical shoots rising from the main limbs. These should be removed, along with any crossing or rubbing wood. Any dead or diseased wood should also be removed. Pruning should take place in the winter.

MYRTUS
Myrtle

Deciduous or evergreen shrubs grown for their foliage and flowers. No initial training or pruning is required, and little is necessary once they are

Malus

established unless they outgrow their allotted space, in which case longer shoots can be trimmed back to within the shrub in spring. It can be renovated by cutting hard back, preferably over several years.

NANDINA
Sacred bamboo

A single species of evergreen shrub, grown mainly for its berries. No initial training is necessary. Once established, it can be left to its own devices, although the removal of some of the older wood each year in spring will help to stimulate the plant. Complete renovation can be carried out by cutting the plant to near ground-level, preferably over several years.

NERIUM
Oleander

Evergreen shrubs or small trees that are grown for their foliage and flowers. In cool climates, they must be grown as container plants and overwintered inside, in a glasshouse or conservatory. Be warned that the sap is toxic and should not be swallowed. It can also cause skin reactions, so take adequate precautions when pruning or handling. There is no initial training for shrubs except to tip-prune them to make them bush out. In the open, they can more or less be left to their own devices but they will need to be cut back if in containers. Reduce all flowered shoots by about half after flowering and cut back any side shoots to just a couple of leaves. Oleanders can be grown as standards. Shrubs can be renovated by cutting hard back to a basic framework, but may take time to recover.

1 Olearias generally need very little pruning, although they can become rather straggly, in which case they can be cut back.

2 If the shrub has completely outgrown its position, it can be cut back hard. It will usually recover from such treatment.

Parthenocissus tricuspidata

Passiflora 'Amethyst'

NOTHOFAGUS
Southern beech
Evergreen and deciduous trees that can grow to enormous size. They are generally grown as single-stemmed trees although they sometimes develop with more than one trunk. These can be left to grow as multi-stemmed trees, but if this occurs as the result of the loss of the leader at some height, this may prove a weak point in the tree. In this case, a new leader should be formed and any rivals removed. Once established, the trees can be left to look after themselves.

OLEARIA
Daisy bush
Evergreen shrubs grown for their foliage and flowers. Initial training is confined to shortening the young shoots to

promote bushiness. Once established, there is no need for pruning, although they may need cutting back if they get leggy or outgrow their allotted space. Taking out some of the oldest wood every year or so should help to keep the plant vigorous. It can be renovated by cutting back hard into old wood.

OSMANTHUS
Osmanthus
Evergreen shrubs grown for their foliage and scented flowers. Initial training is generally not required, and the shrubs can be allowed to develop naturally. However, they can be tip-pruned to make them bush out if necessary. Little established pruning is required other than keeping the bushes within bounds. Any pruning should be done in spring (spring-flowering species

immediately after flowering). They can be cut hard back for renovation purposes.

PAEONIA
Peony
Shrubs and herbaceous plants grown for their flowers and foliage. The shrubby ones are generally referred to as tree peonies. No initial training or pruning is required. Once established, little pruning is required except that they should be deadheaded, cutting back the flowered stem to just above a leaf or shoot. They make rather ungainly shrubs. Removing some of the older growth every few years promotes new, bushier growth. This can be done in autumn or early winter. They can be renovated by cutting hard back but are slow to regenerate, so a yearly routine of removing older material is preferable. Herbaceous plants should not be cut back until the winter, as their foliage often takes on autumn tints and the seed pods are rather attractive.

PARTHENOCISSUS
Virginia creeper
Deciduous climbers that are grown for their foliage, especially for their autumn coloration. They can be vigorous. Initial training consists of training the shoots to spread out as far as possible. Once they reach the wall or support, they are self-clinging, so rarely need any further supports. Established pruning can be restricted to making certain that the climbers stay within bounds. Cut them back when they reach the tops of walls to prevent them from getting into gutters and eaves and under tiles. Also cut them back around windows and vents. Do this in winter. If necessary, they can generally be cut back hard to within 1m (3ft) of the ground for renovation.

PASSIFLORA
Passion flower
Evergreen or semi-evergreen climbers, most of which are not hardy. In cooler areas, *P. caerulea* is the main species grown. It has tendrils and is self-clinging but should be grown over a suitable framework, either against a wall or fence, or over a structure. Initial training consists of spreading out the young shoots to cover as wide an area as possible. Tip-prune these to encourage more shoots to develop. Tie in any wayward shoots. Once developed, cut back flowered shoots to within a few leaves or buds of the main branch. Otherwise, just remove any weak, dead or congested growth unless it is necessary to cut back longer stems to keep the plant within bounds. They do not respond well to hard cutting back, so replant rather than renovate.

1 *Osmanthus delavayi* generally needs no pruning, either initially or when established, other than the removal of dead wood.

2 If the shrub is getting too large for its position, then some of the longer shoots can be cut back. Any wayward shoots can also be removed.

3 Dead, diseased or damaged wood should be removed when it is seen. Any pruning should be in spring, after flowering.

PAULOWNIA
Foxglove tree
Deciduous trees grown for
their foliage and flowers. Initial
training should be directed
towards developing a single-leader
tree, although, if you prefer, it
can be left to develop as a multi-
stemmed tree or shrub. If a single
trunk is desired, train a single
leader, creating a clear trunk up
to 1.2–2m (4–6ft) by removing
shoots as they appear. Once
established, there is no need for
pruning in either the tree or
shrub form. Sometimes suckers
appear and these should be
removed. Renovation is not
easy and it is better to replant in
the unlikely event of this being
necessary.

PEROVSKIA
Russian sage
Deciduous shrubs grown for their
foliage and flowers. After planting
cut back to within one or two
buds of the previous year's
growth. Continue to do this
throughout the plant's life,
cutting it back each spring, so
that the framework of the plant is

Perovskia 'Blue Spire'

kept relatively low to the ground.
Every few years, remove some
of the oldest basal structure to
promote vigour.

PHILADELPHUS
Mock orange
Deciduous shrubs grown mainly
for their fragrant flowers. They
shoot mainly from the base in
the form of a stool, so no initial
training or pruning is required.
Once established, flowered stems
can be cut back to a suitable new
shoot or to the base. Remove a

few of the oldest shoots each
year to promote new growth
and vigour. Carry this out after
flowering. *P. microphyllus* is an
exception, as little or no pruning
is required. Renovation is best
carried out as a continuous
process, but if a shrub does
become overgrown or neglected,
cut out most of the oldest wood
to ground-level and shorten newer
shoots by about half their length.

PHLOMIS
Phlomis
Evergreen shrubs grown for their
foliage and flowers. Be warned:
the "dust" from the leaves and
stems of some species can cause
an allergic reaction, so wear a
mask when pruning. No initial
training or pruning is generally
required. Little pruning is
required after the shrubs are
established other than the removal
of the flower stems back to leaves
or shoots. This can be done in
autumn. They may need shaping
if they outgrow their position.
Cut back overlong shoots to a
suitable shoot within the bush.
This is best done in spring. The
more tender species, such as
P. italica, benefit from the removal
of frosted wood in spring.
Renovate neglected plants by
cutting back hard to a basic
framework.

PHOTINIA
Photinia
Deciduous and evergreen shrubs
and trees grown mainly for their
foliage. Generally, there is no
need for any initial training and
pruning unless you want to train

it as a standard. Once established,
no pruning is required, though it
is possible to enhance the spring
colour of the foliage by cutting
back the tips of the shoots to
a strong bud. This should be
carried out in early spring. For
neglected plants, cut hard back
to a basic framework. Photinias
can be grown as a hedge
and can be trimmed two or three
times a year; this is necessary less
often for an informal hedge.

PHYGELIUS
Phygelius
Two evergreen shrubs or
subshrubs grown for their
flowers. No initial training or
pruning is required, although it
helps to tip-prune to stimulate
bushy growth. Every spring, cut
out any frosted wood back to a
shoot and remove some of the
old wood to a basal shoot or bud.
If neglected, they can become

Photinia × fraseri

Pieris japonica

Potentilla fruticosa

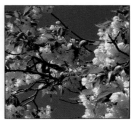

Prunus 'Shirotae'

very straggly and leggy, so try to renovate at least part of the plant each year. If in need of serious renovation, cut all the stems back almost to ground-level.

PIERIS
Pieris

Evergreen shrubs grown for their young foliage and flowers. They need little or no formative training. Generally, there is little need for pruning once the shrub becomes established. If necessary, cut out all frosted wood in spring. Remove the flower heads after the flowers have faded. Renovation can be achieved by cutting hard back to a basic framework.

PITTOSPORUM
Pittosporum

Evergreen shrubs and trees grown for their foliage. Very little initial training or pruning is required except to ensure that trees grow with a single stem. Do not clear the trunk of shoots as it looks better if clothed to the ground. Little subsequent pruning is required unless it is to shape it or keep it within bounds, in which case cut stems back inside the plant in the spring. Renovation, if necessary, can usually be achieved by cutting back hard to a basic framework.

POLYGONUM
Russian vine

Vigorous deciduous climber. They can grow very large, so

need strong supports. Avoid growing through dead trees as the weight and windage could topple the tree. The only initial training involved is to lead and tie in the shoots to their supports, spreading them out so a good coverage is achieved. Generally, the vine becomes such a tangled mass that pruning is impractical. The only thing that may need doing is to cut back the outer limits of the plant to control its spread. This can be done with shears or even a hedge trimmer. If renovation is necessary, reduce the whole plant to within 60–90cm (2–3ft) of the ground to restart it.

POPULUS
Poplar

Deciduous trees mainly grown for their foliage. These are fast-growing and often large trees that are unsuitable for most small gardens. They are all trained as a central-leader tree. Most look best with clear trunks up to 2–3m (6–10ft), but often the wounds left by removing branches will cause more to appear. They should be rubbed out as soon as they appear. Any pruning should be done in early winter, as poplars bleed less when dormant. Once developed, there is little need for further pruning, except for removal of dead branches. Any large-scale work should be left to specialist

tree surgeons. Some poplars produce suckers that should be removed. Some species are very prone to canker, and it is best to avoid pruning these so that there are no open wounds through which the disease can enter. Poplars do not renovate very well.

POTENTILLA
Cinquefoil

Deciduous shrubs grown for their flowers and foliage. Little formative pruning is required, although lightly tipping back the shoots produces a bushier plant. Once established, remove any branches that become overlong and take out one or two of the oldest stems each year in spring to renew the shrub's vigour. Clip over the plant after flowering to tidy it up. Constant renewal is better than cutting the whole shrub back at once. If a plant has become very untidy, it is best to replace it with a new plant.

PRUNUS
Ornamental cherry

Deciduous and evergreen trees and shrubs grown mainly for their flowers but also for their bark and (in deciduous types) autumn foliage. In general, prune deciduous types as little as possible. For initial training, prune as central-leader trees with a clear trunk, or as weeping standards. Suckers may appear from the roots, often some distance from the trunk. Remove these from below ground. Water shoots will often appear on the trunks, especially from around old pruning wounds. Remove these as well by rubbing out as they appear. Any grafted varieties should have any shoots that appear from below the graft removed. Other than that, avoid any pruning unless essential. Evergreens are treated in a similar way, although some can be severely pruned into topiary or hedges.

PRUNING PITTOSPORUM

1 Pittosporums need little pruning. Any dead or, as here, damaged branches should be cut back to a suitable point.

2 Cut out any multiple stems that cause congestion or badly rub against other stems. These can be cut right back to the ground.

3 Cut out any over-vigorous shoots that spoil the shape of the shrub or tree. Also cut out long shoots if they are outgrowing its space.

PYRACANTHA
Firethorn
Evergreen shrubs grown mainly for their berries. Be warned that they are armed with vicious thorns which can penetrate deeply. Wear thick gloves and some form of arm protection when pruning. Pyracanthas can be trained either as free-standing shrubs or as wall shrubs, the latter generally being preferred (especially under windows, as the thorns make them a burglar deterrent). Free-standing shrubs need little attention either initially or when established, except for tidying up if necessary by cutting back overlong stems. Wall-trained shrubs are usually trained against wires, either informally by tying branches in to the wires as and when gaps occur, or more formally by training either as an espalier (with horizontal branches on either side of a central stem) or as a fan. Once established, cut shoots back to a few buds in summer to keep the plant compact against the wall and to prevent overcrowding. They do not always renovate well from hard pruning and it may be better to replace them if necessary. They can be grown as compact, thorny hedges, which need pruning two or three times a year to keep them in shape.

PYRUS
Pear
Deciduous trees grown for their fruit, and for their foliage and flowers. Fruiting varieties are treated under *Fruit Trees*. Among the decorative varieties, one of the most popular is the silver foliage form, especially in its weeping variety (*Pyrus salicifolia* 'Pendula'). The trees are all grown as central-leader trees and should have clear trunks. Weeping varieties may need staking initially to encourage the trunk to grow upright, as they sometimes have a tendency to lean and become lop-sided. Once developed, most pears need little pruning other than the removal of dead or diseased wood. Fireblight can be a problem. Cut out the affected wood and sterilize the tools before using them again to prevent spread of the disease.

Quercus frainetto

QUERCUS
Oak
Deciduous and evergreen trees grown for their foliage and general shape. Most oak trees are likely to develop naturally into central-leader trees unless they are damaged in some way. Remove any growth on their trunks up to the level of the desired lowest branches, usually around 2.5–3m (8–10ft). Very little pruning is required except to remove dead branches, especially from very mature trees, but this is often best left to a specialist tree surgeon, as is cutting back overgrown trees. Oaks can be renovated quite hard but will take a long time to recover their normal shape. Any pruning should take place in winter.

RHODOCHITON
Deciduous perennial climbers. Initial training is confined to pinching out the tips to promote bushiness and spreading the stems wide to produce good coverage. They should be provided with vertical supports such as twigs or strings, as they have leaf stalks that enable them to climb. Once established, no pruning is required other than the removal of dead material. They are relatively short-lived, so replace rather than renovate plants.

RHODODENDRON
Rhododendron, azalea
Evergreen and deciduous shrubs and trees grown for their foliage and flowers. Generally they need little initial training or pruning but are left to develop their natural habit. If necessary, shorten overlong branches to improve the overall shape. Once established, they can be left to their own devices, with no work necessary other than the removal of dead wood. Most benefit from deadheading after flowering, but this can be impractical on large

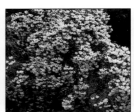
Rhododendron 'Loder's White'

Ribes sanguineum

shrubs. Some produce suckers and these should be removed, especially on grafted specimens. Most are not easy to renovate, with the exception of *R. ponticum*, which will reshoot even if cut back almost to ground level.

RHUS
Sumach
Deciduous trees or shrubs grown for their foliage (especially the autumn tints) and flower heads. There is no need for initial training unless you want to grow the plant as a tree. In this case, choose a strong stem and train it as a central leader with a clear trunk up to 1.2m (4ft) or so. There is very little subsequent pruning required except for the removal of suckers from below ground level. These can be produced in large quantities. Sumachs can be pruned hard back almost to ground-level every spring to produce especially good foliage. They can be renovated in the same way.

RIBES
Currant
Deciduous shrubs grown for their flowers and foliage or for their fruit. Fruiting varieties are dealt with under *Fruit Trees*. Decorative forms need little initial training. Once established, just remove one or two stems of the oldest wood every year after flowering. *R. speciosum* is often trained flat against a wall or fence. It can be grown either with branches tied in at random to fill the available space or trained in a more systematic way as a fan. Renovation is best carried out by regular removal of a few old stems, but they can be cut back hard.

DEADHEADING RHODODENDRONS

1 Rhododendrons generally need little pruning, but keep them neat by pinching out dead flower-heads.

2 Take them out carefully so that the surrounding buds, carrying next year's flowers, are not damaged.

PRUNING SANTOLINA

1 Santolinas can become very straggly and untidy-looking. It is not always possible to renovate them successfully.

2 However, if there are plenty of new shoots in the middle of the bush, then it is possible to prune them hard in the spring.

3 The pruned shrub showing all the new growth waiting to develop. If there are no suitable shoots, dig out the plant and replace it.

Sambucus racemosa

ROSA
Rose
Deciduous shrubs and climbers grown for their flowers. These are dealt with in detail under *Roses*.

ROSMARINUS
Rosemary
Evergreen shrubs grown for their foliage and flowers. No formative training or pruning is required. Once established, no pruning is required except to cut back any overlong shoots. Young shoots can be pinched out for culinary purposes, but spread this around the bush so that the gaps do not show. They can become aged and rather scrawny, in which case it is best to replace them rather than to attempt renovation. This lax growth can to a certain extent be avoided by cutting back the new growth lightly each year to keep the plant compact.

RUBUS
Bramble
Deciduous shrubs grown for their flowers or winter stems. Fruiting forms are dealt with under *Fruit Trees*. Species that are grown for the colour of their winter stems should be cut back to the ground in late spring. For those grown for their flowers, cut out the flowered wood after flowering back to a new shoot. At the same time, remove one or two of the oldest shoots to keep the plant growing vigorously.

SALIX
Willow
Deciduous shrubs and trees grown for their foliage, flowers (catkins) or winter stems. For general use, they can be allowed to develop naturally without any initial training (unless planted as a "living fence", in which case stems can be woven). Once established, little or no pruning is required unless they are to be pollarded or coppiced. For colourful winter stems, the young shoots are usually cut right back in spring. For living fences individual wands are rooted and then woven into the desired shape. Usually side-shoots that develop are cut back to a single bud in the autumn, so that the shape and pattern of the woven wands is still apparent. Willow can be cut back hard for renovation. Small weeping varieties should have their branches thinned each year and

Salix repens

the remaining ones cut back by about half to an outward-facing bud. Large weeping varieties should be initially trained and pruned as a single-leader tree with a clear trunk up to about 2m (6ft). Once established, little pruning is required.

SALVIA
Sage
Evergreen shrubs grown for their foliage and flowers. Prune back the shoots on planting to promote bushiness. Once established, cut back the previous year's growth to a couple of buds in the spring. Also in spring, any dead wood in *S. officinalis* should be removed. If used for culinary purposes, remove leaves and stems throughout the shrub rather than making one area bare. Sage can be cut hard back for renovation, but it is better to keep it under control in the first place.

SAMBUCUS
Elder
Deciduous shrubs grown for their foliage and flowers. Most elders can be allowed to develop naturally for the first two or three years. Thereafter, treatment varies depending on what you want from the plant. For those grown for foliage effect, cut back all the stems to a framework just above soil level in early spring before growth starts. This will promote large and colourful foliage. If

grown for flowers, remove only the oldest stems, cutting back the younger shoots to about half their length. If left unpruned for a couple of years, dead wood starts to accumulate, and this should be removed. They generally respond well to renovative pruning, but very old plants are best replaced.

SANTOLINA
Santolina
Evergreen shrubs grown for their foliage. Newly planted specimens should have their shoots reduced to encourage bushiness. Once developed, clip over in spring to keep the plant compact. In summer, it produces yellow flowers which many gardeners feel spoil the foliage effect. They can be removed as soon as the flower buds start to appear. If the flowers are allowed, trim them off in autumn once they have faded. Straggly plants are best replaced, as they do not respond well to renovation.

Santolina pinnata subsp. *neapolitana*

SCHIZOPHRAGMA
Schizophragma

Deciduous climbers grown for flowers and foliage. They are best grown on walls or strong fences but can be grown over other supports, including trees. They have aerial roots and so are self-supporting, but stems do need to be led to their support from the planting position, which should be well away from the wall (at least 45cm/18in). Spread out the shoots as much as possible to produce good coverage. Once established, little pruning is required although it is a sensible precaution to prevent them from entering gutters, eaves and vents as well as keeping them away from roofs. Take out one or two of the oldest stems each year after flowering to promote constant renewal.

SKIMMIA
Skimmia

Evergreen shrubs grown for their foliage, flowers and berries. They rarely need much pruning other than to remove any dead, damaged or diseased wood. Any pruning is cosmetic. Cut out overlong branches that upset the balance of the bush. It forms a compact bush and rarely needs trimming, but if you do, use secateurs (pruners) rather than shears, which will cut through the large leaves.

SOLANUM
Potato vine

Deciduous shrubs and climbers grown mainly for their flowers.

Sorbus

The sap can cause skin problems so take appropriate precautions when pruning. Climbers can be grown against any kind of support but look particularly good against walls. They are not self-clinging so will need to be tied into wires. Prune back shoots on planting to encourage bushiness, then spread these out to get wide coverage. Tie in shoots as they develop. In spring, prune back side shoots to two or three buds to form a framework of stems. Remove any dead wood. Cut back the oldest stems each year to promote renovation. Drastic renovation is usually unsuccessful. If old, straggly or overgrown, replace with a new plant.

SORBUS
Rowan

Deciduous trees and shrubs grown for their foliage, flowers and fruit. Formative training and pruning consists of growing them as central-leader trees, a habit they generally assume naturally. Clear the trunk to 1.2–2m (4–6ft). Once established, little pruning is

Spiraea × arguta

necessary, except to keep the base of the trunk clear of any suckers. Rowans are difficult to renovate, so replace if necessary.

SPIRAEA
Spiraea

Deciduous or evergreen shrubs grown for their foliage and flowers. Generally, no formative pruning is required. Once established, cut back flowered stems to the next shoot after flowering. Also remove one or two of the oldest shoots each year to promote continuing vigour. Renovation is best achieved by constant renewals as above.

STEPHANANDRA
Stephanandra

Deciduous shrubs grown for their foliage, especially in autumn, and flowers. No initial pruning is required and established pruning is restricted to removing a few of the oldest stems each year after flowering to achieve constant renewal. Stephanandra can sucker, and it may be necessary to remove some suckers annually to prevent the shrub spreading. Renovation can

Syringa × josiflexa

be achieved by cutting back the shrub hard to almost ground-level in early spring.

STEPHANOTIS
Bridal wreath

Evergreen tropical climbers that are mainly grown under glass in cooler countries. Initial training consists of cutting back shoots to promote bushiness. Once established, thin out some of the older wood occasionally to prevent congestion, and cut back any overlong stems if necessary. They do not respond well to hard pruning, so replant rather than cutting back hard.

SYRINGA
Lilac

Deciduous shrubs grown for their flowers. Some form a typical shrub shape while others develop more like small multi-stemmed trees. No initial training is required unless the shrub becomes misshapen. Once established, the main task is to deadhead if you can easily reach all the faded flowers. Take care not to damage the new buds behind the flower head. Also remove suckers as they appear. If it becomes necessary, lilacs can be cut hard back for renovation purposes.

TAMARIX
Tamarisk

Airy deciduous shrubs and trees grown for their flowers and feathery foliage. Initial pruning consists of pruning back shoots to promote bushiness, both in its first and next two seasons. Once established, cut back flowered stems to a strong shoot. Do this after flowering, except with late-flowering varieties, which should be pruned in spring. They can be renovated by cutting back hard to a basic framework.

PRUNING SKIMMIA

1 Skimmias do not usually need any pruning and are spoilt if tightly pruned. However, they do occasionally have dead stems that need to be removed.

2 (*right*) Cut these stems out, along with any damaged shoots, back to sound wood.

3 The shrubs are usually well balanced, but if there are any wayward shoots, remove these as well, cutting back into the bush.

Tilia platyphyllos

THYMUS
Thyme
Low-growing shrubs grown for their foliage and flowers as well as for culinary purposes. No initial training is required. Once established, cut back flowered stems, but do not cut back into old wood. If picking for the kitchen, only cut the new growth or gaps will appear. Some of those with decorative foliage may well have shoots that revert back to the original green. Cut these out as soon as they appear. If plants get too old and straggly, replace them, as cutting back hard is seldom successful.

TILIA
Lime
Deciduous trees grown for their foliage and flowers. Their size means they are usually best in large gardens, unless they are pleached. Formative training is as a single-leader tree, with a trunk cleared of shoots and branches to about 2–3m (6–10ft). Little subsequent pruning is required unless there is a problem with the tree, when professional tree surgeons should be called in. The trees can be easily pleached to provide screens or covered walkways. Renovation should always be carried out by professionals.

TRACHELOSPERMUM
Star jasmine
Evergreen climbers grown for their foliage and flowers. They are twiners and should be provided with a vertical support. Initial

Trachelospermum asiaticum

training consists of spreading out the shoots so that the whole of the support will be covered, and tying them in to get them started. Little or no pruning is required once established. Cut back shoots in spring by half for renovation. Extremely overgrown plants are best replaced.

ULMUS
Elm
Deciduous trees grown for their foliage and shape. These are mainly very big trees and any serious pruning needs to be undertaken by a professional tree surgeon. Initially they should be trained and pruned, if necessary, as single-leader trees, clearing the trunk from 2–3m (6–10ft) and maintaining a balanced shape. Little further pruning is required. Renovation should be undertaken by professionals.

VIBURNUM
Viburnum
Deciduous and evergreen shrubs grown for their flowers, foliage and (sometimes) fruit. All need little initial pruning The deciduous winter-flowering types, such as *V.* × *bodnantense*, should be

Viburnum opulus 'Xanthocarpum'

pruned once established by removing some of the oldest growth from the base each year in spring. Others require the minimum of pruning, although those that sucker or layer should have any suckers removed to prevent the shape of the plant being compromised. Most can be cut back hard for renovation purposes. *V. tinus* can be trained as an attractive standard.

VINCA
Periwinkle
Evergreen shrubs grown for their foliage and flowers as well as for ground cover. Initial training is unnecessary, but once established it is likely to be necessary to cut back long shoots to keep the plant compact and to prevent them rooting outside their allotted space. Ground cover can be sheared or strimmed over to keep it neat and compact to the ground. Those grown through hedges can be cut back when the hedge is cut. Alternatively, reduce long, arching stems as necessary. Renovation consists of cutting plants hard back to the ground.

VITIS
Vine
Deciduous climbers grown for their foliage and/or fruit. The fruiting varieties of grapes are dealt with under *Climbing Fruit*. The decorative forms need to be supported by a strong trellis or pergola, although they can also be trained through trees. Cut

Vitis vinifera 'Purpurea'

back the original shoots to encourage more, and tie the resulting shoots in to the support to ensure maximum coverage. Continue to tie in as the plant develops. Once the space is covered, cut back all side shoots to one or two buds each winter. If the vines are particularly vigorous, it may be necessary to repeat this in summer. If they are grown solely for their leaves, remove flowers as they appear. Overgrown plants can be renovated by cutting back hard, even right to the base if necessary.

WEIGELA
Weigela
Deciduous shrubs grown mainly for their flowers. Formative pruning is not generally required. Once the plant is established and starts flowering, cut back the flowered stems after flowering to a strong shoot. If the shrub becomes misshapen with overlong stems, reduce these in length. In spring, cut out one or two of the oldest stems to promote constant rejuvenation. On variegated and coloured foliage forms, cut out any stems that bear plain green leaves. Renovate by cutting back hard almost to ground-level.

WISTERIA
Wisteria
Deciduous climbers grown for flowers and foliage. For further details of pruning and training, see *Ornamental Climbers and Wall Shrubs*.

Wisteria floribunda

Fruit Trees

Fruit trees have been grown since gardens were first cultivated. Simple pruning has always been undertaken to make fruit trees as productive as possible. However, in recent times, different rootstocks have been produced to control the size and shape of the tree, and with that new methods of pruning have been devised that increase control over the tree and its fruiting capacity. So, now, instead of a normal tree that would take up all of a small garden, you can choose from a variety of shapes, from poles to fans. These can be grown as free-standing trees or trained against walls or fences, or even planted in pots. Now anyone can grow a fruit tree, even with only a balcony.

Although pruning a fruit tree initially appears very daunting, once you have become more familiar with the process, it becomes second nature. Bear in mind that you only need acquire those techniques which apply to the trees you have. However, ignore them and the trees will soon become overgrown and the amount and quality of fruit considerably reduced.

You can simply buy any tree and plant it, but after a few years the results can be disappointing. However, if you learn to prune your trees and attend to them regularly they will provide a lifetime's supply of fruit, well repaying your original investment. The following pages show a range of ways to train and prune various types of hardy fruit tree.

LEFT There is great satisfaction to be gained from growing your own apples: nothing tastes quite so sweet as your own fruit that has been freshly picked from the tree.

Fruit tree shapes

While the typical mental image of a tree is usually a large plant with a solid trunk and a rounded system of branches, there is also a wide variety of forms in which fruit trees in particular can be trained.

Size

There are several reasons for choosing a particular shape of fruit tree. The first is size. A fully grown apple tree, for example, can take up a lot of space, especially in a small garden, but a dwarf pyramid can be fitted into a limited space, while cordons can be grown along a fence or even as a hedge.

Productivity and quality

The second reason for training fruit trees is for improved productivity and quality. A fan grown against a wall will not only produce a large crop but will supply individual fruits with the maximum amount of light for even ripening. The upper branches of a standard tree can shade the lower branches, and these in turn will shade the ground beneath it, limiting what you can grow there. A free-standing fan or cordons that are trained against wires will be far less limiting. Training trees against

ABOVE Espaliered fruit trees are decorative as well as productive and can be used to create effective screens between areas of the garden.

walls also provides protection and warmth for more tender fruits such as peaches or nectarines.

More varieties

When choosing the shape of your tree you should also think about the number of varieties you require. For example, a fan might occupy the whole of one wall, but in the same amount of space you could grow half a dozen cordons or more. These will not necessarily yield more fruit but

could provide variety, giving you a lot more choice in terms of flavour and timing of harvest.

Decorative qualities

Do not overlook the decorative aspect of trained fruit trees. A tall pear espalier growing against the end of a house can be stunning, as can fans on a smaller scale. Free-standing cordons and espaliers produce excellent screens, and can be used as dividers in a kitchen garden.

Choosing trees

Before buying a tree consider the above aspects and think about where you are going to plant it and what the best shape is for the space available. It is also worth bearing in mind that basic shapes, such as standards, require far less pruning than more complicated ones. Something that is often forgotten is that the fruit on larger forms may be out of reach, so if you are not happy on ladders or steps, then these are not for you.

ABOVE Fans are a decorative form which look particularly good when grown against walls. They look attractive, both in blossom and in fruit.

ABOVE Fruit trees can be grown in containers. Here, pear trees have been trained in the form of multiple cordons in terracotta pots.

ABOVE Pole apples are a relatively new introduction. They are particularly suitable for small gardens because they take up little space.

FRUIT TREE SHAPES

The shapes of your fruit trees should be chosen according to their suitability for your available garden space. The more decorative shapes are again dependent on space, but are also a matter of personal preference with regard to how they fit in with the design of the garden as a whole. Obviously, the larger decorative shapes will produce more fruit.

BUSH TREE This is the most practical "tree" shape for most domestic gardens. The size is not too large, making it relatively easy to pick the fruit as well as to carry out pruning.

STANDARD This is the largest of the fruit tree shapes and is not often grown these days. Standards are very large, open trees that need ladders to access them.

SEMI-STANDARD This is similar to a standard except it is smaller. They still need ladders to reach the fruit and for pruning. They have the advantage of looking like a "tree".

SPINDLE BUSH A small, bush-like fruit tree that has its branches spaced for maximum light. Most can be reached from the ground, although taller ones need steps.

DWARF PYRAMID The smallest of the tree shapes and eminently suitable for a small garden. Fruit can be reached and pruning can done from the ground.

FAN This a very good fruit tree shape for walls, fences or even free-standing wirework. Fans are highly decorative and can also be very productive.

CORDON This takes up very little space and can be surprisingly productive. A row of different varieties can easily be accommodated in a small garden.

DOUBLE CORDON This is similar to a cordon, but is upright and has two main stems. Double cordons are obviously more productive than single ones.

POLE This is rather like a single cordon except that it can be much taller. Poles are very useful for small gardens and some can be grown in containers.

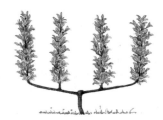  

MULTIPLE CORDON This is very similar to the double cordon except that it has four or five upright stems. These can look very decorative, especially once they have aged.

ESPALIER This is one of the most productive of the more decorative shapes. If used against the end of a house, it can produce enough tiers to reach the eaves.

STEPOVER A delightful way of growing apples and pears, making good edging for paths or for dividing areas. In essence, it is a one-tiered espalier.

Rootstocks

There is much more than meets
the eye in the production of a fruit
tree. While most other plants
are grown from seed or by some
vegetative means, such as cuttings
or division, this does not apply to
apples and many other fruit trees.
The only way to propagate them is
to graft a bud or cutting on to a
rootstock. Always check with your
supplier before buying a fruit tree
that it is on a rootstock suitable for
your needs.

A matter of size

The type of rootstock will determine
the characteristics of your tree. The
graft or scion will determine
the type of tree (e.g. 'Bramley'
or 'Golden Delicious'), while the
rootstock will determine the vigour
and hence the ultimate size of the
tree. Much research has been carried
out into rootstocks and there is an
increasing number of them. Until
relatively recently, for example,
cherry trees could only be grown on
non-dwarfing stock and were often
very large.

PLANTING A FRUIT TREE

1 Thoroughly prepare
the earth, both around the
position of the hole and in
the bottom of the hole itself.
Add plenty of well-rotted
organic matter.

2 Check that the rootball is
not pot-bound and the roots
are not tangled. If they are
tangled, gently tease them
out, handling them as little
as possible.

3 Place the young tree into
the hole and check that
the surrounding soil is
approximately level with that
in the container. Do not put
the graft below ground.

4 Knock a post in at an
angle to avoid damaging
the roots. Cut off any extra,
so that it does not present
a hazard.

5 Firmly secure the tree
to the post, using a proper
tree tie. Do not use string or
anything that can cut into or
chafe the trunk.

6 The tree is now ready for
its initial pruning. The shape
should be rectified to ensure
that it grows evenly. The
ground should be mulched.

ABOVE An apple on M9 rootstock, which is a
dwarfing stock suitable for many bushes and
decorative forms in the small garden.

ABOVE An apple on M26 rootstock, a semi-
dwarfing stock that can be used for slightly
larger decorative forms, like fans and espaliers.

ABOVE An apple on M27, which is the smallest
of the rootstocks, used for dwarf pyramids,
cordons and other restricted-size forms.

Other qualities

As well as determining final size and shape, rootstocks also influence resistance to pests and diseases. Certain rootstocks are also more suited to certain conditions. Some are more tolerant of drought or can stand cold weather better. In general, one need not worry much about these aspects, as trees sold in your area will probably be suited to local conditions. But bear this in mind if ordering from a nursery.

Planting

In general, fruit trees are sold as "whips", which have a single, upright stem, or "feathered", which have developed side shoots. Planting fruit trees is basically no different from planting any other tree. The ground should be thoroughly prepared and drainage improved if there is the chance that the planting hole will turn into a sump which will retain water. It is important to ensure that the tree is planted at the correct depth. If the junction between the rootstock and the scion is below ground, then the scion is likely to produce suckers that will produce a tree much larger and more vigorous than you had hoped. So, it is important to ensure that the graft is above ground. Make certain that the correct support is in place before planting and then tie in the tree to it.

GRAFTED ROOSTOCKS
This is the rootstock of a grafted fruit tree, showing the junction between the rootstock and the scion, which will form the basis of the tree.

Apple rootstocks

M27	extreme dwarfing stock	bush tree, dwarf pyramid, cordon
M9	dwarfing stock	bush tree, dwarf pyramid, cordon
M26	semi-dwarfing stock	bush tree, dwarf pyramid, cordon
MM106	semi-dwarfing stock	bush tree, spindle bush, cordon, fan, espalier
M7	semi-dwarfing stock	bush tree, spindle bush, cordon, fan, espalier
M4	semi-vigorous stock	bush tree, spindle bush
MM4	vigorous stock	standard
M2	vigorous stock	standard
MM111	vigorous stock	semi-standard, standard, large bush, large fan, large espalier
M25	vigorous stock	standard
MM109	vigorous stock	standard
M1	vigorous stock	standard

Pear rootstocks

Quince C	moderately dwarfing stock	bush tree, cordon, dwarf pyramid, espalier, fan
Quince A	semi-vigorous stock	bush tree, cordon, dwarf pyramid, espalier, fan
Pear	vigorous stock	standard, semi-standard

Cherry rootstocks

Tabel/Edabritz	dwarfing stock	bush tree
Gisela 5	dwarfing stock	bush tree
Colt	semi-vigorous stock	semi-standard
GM61.1	semi-vigorous stock	semi-standard
Mazard	vigorous stock	standard
Mahaleb	vigorous stock	standard

Plum, gage and damson rootstocks

Pixy	dwarfing stock	bush tree, pyramid
Damas C	moderately vigorous stock	bush tree
St Julien A	semi-vigorous stock	bush tree, fan, pyramid
Brompton A	vigorous stock	semi-standard, standard
Myrobalan B	vigorous stock	semi-standard, standard

Apricot, peach and nectarine rootstocks

St Julien A	semi-vigorous stock	bush tree, fan
Brompton A	vigorous stock	bush tree
Peach seedling	vigorous stock	standard, bush tree
Apricot seedling	vigorous stock	standard, bush tree

Basic techniques

As with most aspects of gardening, there are many ways of achieving the same end when it comes to pruning fruit trees. However, there are certain basic rules which apply, especially in connection with how the tree bears fruit.

Basic cuts

The general rules of good pruning apply as much to fruit trees as they do to ornamental ones. Cuts on both smaller shoots and larger branches should be close to a bud or junction so that no die-back occurs on the "snag" (the piece beyond the bud). If you cut between two buds, the section above the remaining bud will invariably die and may cause more extensive problems. The cut should gently slope away from the bud.

The second point to remember is that large branches are heavy, so if you cut straight through one from above, as you approach the bottom of the cut the weight of the branch will cause it to fall and tear back beyond the cut, potentially causing certain problems. Always make a cut

ABOVE It is often necessary to thin out some of the foliage on a fig bush in order to expose the developing fruit to sufficient sunlight to ripen well.

on the underside of the branch first, then make the downward cut. When the branch falls it will now only split as far as your undercut. Once the branch is removed, you can trim back the stub.

The jury is still out as to whether to paint the larger cuts with a sealant. It was once a widespread practice and then became frowned upon, but has been partially revived by some growers in recent years.

ABOVE Upright posts should be knocked into the ground before the tree is planted as they will break the roots if inserted later.

ABOVE If the crop is heavy, you may need to thin out some of the apples in mid-summer to allow the remainder to develop properly.

ABOVE Cutting back the new growth on a pear to reduce its vigour and to promote the formation of fruiting spurs.

ABOVE Spur-bearing fruit trees. Some apple trees produce fruit on older wood and this is normally pruned to form clusters of spurs.

ABOVE Tip-bearing fruit trees. Other trees produce their fruit on the tips of the shoots and must be pruned in such a way that these are not removed.

With so much controversy surrounding the practice, you can make your own choice. The simplest way, which appears as sound as any, is to make clean cuts and leave them alone, apart from paring round the wound with a knife to tidy up any jagged bark.

Initial training

During the first few years after planting it is important to train the tree so that it assumes the desired shape. The basic shape of a cordon might be simple but that of a large fan may take a number of years to complete. Even the less obviously contrived forms such as standards and bushes need initial attention, as they are not quite as natural-growing as they look. These need well-spaced branches and open centres if all the fruit is to have equal access to light and air.

MAIDEN WHIP In the first year only the main stem develops above the graft. Trees sold in this form are known as maiden whips.

FEATHERED WHIP During the second or subsequent years the maiden whip produces side shoots and is known as a feathered whip.

LATERALS OR SIDE SHOOTS (*top*) This is a new lateral or side shoot with just one year's growth.

(*above*) This is the same lateral in its second year, showing the old and new wood.

Blossom and fruit

Which parts of the plant carry blossom and then fruit varies according to type, and this has a direct bearing on how trees are pruned. For example, most apples produce fruit on short shoots, usually occurring in clusters called spurs. These are usually three years old or more. On the other hand, some varieties produce fruit towards the tips of longer shoots. It follows that the removal of longer shoots in the case of tip bearers would reduce the crop. This is why tip bearers such as 'Worcester Permain' apple cannot be trained as cordons, as the pruning required to maintain the shape would entail removing the fruiting wood. Some trees (e.g. fruiting sour cherries and peaches) produce fruit only on the previous year's growth, so have to be pruned to encourage plenty of new growth.

General pruning

As well as pruning for fruit, it is also important to consider the general shape of the tree. Any dead or damaged branches should be removed. Along with these, any weak growth, or branches that cross over others, rubbing or crowding them, should be cut out.

Timing

Timing varies according to the type of fruit and the method of training. Generally, standard and bush fruit only need pruning once a year, while the more complex shapes, such as fans, need pruning twice a year.

Renovating fruit trees

If trees are looked after well and pruned regularly, they will continue to fruit freely for many years. However, you may sometimes inherit trees that have been neglected for a variety of reasons or you may not have been as diligent as you might have, and the trees become overgrown and congested. In such cases, the trees do not fruit as prolifically as they once did and those fruits that are carried are much smaller than they should be and are often diseased.

Past it

Not all fruit trees are worth renovating. If they are very ancient, diseased and/or broken, they are best removed and replaced with new ones. If you want to use the tree for shade only, rather than as a fruiting specimen, then it may have a few years of life left in it, but there is always the danger that it may suddenly collapse, causing damage to other plants and possibly even injuring somebody.

First year

It is best to stagger renovation over a period of two to three years so that the tree has a chance to recover from each stage and does not get over-stressed. The first thing to do – as with all pruning jobs – is to look for any dead wood and remove it. At the same time, cut out any dead, diseased, or damaged wood. This will not impose any stress on the tree, so you can go further in the first year. The next problem to tackle is overcrowding. Firstly, you will need to take out any branch that crosses any other branch, especially if it rubs against it. Stand back and assess the tree, noticing whether there is any over-crowding. If necessary, remove some of the branches, especially in

RENOVATING A FRUIT TREE

1 Sometimes a fruit tree can become overgrown, usually through neglect. This is not only unsightly, but it also reduces the tree's productivity.

2 The first task when renovating is to cut out all the dead, diseased or damaged wood. Next, take out any of the older wood that is causing congestion or rubbing other branches.

3 Take out all the "suckers" – new, straight growth, which, if it is allowed to develop, will make the crowding and unproductivity of the tree worse.

4 Cutting back the new growth in this way will encourage new fruiting spurs to develop and increase the tree's fruiting potential.

5 The centre of the tree should now be opened up slightly, so that it is not too crowded and light can enter. This will improve the ripening of the fruit.

6 The same tree the following summer showing the vigorous growth as a result of the renovation. It will need further pruning in spring to contain it.

SPUR-THINNING FRUIT TREES

It is important after a few years to ensure that spurs do not become too crowded, as this will cause a drop in the amount and quality of the fruit being produced. It then becomes important to thin them.

BEFORE PRUNING Once a tree has been bearing fruit for a number of years, the clusters of spurs can become very crowded and productivity can drop.

AFTER PRUNING Reduce the number of spurs by cutting out a number of the older ones, leaving enough to produce the following autumn's fruit.

ABOVE Rows of well-maintained trees in an orchard. Note how pruning has kept the centre of the trees open.

the middle of the tree, so that light can enter and air circulate. If there is a lot to be removed, concentrate on the centre for the first year and thin round the periphery the following year. By now the tree should be beginning to look less neglected and will have gone some way to recovering its proper shape.

Below the tree

If you have a neglected tree, it is important to deal with the ground beneath as well as pruning it. Clear away any brambles and other tough growing weeds. Lightly fork the ground and add plenty of garden compost, manure or other fertilizer. Top-dress with a mulch to improve its moisture-retentiveness. Apply the mulch in a doughnut-like ring around the trunk, making sure it does not touch the trunk. Contact could lead to rotting and/or the production of suckers.

Second year

The shape of the tree has been improved overall, and now it is time to improve the fruiting. Thin out overcrowding around the edges of the tree, if this was not done in the first year. Also, remove much of the new upright growth from the main branches, so that the tree presents a "clean" look. (These whippy growths are often known as "suckers" due to their similarity in appearance to the true suckers that appear from the ground.) Shorten growth at the ends of the branches, cutting back to a replacement bud. The clusters of fruiting spurs are likely to be overcrowded and these will need thinning.

PRUNING A YOUNG PEAR TREE

1 The best way to avoid the need to renovate fruit trees is to start pruning correctly from an early age. Here, young pear trees are being prepared.

2 The central leader of the young pear tree is removed so that the tree bushes out rather than growing tall and lanky.

3 The longer laterals or side shoots are cut back by about half so that they branch, thus creating a well-balanced fruit tree.

4 The shorter laterals towards the top of the leader should now be cut back to a growth bud.

5 Side shoots that are not required for the main structure of the tree should be tipped to encourage fruiting spurs to develop.

APPLES (*Malus domestica*)
Apple standard and semi-standard

The apple standard used to be the preferred type of tree for most commercial growers and for many gardeners. They have fallen out of favour because they take up a great deal of space, besides being awkward to prune, spray, net and pick. However, they still have their devotees, as in the garden they cast incomparable shade for sitting under. The semi-standard, a shorter version, is not so vigorous and has much to recommend it. Both types are free-standing trees. To the uninitiated they can look like unpruned natural trees, so fit in well with many garden settings.

Supports
Drive a stout stake into the ground before planting the tree (doing it after planting risks damage to the roots). In exposed positions, a stake on either side is more secure. Attach to the tree with proprietary tree ties (not string or old nylon tights, which can dig into the bark).

Initial training
Start with a feathered tree, staked. As it grows, gradually remove the lowest side branches to create a bare trunk. Continue to do this until the

ABOVE The medium-size fruit of the apple 'Katja' is best eaten straight from the tree because it quickly loses its flavour.

trunk has reached the required height. Now remove the leader. The main branches then develop from this point and any remaining branches on the trunk can be removed. Ensure that the branches are well spread and remove any that

cross. Shorten the shoots that develop on these branches so that the tree branches out. Keep the centre of the tree open.

Established pruning
Usually only winter pruning is required for standards. The method depends on whether the variety is spur-bearing or tip-bearing. On the former, remove any excessively vigorous and/or badly placed wood, along with any branches that are crossing or rubbing. The leaders of all branches can be reduced by one-quarter to one-third of the previous season's growth. Check the spurs: if any are overcrowded, remove the older and less productive wood. On tip-bearers, either leave the young wood unpruned or just remove the tip back to a bud. Take out older wood back to young shoots to ensure renewal and continued fruiting. Again, also take out any crossing or rubbing branches as well as any that are too vigorous or are misplaced. In both cases try to keep the centre reasonably open.

ABOVE 'Laxtons' Epicure' apples. There are lots of varieties of apple available to gardeners that cannot be bought at the supermarket.

Varieties

Dessert	
'Blenheim Orange'	'Laxton's Fortune'
'Braeburn'	'Laxton's Superb'
'Cox's Orange	'Lord Lambourne'
Pippin'	'Millers Seedling'
'Discovery'	'Ribston Pippin'
'Egremont Russet'	'Starking'
'Fuji'	'Sturmer Pippin'
'Gala'	'Worcester
'George Cave'	Pearmain'
'Golden Delicious'	
'Granny Smith'	**Cooking**
'Idared'	'Bramley's Seedling'
'James Grieve'	'Grenadier'
'Jonagold'	'Howgate Wonder'
'Jonathan'	'Lord Darby'
	'Newton Wonder'

TRAINING AN APPLE STANDARD

There is not a great deal to do when training a standard or semi-standard apple. However, the training that is required is very important because the initial structure will be with the tree for life unless branches become diseased or damaged. Both tip- and spur-bearers are started in the same way, but they are treated differently from the third year onwards.

SPUR- AND TIP-BEARERS Plant a young feathered tree and remove any laterals below what will be the lowest branches. Grow on until the top branches are formed at the height you want them and then remove the leader. Cut back the branches to get them to bush out.

SPUR- AND TIP-BEARERS As the tree develops, remove any sub-branches that cross over or rub against each other, cut back new growth on the main branches by half, and cut back any side shoots not required as branches to about four buds.

SPUR-BEARERS Once the fruit tree is established, cut back new shoots to about five buds. Continue to remove any misplaced shoots on branches. Thin the clusters of spurs if they become overcrowded. Occasionally, replace older sub-branches by cutting back to a strong shoot.

SPUR-BEARERS Continue to cut back the new growth of the main leaders by a quarter to one-third. Develop the fruiting spurs by cutting the shoots not required for branch development back to four buds. Continue to remove any crossing or misplaced shoots or branches.

TIP-BEARERS Tip-bearing apples should only have the new growth on the main branches cut back by a quarter. Do not prune any of the other shoots unless they are crossing or misplaced, in which case they should be removed or cut back to a suitable shoot or growth bud.

TIP-BEARERS Once tip-bearing trees have become established, little or no pruning is required. Just cut back the tips. Cut out any crossing or congested wood, especially towards the centre of the tree, which should be kept as open as possible.

Apple bush tree

Bush trees are similar in form to standards and semi-standards but are smaller. This makes them useful to anyone with a small garden. A well-developed bush is still tall enough to sit under and looks like a smaller version of a fully grown tree, which may be important for the design of the garden. Again, like standards and semi-standards, bush trees are suitable for both spur- and tip-bearing varieties.

Supports

Choose a stout stake, and insert this into the ground before the tree is planted. Avoid doing it after planting as this can damage the roots. In exposed positions, a stake on either side is more secure. Use proprietary tree ties, as these are designed to expand so that they do not rub and bruise the bark.

Initial training

You will need to start with a feathered tree, which is staked. As the young tree grows, gradually remove the lowest side branches in order to

ABOVE Bush trees are the best type of apple if you want a "tree-shaped" tree. They are relatively small, even on larger rootstock.

ABOVE There is nothing quite as rewarding as growing your fruit. This apple will taste as good as it looks.

create a bare trunk. Do this until the trunk has reached the height you want. You should now remove the leader. The tree's main branches now develop from this point and any remaining branches on the trunk

should be removed. As usual, ensure that the branches are well spread and remove any that cross. Shorten the shoots that develop on the branches so that the tree branches out. Keep the centre of the tree open.

Established pruning

You will usually only need to prune bush trees in the winter. The method you use depends on whether the tree is spur-bearing or tip-bearing. For spur-bearing apples, remove any overly vigorous and unwanted wood, as well as any branches that are crossing or rubbing. The leaders of all the branches can be reduced by about a quarter to one-third of the previous season's growth. If any of the spurs are overcrowded, then remove the older and less productive wood. For tip-bearing apples, either leave the young wood unpruned or just remove the tip back to a bud. Remember to take out older wood back to young shoots to ensure renewal and continued fruiting. As usual, take out any crossing or rubbing branches, and any that are too vigorous or misplaced. Try to keep the centre of both types reasonably open.

ABOVE An apple bush tree can make a decorative, as well as productive, feature in a domestic garden. This variety is 'Pruniflora'.

TRAINING AN APPLE BUSH TREE

Bush trees are ideal for the small garden as they do not need a great deal of training or pruning once they are established. Both initial training and the pruning are very similar to that of standard and semi-standard trees, except that the tree is on a smaller scale. Both tip- and spur-bearers are started in the same way, but from the third year onwards they are treated differently.

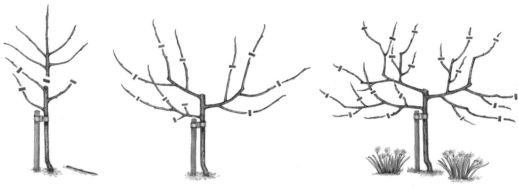

SPUR- AND TIP-BEARERS In winter, plant a young feathered tree. Grow on until the top branches have reached the required height. Remove the leader and prune back the branches so that they will divide. Remove any laterals below what will be the lowest branches.

SPUR- AND TIP-BEARERS Remove any shoots that cross over or rub, and cut back new growth on main leaders by half. Any side shoots not required as branches should also be cut back to about four buds.

SPUR-BEARERS Cut back new shoots to about five buds, once the bushes are established. Continue to remove any misplaced shoots or branches. Thin the clusters of spurs if they become overcrowded. Occasionally replace older sub-branches by cutting back to a strong shoot.

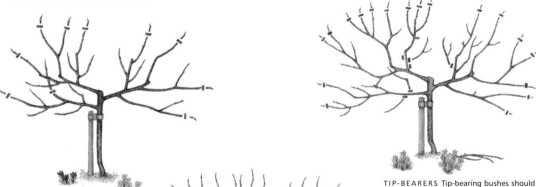

SPUR-BEARERS Continue to cut back the new growth of the main leaders by a quarter to one-third. Develop the fruiting spurs by cutting the shoots not required for branch development back to four buds. Continue to remove any crossing or misplaced shoots or branches.

TIP-BEARERS Tip-bearing bushes should only have the new growth on the main branches cut back by a quarter in their third year. Do not prune any of the other shoots, except if they are crossing or misplaced when they should be removed or cut back to a suitable shoot or growth bud.

TIP-BEARERS Once tip-bearing bush trees have become established little or no pruning is required. Just cut back the tips. Cut out any crossing or congested wood, especially towards the centre of the tree which should be kept as open as possible.

Apple spindle bush

This form of training and pruning is derived from commercial practice. It offers an effective way of producing heavy crops on small trees, but it is not the most elegant of forms for the domestic garden, and is really used only by gardeners who want to produce the maximum number of apples in a small space, without worrying too much about the tree's appearance. The basic principle involves developing horizontal branches that will produce more fruiting buds and hence a heavier crop.

ABOVE Spindle bushes allow a number of varieties to be grown within a small space, giving the appearance of a small orchard.

Supports

A stake that is as tall as the fruit tree will eventually grow is required. It should be inserted into the ground before the tree is planted so the tree roots are not damaged when the stake is driven into the ground. Tie the tree to the stake at several points as it develops. The stake can be left in place even once the tree has reached maturity.

Initial pruning

Plant a feathered tree against the stake and cut the leader off at around 1m (3ft) from ground level. Reduce the number of laterals to three or four. The lowest should be about 60cm (2ft) from the ground. The laterals should be well spaced, both around and up the trunk. During the first summer these laterals will develop new leaders which should be gently pulled down to as near the horizontal as possible. Hold them in place by tying them to pegs in the ground or staples towards the base of the stake. Make certain that the string does not cut into the branches. As a new leader is formed tie it in to the stake and allow further well-placed laterals to develop. You can encourage this

process by cutting back the leader each winter by about one-third to a bud on the opposite side to that from which growth emerged the year before. Allow the side branches to develop, removing any vigorous or crossing growth. Aim to keep the branches horizontal and open to the light and air. When the leader has reached the desired height of around 2–2.2m (6–7ft) (the highest that can be comfortably reached without a ladder), cut it back to two buds each year.

TRAINING AN APPLE SPINDLE BUSH

Spindle bush trees can look rather more complicated to train and prune than other fruit tree shapes, largely because of the strings, but, in fact, they are not at all difficult and the resulting productivity can be well worth the effort.

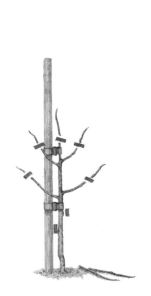

YEAR ONE, WINTER Spindle bushes are started by planting a young feathered tree. It should be secured to a strong, firm stake that is taller than the young tree. Take out the leader at about 1m (3ft) above the ground. Cut out the bottom laterals up to about 60cm (2ft).

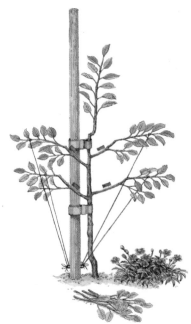

YEAR ONE, SUMMER During the tree's first summer, pull the remaining laterals gently down and tie them to staples at the bottom of the stake, or to pegs that have been inserted into the ground. Tie the new leader to the stake as it develops.

Established pruning

Once the tree has reached its ultimate height, prune back the leader each year to one or two buds. It should be possible to remove the strings that are holding down the branches without the branches springing back up again. Any replacement branches should be tied down so that they do not follow their natural inclination to grow upwards.

Also continue to prune out any vigorous or crossing growth. Each year allow some new growth to develop to replace some of the older wood, which can then be removed.

ABOVE Rows of commercially grown spindle bushes show how relatively short they are, making them easy to prune and pick.

ABOVE A spindle tree coming into production. It would be better to tie the strings to pegs in the earth rather than to the trunk.

SUBSEQUENT YEARS Repeat these two processes each year until the spindle bush reaches the height to which you want it to grow, usually around 2–2.2m (6–7ft). Cut out any shoots that attempt to grow vertically or upset the balance of the tree.

ESTABLISHED PRUNING Once the tree has reached its ultimate height, prune back the leader each year to one or two buds. Cut out some of the older wood each year to promote new, more productive wood, and remove any crossing or rubbing wood. The strings can be removed once the tree has matured.

Apple dwarf pyramid

For the gardener with a small garden who likes to grow apples on a tree, as opposed to artificial shapes such as cordons or fans, the dwarf pyramid offers the ideal solution. The trees are on a dwarfing stock, which prevents them from becoming too vigorous, and are usually restricted to a maximum height of 2m (6ft) with a spread of around 1.2m (4ft). Because of the restricted size, the range of varieties is usually confined to spur-bearing apples, but this still provides the gardener with a far wider range of varieties than is normally found in either the supermarket or at a greengrocer.

Supports

A stout pole or stake should be inserted in the ground before the tree is planted (doing it afterwards can damage the roots). The stake should protrude at least 2m (6ft) above the ground. Use proprietary tree ties, rather than string, to attach the trunk to the stake.

Initial training

The tree is trained into a cone shape with the branches getting progressively shorter towards the top of the trunk. Start with a feathered tree with well-spaced laterals. Remove any misplaced side shoots or those that point sharply upwards. Cut back each remaining lateral to about 15cm (6in) from the trunk, if possible to an outward- (not upward-) facing bud. Reduce the length of the leader to a bud about 75cm (30in) above the ground. Take out any laterals that are below about 45cm (18in) from the ground. In the summer, remove entirely any vigorous vertical growth that appears. Leave the main leader unpruned but reduce the side shoots of the main branches to about 10cm (4in). During the second winter shorten the previous season's growth of the leaders to about 20cm (8in), cutting

ABOVE Dwarf pyramids are small enough to be easily grown in large containers, which are ideal for a courtyard or patio. The pruning involved is no different from that of dwarf pyramids planted in the open ground.

TRAINING AN APPLE DWARF PYRAMID

Dwarf pyramids are some of the best shapes and size of apple tree to grow in a small domestic garden, making it possible to grow several different varieties. In general, dwarf pyramids start to produce apples very quickly.

YEAR ONE, WINTER Plant a feathered tree. Remove the leader about 75cm (30in) above ground-level. Take out any laterals below about 45cm (18in) above the ground. Cut back all other laterals to about 15cm (6in).

YEAR ONE, SUMMER Cut back the side shoots on the main branches in the following summer to about 10cm (4in). Leave the main leader and those of the branches unpruned.

ABOVE The central leader is cut back after planting in its first winter. It is cut back to a good bud, about 75cm (30in) above the ground.

to a downward-facing bud. The main leader should also be cut back by about two-thirds, to a bud on the opposite side to that from which growth emerged the previous year. In the second summer reduce the new growth of the main branch leaders to about 20cm (8in) and that of the side shoots to about 15cm (6in).

Established pruning

Once the tree has attained its outline, probably in its third year, it will need pruning twice a year to keep it compact. In summer, cut back the new growth of all main stems to about six leaves. Cut back all new shoots to about half this. At the same time reduce any new growth from the clusters of spurs to one

ABOVE Once established, new side shoots are cut back to one bud to help promote the growth of the spurs which produce the fruit.

leaf. In the winter, cut back new growth to one bud in order to promote new spurs. Also, cut back the main leader to one bud of its new growth. As the tree ages, thin out the older clusters of spurs as they become overcrowded.

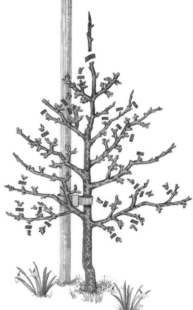

YEAR TWO, WINTER In the following winter, reduce the new growth of all the branch leaders to about 20cm (8in). The new growth of the main leader should be cut back by about two-thirds.

YEAR TWO, SUMMER In the second summer, leave the main leader as it is, but again cut back the new growth of the branch leaders to about 20cm (8in) and that of the side shoots to about 15cm (6in).

ESTABLISHED PRUNING Once established, the apple tree bush will need pruning both in summer and again in winter, otherwise it will rapidly become overgrown. Follow the instructions in the main text above.

Apple cordons

The technique of training apples on wires as cordons allows a number of different varieties to be planted in a relatively small space. Admittedly, the quantities of fruit produced are not large, but it allows cropping over a long period, if the varieties are selected carefully. Cordons can also be very decorative. They make excellent screens and internal hedges.

Supports

Cordons can be planted against walls or fences or as free-standing screens trained against wires stretched between upright posts. The wires should be held away from walls and fences by about 10cm (4in) and should be spaced about 60cm (2ft) apart. The bottom wire should be about 30cm (12in) from the ground. Free-standing cordons can be supported on horizontal wires stretched between posts that are firmly embedded in the ground about 2–2.5m (6–8ft) apart.

Initial training

Plant a feathered whip so that the trunk is at an angle of about 45 degrees to the wires. Tie it in to a cane which has in turn been tied to the wires at the same angle. Cut back

PRUNING AN ESTABLISHED APPLE CORDON

1 Established cordon apples against a fence. They take up very little space and enable the gardener to grow several different varieties.

2 In the winter, prune back any new side shoots to one or two buds.

3 New growth on existing side shoots should also be cut back to one or two buds in the winter.

4 In summer, cut back the main leader once it has reached the top support. Do this every summer, cutting back to one or two buds.

5 In summer, you should also cut back any new shoots to two or three leaves.

6 Any new shoots on existing side shoots should be cut back to one leaf.

the laterals to about three or four buds. The following summer cut back any new laterals to four leaves and any sub-laterals to one or two leaves.

Established pruning

Continue to summer prune, reducing new growth on the sub-laterals to one leaf and any new laterals to two or three leaves. When the leader reaches the desired height cut it back

to one bud in winter or late spring. In the winter thin over-crowded clusters of spurs, taking out the older ones.

Pole or pillar apples

These are a modern innovation, and are essentially intended to be grown in containers. They are in effect vertical cordons, and should be pruned in the same way as conventional cordons.

ABOVE Well-maintained cordons bearing a good crop of apples. Cordons are an easy height for pruning and for picking fruit.

ABOVE Cordon apples in winter after they have been pruned. These have been grown in the open against a wire and pole support.

ABOVE A pole or pillar apple takes up very little space, thus allowing the gardener to grow several varieties even in a small garden. Prune as for cordons.

Multiple cordons

Cordons can be grown with two, three or more stems, either vertical or tilted at an angle of 45 degrees. Cut off the leader of a whip just below the bottom wire and allow two laterals to develop. Train these to the vertical, tying them to canes on the wires. Once established, prune as for two separate cordons. For a three- or five-stem cordon, allow three or five laterals to develop. Train the central one vertically, and the others at an angle and then vertically.

TRAINING A SINGLE CORDON

The initial training and regular established pruning of cordons is crucial. If these are neglected in any way the plant will quickly revert to a tree- or bush-like habit and outgrow its position within the design of the garden. The work required is not arduous, but it should be carried out every winter and summer.

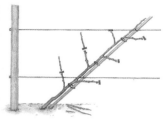

YEAR ONE, WINTER Plant a feathered whip at an angle of approximately 45 degrees. Cut back any side shoots to about three or four buds. Leave the leader uncut.

YEAR ONE, SUMMER In the first summer, cut back any new shoots on the existing side shoots to one or two leaves. Prune back any new side shoots to about four leaves.

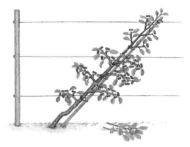

ESTABLISHED PRUNING, SUMMER Once established, the summer pruning consists of cutting back new growth on existing side shoots to one leaf and new side shoots to two or three leaves.

ESTABLISHED PRUNING, WINTER In winter or late spring, remove any growth on the leader to one bud. After a few years, once the clusters of spurs become congested, remove some of the older ones each year.

PRUNING MULTIPLE CORDONS

TWO-STEMMED CORDON A two-stemmed cordon with vertical stems. It is treated in exactly the same way as an ordinary cordon.

THREE-STEMMED CORDON A three-stemmed cordon in which an extra stem is grown in the middle, producing more fruit from one plant.

FOUR-STEMMED CORDON Four stemmed cordons are very decorative, but they obviously take up a lot of extra space.

ANGLED CORDON A two-stemmed cordon can be grown at 45 degrees in the same way as normal cordons.

Apple espalier

An apple espalier can be created against either a wall or fence, where it looks attractive, or free-standing against wires, to form a decorative as well as productive screen or hedge. Initially, strong supports are needed, but many established ones become totally free-standing and any support can be removed. Try to keep the shape as symmetrical as possible, with the "arms" on either side of the main stem at the same level and of the same length. This method of training is suitable only for spur-bearing apples.

Supports

Fix three (or more on a tall wall) parallel wires to a wall, fence or strong posts. The wires should be taut and between 45cm (18in) and 60cm (24in) apart. They should be held clear up to 15 cm (6in) of a wall or fence. The bottom wire should be 45–60cm (18–24in) from the ground.

Initial training

Start with either a feathered tree or a maiden whip. The former should have a good pair of opposite shoots and a strong leader or a suitable shoot

ABOVE A free-standing espalier trained against wires. Espaliers are both decorative and productive. The variety here is 'St Edmund's Pippin'.

that can be trained as a leader. The whip should be allowed to develop two strong, opposite shoots by cutting the leader back to a bud about 5cm (2in) or so above the first wire, so that new shoots will develop just beneath the wire. The first summer after planting, train what will be the horizontal shoots against canes at an angle of 45 degrees. Tie in the new

leader vertically. Cut back any other side shoots to two or three leaves. The following winter, lower the bottom branches to the horizontal. Remove any other side shoots. Also during the second winter, cut back the vertical leader to just above the second wire. Repeat the process in subsequent years until all the wires are filled. Cut back the leader.

PRUNING A YOUNG ESPALIERED APPLE

1 A young espalier showing the developing first tier and the laterals that will form the second tier, ready to be lowered into position.

2 New shoots growing on existing side shoots should be cut back to one or two buds above the base of the new wood.

3 Completely new side shoots should be cut back to three or four buds and the tip of the branch should be tied to the support.

TRAINING AN APPLE ESPALIER

It is not especially difficult to train and prune an espaliered apple, but work must be carried out regularly each winter and summer, otherwise the espalier will soon become overgrown and out of shape. The basic principles are the same as those for training a cordon, but you will be working mainly on a horizontal plane, as the espalier is trained against a wall or fence.

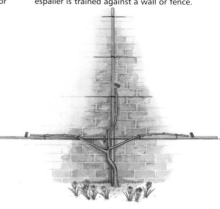

YEAR ONE, WINTER In winter plant a maiden whip against a cane that is tied to the wire supports. Cut it off just above the lower wire.

YEAR ONE, SUMMER As the two side shoots develop, tie them in to canes tied to the wires at an angle of 45 degrees. The new leader should be tied in vertically. Any other side shoots should be cut back to two or three leaves.

YEAR TWO, WINTER During the second winter, gently lower the two bottom branches to the horizontal and tie them to the wire to form the bottom tier. Cut the leader just above the second wire and remove all other side shoots.

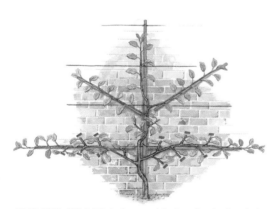

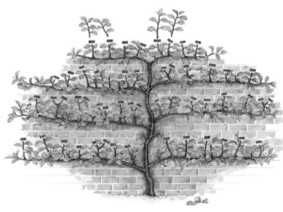

YEAR TWO, SUMMER As the second-tier branches develop, tie them in at an angle of 45 degrees. Tie the leader to the vertical cane. Cut back the side shoots on the lower tiers to three leaves. Tie in the tips of the bottom tier as they grow.

SUBSEQUENT YEARS, SUMMER AND WINTER Continue to tie in and lower the various tiers as they develop, one level a year. Prune new shoots back to three leaves if needed; if not, cut them out. Prune new shoots on old ones back to one leaf in summer. In winter, thin the spurs if necessary.

Established pruning

Remove the canes and tie branches directly to the wires. Prune each summer, cutting back the new growth on the side shoots to one leaf, to promote the growth of fruiting spurs. Once established, remove any new growth springing directly from the main branches. In winter, thin out the clusters of spurs if necessary, cutting out the oldest and any unproductive spurs.

New shoots arising from the main trunk can be cut back initially to three leaves and then treated as a spur as on the tiers. It is important that you only allow one or two to develop between each tier.

Apple fan

Fans are an attractive way of growing apples against walls or large fences, but they do need considerable space and a strong support. Avoid excessively windy positions for free-standing fans, as they will not be stable when in full leaf.

Supports

Use five to seven parallel wires, about 30cm (12in) apart. They should be pulled taut and held 10–15cm (4–6in) away from the wall to allow air to circulate and prevent the tree from rubbing against the wall. The bottom wire should be about 45cm (18in) above ground-level. For a free-standing fan, the posts must be solidly set in the ground, 2–2.5m (6–8ft) apart.

Initial training

Buy a feathered tree that has two strong shoots just below the proposed position of the bottom wire. Cut off the leader just above the upper of these two. Tie the laterals to canes, then attach these to the wires at an angle of about 40 degrees or so. Shorten the shoots back to about 45cm (18in) to a bud on the underside. This will stimulate the production of side shoots later that year. Tie these in to new canes as they develop. The top bud will produce a new leader for each of the main arms and this should be tied in along the cane in the same direction. Cut out any unwanted shoots, aiming to keep both sides balanced. Remove any new growth from the main trunk. Cut back the tips of laterals on either side of the main stems so that they in turn branch out. Remove any growth that projects from the fan. Over the next three years or so, gradually allow the fan to develop so that it branches more towards the periphery and covers the entire space evenly.

TRAINING AN APPLE FAN

Fans, like most decorative forms of apple, need a lot of care and attention in order to prevent them from becoming overgrown and out of hand. An apple trained in this way will need attention both in the summer and in the winter.

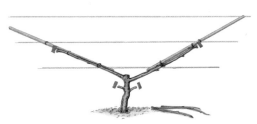

YEAR ONE, WINTER Start with a feathered tree which is planted in winter. Cut off the leader just below the bottom wire and tie in two laterals to canes attached to the wires at 40 degrees. Cut these back to about 45cm (18in). Shorten any other remaining laterals to a couple of buds.

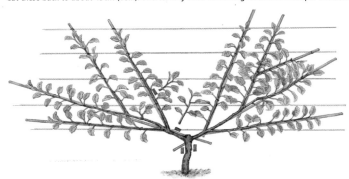

YEAR ONE, SUMMER In the following summer tie in the side shoots that develop on the laterals to form an even spread of branches, but remove any that crowd the space. Now remove any side shoots that you cut back in the winter from the main trunk.

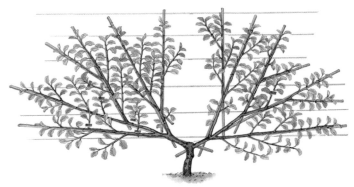

SUBSEQUENT YEARS, SUMMER Continue to tie in the developing side shoots so that a fan-like framework of branches is developed. Cut out their tips so that they continue to branch. Cut back any unwanted shoots to two or three leaves to create fruiting spurs.

Established pruning

Once the branches have matured, remove the canes and tie the stems directly to the wires. Prune each summer, cutting back the new growth on the side shoots to one leaf. Also cut out any new growth at the ends of the main branches to restrict further growth and to promote the production of fruiting spurs. Once established, remove any new growth that crowds the existing fan. In winter, thin the clusters of spurs if necessary, cutting out the oldest and any unproductive ones. Keep the fans tied back firmly to their supports because they can easily be blown away from the wall or wires, causing damage to the tree.

RIGHT Fans for growing apples are not as common as for other fruit, but nonetheless they are a valid decorative and productive way of growing them.

ESTABLISHED PRUNING, SUMMER AND WINTER In summer, reduce any new shoots on the spurs to one leaf and either cut out new shoots or reduce them to two or three leaves to create more spurs. In winter, thin out the clusters of spurs if necessary by removing the older ones.

Apple stepover

This is essentially a decorative way of growing apples, although it will produce quite a surprising amount of fruit once it is mature, especially if the arms are long. Stepover apples are mainly used for edging paths in a kitchen garden, and look especially attractive in parterres or walled gardens. They are usually grown no more than 30–60cm (1–2ft) above the ground, and derive their name from the fact that they are low enough to step over. Any variety of apple that is spur-fruiting and is grown on a dwarfing stock can be used to create a stepover.

Supports

Short stout posts should be driven into the ground at about 2m (6ft) intervals. Stretch a wire between them about 45cm (18in) above the ground. Several stepovers can be planted in a long line, so continue the posts and wire as far as is needed, even around a vegetable plot.

Initial training

Stepovers are generally grown with two arms, one on either side of the trunk. They can be considered a multiple cordon on which the horizontal arms are not turned vertically, or as an espalier that has only the bottom tier of branches. Sometimes, however, they are grown with a single arm, turned to left or right. This is more like a single cordon that has been laid horizontally rather than at an angle of 45 degrees. The two-branch stepover can be trained in the same way as a double cordon, except that instead of turning the arms into an upright position, continue to train them horizontally, tying them to the wires on either side of the trunk. This method is almost identical to growing the first tier of an espalier, except that the main leader is cut off immediately above the top of the two laterals.

TRAINING AN APPLE STEPOVER

In essence, a stepover is simply the bottom tier of an espalier-trained apple. It is trained in exactly the same way and is pruned once it is established in the same fashion as an espalier. It is important to prune the stepover regularly or it will grow out of character very rapidly. Avoid planting them where children might use them as a high jump.

YEAR ONE, WINTER Plant a maiden whip in winter and cut off the leader below the wire support and just above two strong buds, which will develop into the arms

YEAR ONE, WINTER If a one-sided stepover is required, the leader should not be cut but moved though 45 degrees and tied in. During the following summer, it can be eased down into a horizontal position. Further pruning is the same as for a double-sided stepover.

YEAR ONE, SUMMER As the two top shoots develop during the first summer, tie them to canes at an angle of approximately 45 degrees. Remove any side shoots that develop below these two.

YEAR TWO, WINTER During the second winter, gently lower the canes and tie the two arms into the horizontal wires. If the tips have reached the full extent of the support, cut them out, otherwise leave.

SUMMER PRUNING AN APPLE STEPOVER

1 A stepover of 'Kidd's Orange Red' apples in late summer. The side shoots have grown during the summer and are now ready to be pruned.

2 The main summer job is to reduce all new side shoots from the main stems back to three or four leaves. In the case of new side shoots on old growth, cut them back to one or two leaves.

3 The summer pruning is completed. The longer side shoots will be reduced in the winter when the tree is dormant.

4 A stepover in winter showing all the side shoots shortened back to the fruiting spurs. Any clusters of spurs that were overcrowded have been thinned.

The single stepover is developed either in the same way from a maiden whip or feathered tree (remove all the laterals except one), or by choosing a flexible single whip. Plant the tree near to one of the posts. Tie the section above the proposed bend to a cane and gradually pull this through an angle of 90 degrees, tying the cane to the wire with ever-decreasing lengths of string until it reaches the horizontal. The initial training then follows that of a cordon.

Established pruning

The subsequent pruning is exactly the same as if you were pruning a cordon, except that the length of the leader can be as long as you like. The tip is usually removed just before it meets the tip of the leader coming from the next stepover, if there is one, so that a continuous hedge is created.

YEAR TWO, SUMMER During the following summer, cut back all side shoots to three or four leaves. Remove any side shoots that appear on the main vertical trunk.

ESTABLISHED PRUNING, WINTER AND SUMMER Once established, cut new growth back to one bud each winter and thin the spurs. In summer, cut back any new growth on the spurs to one or two leaves and take out any other unnecessary shoots that cause crowding.

PEARS (*Pyrus communis*)
Pear bush tree

Pears used to be grown as standard trees, which would eventually become rather large. Free-standing pear trees can still be seen in gardens, although many are now getting rather aged. Nowadays if you want to grow pears as free-standing plants, bushes are the usual form, or dwarf pyramids if you want something really small. Generally, pear trees are more upright-growing than apples, but the training and pruning are very similar.

Supports

Insert a strong stake into the ground in the planting hole before planting the tree. If you plant the tree first, it is only too easy to damage the roots, hidden by the soil, by driving the stake through them. Secure the trunk of the tree to the post with a proprietary tree tie that is designed not to rub and damage the bark.

Initial training

Start with a feathered tree, staked. As it grows, gradually remove the lowest side branches to create a bare trunk.

Varieties

European Pears	'Louise Bonne of Jersey'
'Bartlett'	'Merton Pride'
'Beth'	'Onward'
'Beurré Hardy'	'Ubileen'
'Black Worcester'	'Williams
'Comice'	Bon Chrétien'
'Concorde'	
'Conference'	
'Doyenné du Commice'	
'Durondeau'	
'Glou Morceau'	
'Jargonelle'	
'Joséphine de Malines'	

ABOVE An attractive group of 'Williams Bon Chrétien' pear blossoms, illustrating how they are concentrated on a cluster of spurs.

Continue to do this until the trunk has reached the required height. Now remove the leader. The main branches then develop from this point and any remaining branches on the trunk can be removed. Ensure that the branches are well spread and remove any that cross. Shorten the shoots that develop on these branches so that the tree branches out. Keep the centre of the tree open, countering the natural tendency of pears to grow upright.

PRUNING A FEATHERED PEAR BUSH

1 The young feathered pear bushes in this nursery bed are now ready for transplanting to their final positions.

2 Cut off the leader above a strong bud at the height where you want the trunk to finish, using a sloping cut away from the bud.

3 Cut out any over-strong growth that might form a new leader or unbalance the tree. Remove any laterals low down on the trunk.

4 Cut back the remaining side shoots by about half to promote a branched shape. Cut to an outward-facing bud.

TRAINING A PEAR BUSH TREE

The development of a pear bush does not differ greatly from that of a similarly shaped apple tree. Also, like the apple, once established it needs far less pruning than the more decorative forms of pear tree. Unless they are deliberately kept small, pear bush trees will usually need steps or even a ladder in order to prune them and pick the fruit.

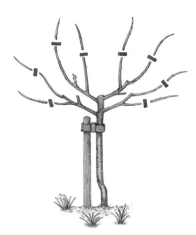

YEAR ONE, WINTER In the first winter cut off the leader at the height you want the top of the trunk to be or leave for further years until it reaches it. Remove the lowest laterals and cut back the remainder by up to a half.

YEAR TWO, WINTER In the second winter shorten the new branch leaders and side shoots to promote more branching. Remove any crossing or crowding branches, especially towards the centre which should be kept open.

SUBSEQUENT YEARS, WINTER Continue in the same fashion until the tree fills out to its final shape. Once this has been achieved there is little pruning except to thin the spurs if they become congested.

Established pruning

Generally only winter pruning is required for pear bushes. Once established, bush trees do not grow particularly vigorously and pruning is restricted mainly to thinning spurs. But you should remove any excessively vigorous and unwanted wood, along with any branches that cross or rub against each other. If the leaders are over-long reduce them by about a quarter to one-third of the previous season's growth. Check the spurs. Any that are overcrowded should have their older and less productive wood removed.

ESTABLISHED PRUNING, WINTER (*right*) Once the tree is established it requires no summer pruning and very little winter pruning. Just remove any dead or damaged wood and thin the spurs if necessary. If the leaders are over-long, reduce them by a quarter to one-third of the previous season's growth.

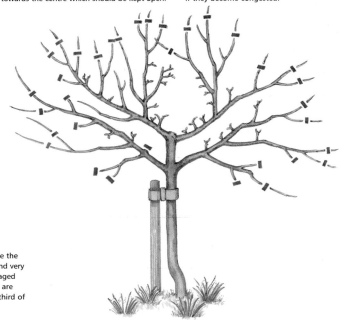

Pear dwarf pyramid

Dwarf pyramids are the best tree-shaped pear trees for the small garden. They take up relatively little space and they do not require a ladder for pruning, netting or harvesting. They are excellent for mixing with dwarf pyramid apples for making a small but productive fruit garden. The basic principle is to create cone- or pyramid-shaped trees on which even the lowest branches receive plenty of air and light.

Supports

A strong pole or stake should be inserted in the planting hole first, so that the roots of the tree can be

ABOVE Mid-summer and these 'Williams Bon Chrétien' are developing well. The fruit has been thinned so that each pear has the space and supply of energy to develop fully.

spread around it before the hole is filled in (doing it afterwards can damage the roots). The stake should protrude at least 2m (6ft) above the ground. It is important to use proprietary tree ties, rather than string, to support the trunk.

Initial training

Start with a feathered tree with good, well-spaced laterals. Remove any misplaced side shoots or those that point too sharply upwards. Cut back remaining laterals to about 15cm (6in) from the trunk, if possible to an outward- (not upward-) facing bud. Reduce the length of the leader to a bud about

TRAINING A PEAR DWARF PYRAMID

Dwarf pyramids are the smallest of the tree forms of pears and are ideal for use in small gardens. However, it is important to keep them well-pruned or they will grow into rather untidy trees and eventually outgrow their space. Dwarf pyramids should normally be kept low enough so that they can be pruned and picked from the ground.

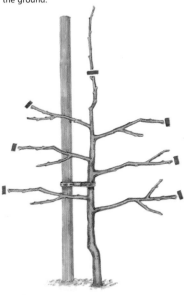

YEAR ONE, WINTER Plant a young feathered tree in winter. Cut the leader back to about 75cm (30in) from the ground. Remove the laterals below about 45cm (18in) and prune the remainder back to about 15cm (6in).

YEAR ONE, SUMMER In the following summer, remove any vigorous vertical growths (except the leader) and shorten any side shoots on the main laterals to about 10cm (4in). Leave the tips of the laterals unpruned.

YEAR TWO, WINTER In the second winter, cut back the new growth on the main laterals to about 20cm (8in), preferably to a downward-facing bud. The leader should also be reduced, cutting back the new growth by about two-thirds.

ABOVE A cluster of 'Conference' pears that are on the verge of ripening. They are best eaten straight from the tree.

75cm (30in) above the ground. Remove any laterals that are below about 45cm (18in) from the ground. In the summer, remove any vigorous vertical growths that appear. Leave the main branches unpruned but shorten the side shoots to about 10cm (4in). During the second winter, shorten the new growth of the main branches to about 20cm (8in), cutting to a downward-facing bud. The main leader should also be cut back by about two-thirds, to a bud on the opposite side to that from which growth emerged the previous year. In the second summer reduce the main branches to about 20cm (8in), and their side shoots to about 15cm (6in).

Established pruning

Once the tree has attained its outline, probably by its third year, it will need pruning twice a year to keep it compact. In summer cut back new growth on all main branches to about six leaves. Cut back all new shoots to about half this. At the same time, reduce any new growth from the clusters of spurs to one leaf. In winter, thin out the older spurs as they become crowded, and cut back the main leader to one bud of the new growth.

YEAR TWO, SUMMER During the second summer, cut back all the new growth on the lateral side shoots to about 15cm (6in). The main branches themselves should have the new growth cut back to about 20cm (8in). Leave the leader.

ESTABLISHED PRUNING, WINTER AND SUMMER Prune in winter by cutting the new growth on the main leader back to one bud, and thin the clusters of spurs if necessary. In summer, cut back new growth on main branches to about six leaves and new side shoots to three leaves. The new growth on spur clusters should be cut back to one leaf.

Pear espalier

Espaliered pears can be a very decorative feature in the garden, especially when mature. They look particularly good on walls, and some old specimens are seen on the gable ends of houses, where they can have five, six or even more tiers.

Supports
Attach three (or more on a tall wall) parallel wires to a wall, fence or strong posts. The wires should be taut, between 45cm (18in) and 60cm (24in) apart and held at least 10cm (4in) clear of the wall. The bottom wire should be 45–60cm (18–24in) above the ground.

Initial training
Purchase the tree either as a feather or a maiden whip. The former should have a good pair of opposite laterals and a good leader or an upper shoot that can be trained as a leader. The whip should be encouraged to develop two good,

ABOVE A pear espalier growing against a fence. They can also be trained against walls or grown free-standing on a post-and-wire structure.

ABOVE An abundant crop of luscious-looking pears is the result of careful training and good pruning techniques.

opposite shoots by cutting the leader back to a bud about 5cm (2in) or so above the first wire, thus encouraging new shoots to develop just beneath the wire. Train these new shoots as shown in the illustrations. What will eventually be the horizontal branches are trained at an angle of 45 degrees against canes in their first summer, then lowered during the second winter to the horizontal. Remove any other laterals. Also during the second winter, cut back the vertical leader to just above the second wire. Repeat the process in subsequent years until all the wires are filled. Cut back the leader.

Established pruning
Remove the canes and tie the branches directly to the wires. Prune each summer, cutting back the new growth on the side shoots to one leaf, also pruning back any new growth at the ends of the main branches both to restrict growth and to promote the production of

fruiting spurs. Also remove any new growth springing directly from the main branches. In winter, thin out the clusters of spurs as necessary, cutting out the oldest and less productive ones.

ABOVE In fruitful years the pears may be produced in thick clusters and it can be an idea to thin them out when they reach this size.

TRAINING A PEAR ESPALIER

Espaliers are a tiered system of growing pears. They normally have three or four parallel branches on either side of the main trunk but they can go up to any height you like, and are sometimes trained as a decorative feature to cover the whole of the end of a house or barn, creating a splendid visual display as well as a productive tree.

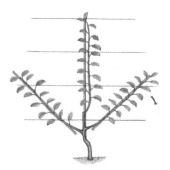

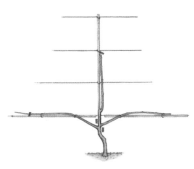

YEAR ONE, WINTER In winter plant a maiden whip against a cane tied to the wire supports. Cut it off just above the lower wire, leaving two good buds to develop into the side shoots.

YEAR ONE, SUMMER In the first summer after planting, as the two side shoots develop, tie them in to canes tied to the wires at an angle of 45 degrees. The new leader should be tied in vertically. Any other side shoots should be cut back to two or three leaves.

YEAR TWO, WINTER In the second winter, gently lower the two bottom branches to the horizontal and tie to the wire to form the bottom tier. Cut the leader just above the second wire and remove all other side shoots.

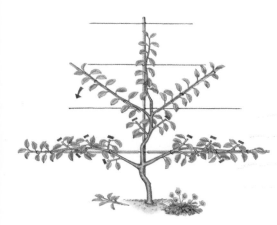

YEAR TWO, SUMMER As the second-tier branches develop, tie them in at 45 degrees. Tie the leader to the vertical cane. Cut back any side shoots on the lower tiers to three leaves. Tie in the tips of the bottom tier as it grows.

SUBSEQUENT YEARS, WINTER AND SUMMER Continue to tie in and lower the various tiers of the espalier as they develop, working on one level a year until the espalier is established. Prune new shoots back to three leaves if they are needed for the overall shape; if they are not needed, cut them out completely. Prune new shoots on old ones back to one leaf in the summer. In the winter, thin the spurs if this is necessary.

Pear fan

This is not such a popular method of training pears as an espalier, but when done well it can be an attractive way of clothing a wall or tall fence. Fan-trained pears need a lot of space to look their best. Alternatively, they can be free-standing, trained on wires.

Supports

Use five to seven parallel wires set about 30cm (12in) apart. They should be pulled taut and held at least 10cm (4in) away from the wall to allow air to circulate and prevent the tree from rubbing. The bottom wire should be about 45cm (18in) from the ground. If free-standing, the posts must be solidly set in the ground, 2–2.5m (6–8ft) apart.

Initial training

Select a young feathered tree with two strong shoots that will lie just below the position of the bottom wire. Cut off the leader just above

ABOVE A splendid free-standing pear fan, growing against a support of wires and posts. Trees trained in this way can also be grown against walls and fences.

these two laterals. Tie the laterals to canes, and tie the canes to the wires at an angle of about 40 degrees. Shorten these shoots back to about 45cm (18in) to a bud on the underside. This will stimulate new

side shoots later that year, which can also be tied in against canes as they develop. The top bud on each lateral will produce a new leader, and this should be tied in along the cane in the same direction as this main stem.

ABOVE A 'Doyenné Du Comice' pear showing how a fan is spread out to expose the fruit. Some of the older wood will need to be removed.

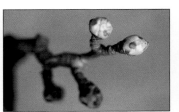

ABOVE A pear shoot showing the cluster of spurs that provides blossom and fruit. This has the right number of buds and is not too congested.

ABOVE Pear fans can also be trained against more permanent supports, as on this sturdy piece of trellis.

ABOVE If the pear crop is potentially heavy, it may be necessary to thin them at this stage to ensure that the rest develop properly.

TRAINING A PEAR FAN

Pears make great subjects for training as decorative fans. The process is very similar to that of apple fans; indeed, the principle behind all fans is very much the same. They will take several years to develop fully, but the result is very rewarding and well worth the effort. Unless they are enormous, most fans can be pruned and the fruit picked easily from the ground.

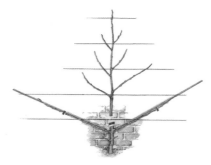

YEAR ONE, WINTER Plant the tree and cut off the leader below the bottom wire so that the top two laterals form the bottom branches. Tie these to canes at about 40 degrees and shorten to about 45cm (18in).

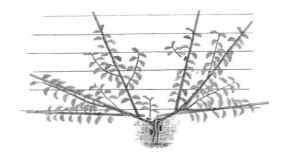

YEAR ONE, SUMMER In the first summer tie in the developing sub-laterals and the new branch leaders, creating an equal spread of branches on either side of the main trunk. Remove any unwanted young shoots from the main branches.

Cut out any unwanted shoots, aiming to keep both sides balanced. Remove any new growth from the main trunk. Cut back the tips of sub-laterals on either side of the main stems so that they in turn branch out. Remove any growth that projects out from the fan. Over the next three years or so gradually allow the fan to develop so that it branches more towards the periphery and covers the space evenly.

SUBSEQUENT YEARS (right) Continue in the same vein until all the space has been filled. Remove any shoots that stick out at the front or back and any others that cause crowding, especially in the centre of the fan. Aim to get an even coverage.

Established pruning

The fan will look better if, once the branches have matured, the canes are removed and the stems tied directly to the wires. Each summer, prune the fan by cutting back the new growth on the side shoots to one leaf, and also cutting out any new growth at the ends of the main branches, both to restrict growth and to promote the production of fruiting spurs. Once established, remove any new growth that may crowd the existing growth. In winter, thin out any congested clusters of spurs, cutting out the oldest and any unproductive ones.

ESTABLISHED PRUNING, SUMMER AND WINTER Once established, remove the canes and tie directly to the wirework. Summer prune the new growth on the side shoots back to one leaf. Cut out any new growth at the ends of the main branches. Continue to remove shoots that cause crowding or congestion. In winter thin overcrowded clusters of spurs.

PLUMS *(Prunus domestica)*
Plum bush tree

Plum bushes are the ideal size for producing large quantities of plums in the garden. They are smaller than a standard or semi-standard but are still large enough to require the use of a ladder for pruning, netting and picking. Plum pruning is mainly undertaken in mid-summer (and in early spring during the formative years). Avoid pruning in winter, as the open wounds provide an entry point for certain diseases such as silver leaf and canker.

Varieties

Dessert	Cooking
'Ariel'	'Belle de Louvain'
'Cambridge Gage'	'Czar'
'Coe's Golden Drop'	'Early Rivers'
'Early Laxton'	'Laxton's Cropper'
'Greengage'	'Pershore Yellow'
'Jefferson'	
'Kirke's Blue'	
'Marjorie's Seedling'	
'Merton Gem'	
'Oulin's Gage'	
'Victoria'	

TRAINING A PLUM BUSH

Plum bush trees are suitable for the larger garden, especially where the gardener wants to have a large crop of plums, perhaps for jam or freezing. Once trained, very little pruning is necessary to keep the trees in shape and productive. Any pruning should be restricted to the summer to avoid disease which can enter through wounds in the tree.

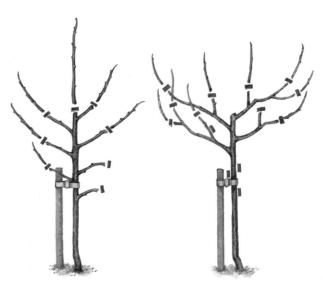

YEAR ONE, WINTER Plant a feathered tree in winter. In early spring, remove the leader at the point where you want the top branch to begin, around 1.5m (5ft) from the ground. Reduce all the remaining laterals by about two-thirds to outward-facing buds.

YEAR TWO, SPRING In the following spring, select four or so of the top laterals to become the main branches and remove all the others completely. Remove any shoots from the main branches that are misplaced or causing crowding. Cut back the new growth on the main branches and their shoots by about half to two-thirds to outward-facing buds.

ESTABLISHED PRUNING, SUMMER Once established, only prune in mid-summer. This is restricted to removing dead or damaged wood and taking out any crossing or congested branches. Also cut out any vigorous vertical growths that appear anywhere on the tree.

ABOVE Clusters of ripening plums. One or more of these could have been removed at an earlier stage to allow the others to fill out more.

Supports

Knock a short stake into the planting hole and spread out the roots. Do not plant the tree and then put in the stake as you may damage the roots beneath the soil. Use a proprietary tree tie to connect the two. In windy areas use two stakes, one on each side of the tree.

Initial pruning

Buy a feathered tree and plant it against a stake. In early spring, shorten the leader at about 1.5m (5ft) from the ground, immediately above a bud, which will produce the top branch. Reduce all laterals by about two-thirds, to outward-facing buds. The following spring, remove all laterals up to about 60cm (2ft) above the ground to produce a tree with a clear trunk. Also, either remove any branches that are misplaced, crowded or crossing other branches completely or cut them back to a bud that will produce a better-placed replacement branch. Remove any shoots from the main branches that are misplaced or causing crowding, especially towards the centre of the tree. Cut back the tips of all remaining shoots by half to two-thirds, to outward-facing buds.

Established pruning

By the third year, the plum bush tree should have achieved its mature size. From now on, prune only in mid-

ABOVE Trees with heavy crops may need their branches to be propped up with poles to prevent them breaking.

summer. In fact, there is not a great deal of pruning to be done except to remove dead, diseased or damaged wood, as usual, along with any weak or crossing wood. You should also remove any upright growths (suckers) that appear on the main or subsidiary branches.

ABOVE Greengages are another type of plum and are treated, as far as the pruning is concerned, in exactly the same way as a plum.

ABOVE A good crop of damsons in late summer. Damsons and bullaces are best grown as bush trees and pruned in the same manner as other plums.

Plum pyramid

For the small garden, a pyramid is the ideal way of growing plums. A pyramid is a short, conical tree on which the branches decrease in size as they progress up the tree. The pyramid shape ensures that even the lower branches receive plenty of light with good air circulation. The short stature also makes a plum pyramid easy to prune, net and pick, while providing a reasonable crop of fruit.

Supports

A single stake should be placed in the ground before the tree is planted. Putting the stake in after the tree may result in the roots hidden beneath the surface being damaged. Use a proprietary tree tie to attach the trunk to the stake.

Once the tree has become established, the stake can be removed except in very exposed positions. Regularly check that the tie is not too tight and cutting into the growing trunk.

Initial training

Choose a feathered tree and plant it in the winter. In early spring, remove all laterals up to about 45cm (18in) from the ground. Cut out the tip of the leader at a height of about 1.5m (5ft). Reduce the remaining laterals by about half, cutting to an outward-facing bud. In the following mid-summer, cut back all sub-laterals to about 15cm (6in) and take back the new growth of the main branch stems to about 20cm (8in), cutting to an outward-facing bud. In the following early spring, cut back the previous year's growth on the main leader by about two-thirds.

Established pruning

Once the tree is mature, prune only in summer to avoid diseases such as

ABOVE 'Victoria' plums are one of the most popular varieties. They can produce heavy crops which may mean the branches require props.

ABOVE A lovely crop of succulent plums are the reward of well-tended trees. Compact trees will make these easy to harvest from the ground.

TRAINING A PLUM DWARF PYRAMID

Some varieties of plum lend themselves to being grown on a dwarfing stock and can be grown as dwarf pyramids. Check that you buy a suitable variety. These are particularly useful in a small garden where just a small quantity of plums is required. Because of their small size it may be possible to grow several varieties of plum as pyramids in a small area.

YEAR ONE, WINTER
Plant a feathered tree in winter. In early spring, cut out its leader at about 1.5m (5ft) from the ground. Cut out all the side shoots below about 45cm (18in) and then reduce all remaining laterals by about half.

YEAR ONE, SUMMER The following mid-summer you will need cut back the new growth on the main branches to about 20cm (8in) to an outward-facing bud. You should also cut back all the sub-laterals to around 15cm (6in).

YEAR TWO, SPRING
In the second spring cut back the new growth made by the leader by about two-thirds. No other pruning is required at this time of the year.

ESTABLISHED PRUNING, SUMMER The tree may be mature by the third spring or it may need another year. Once mature little pruning is required unless there is vigorous growth. This should be cut back to a few leaves in summer. You may also need to remove any dead, diseased or damaged wood and thin out any congested areas by taking out older wood.

silver leaf. The main pruning can be restricted to removing any dead, diseased or damaged wood and thinning any congested areas by taking out the older wood. If the tree is reasonably vigorous, you may still need to reduce the new growth on all the main branches to 20cm (8in) and on the side branches to 15cm (6in). Once the main leader has reached its ultimate height, it should be cut back to one bud of the previous year's growth in late spring.

LEFT A good crop of 'Opal' plums. In early summer, the plums have been thinned so that those remaining have space and sufficient energy to develop fully.

Plum spindle bush

While pyramids are probably the best form of plum tree for the small garden, if you are keen to get maximum cropping from your trees it is possibly a good idea to follow the trend in commercial growing, which concentrates on spindle bushes. If you already grow apples by this method you will be well aware of the technique as it is essentially the same. The idea is to keep the branches as near to the horizontal as possible.

Supports

A permanent stake that is as tall as the tree will grow is required. Insert it before planting the tree so that the roots are not damaged as you drive it into the ground. The tree can be tied to it in several places as it develops, and the stake can be left in place even after the tree matures.

ABOVE Spindle bushes are relatively small and allow a number of different varieties to be grown in a small garden. It is advisable to check with your supplier as to which varieties are suitable for training in this way.

ABOVE 'Victoria' plums are a very popular variety. The luscious fruit on this tree is the result of attentive pruning.

ABOVE A fine crop of damsons. These are pruned in exactly the same way as plums. Some have a tendency to produce suckers, which should be removed.

TRAINING A PLUM SPINDLE BUSH

A spindle bush creates a good open tree, which allows the sun to enter and ripen the fruit. Spindle bushes are no more difficult to train than any other plum trees, although the tethering strings can make them look tricky. As with all plums, it is advisable to keep the majority of pruning to mid-summer if possible.

YEAR ONE, WINTER Plant a young feathered tree in winter. In early spring, remove the laterals below about 60cm (2ft), as well as any that are misplaced or at too steep an angle. Leave the rest intact.

YEAR ONE, SUMMER In mid-summer, you will need to remove the leader at about 1m (3ft) above ground-level and reduce all the laterals to about half their length.

SUBSEQUENT YEARS, SUMMER As the branches develop, gradually pull them down to the horizontal using strings tied to pegs. Remove any vigorous vertical growth. As the new main leader develops, tie it in to the stake. Allow other well-placed laterals to develop. From now on, prune only in mid-summer, allowing the side branches to develop and removing any vigorous or crossing growth.

ESTABLISHED PRUNING Once the bush is established, cut back the leader to two buds each summer. Cut out any vigorous growth and any crowding laterals, but tie down any new growth that makes a useful lateral.

Initial pruning

In the winter, plant a feathered tree against a stake. The following early spring, remove completely all laterals below about 60cm (2ft) above ground-level. Leave the remainder of the laterals, including the leader, except for any that are at too sharp an angle to the trunk or that are misplaced, causing crowding or crossing. In mid-summer cut the leader off at around 1m (3ft) and reduce the length of the laterals by about half. As the new branch leaders develop, gently pull the stems down as close to the horizontal as possible, holding them in position by tying them down to pegs in the ground or hooks towards the base of the stake. Make sure that the string does not cut into the bark. Remove any vigorous growth from the laterals. As a new main leader is formed, tie it in to the stake and allow further well-placed laterals to develop. From now on only prune in mid-summer. Allow the side branches to develop, removing any vigorous or crossing growth. Aim to keep the branches horizontal and open to the light and air.

Established pruning

All pruning of established bushes should be done around mid-summer to avoid fungal diseases such as silver leaf. When the leader has reached the desired height of around 2–2.2m (6–7ft) – the highest that can be comfortably reached without a ladder – cut it back to two buds each year. Once the main branches are established in a horizontal position and no longer spring back, the strings can be removed. Continue to tie down any new growth that follows its natural tendency to grow upwards. Also continue to prune out any vigorous or crossing growth. Each year allow some new growth to develop on the spindle bush in order to replace some of the older wood, which should be removed.

Plum fan

Fans take up a lot of space and not everybody has a wall or fence large enough to accommodate one, but if you do it is a very decorative way of growing plums as well as a good method of lessening the effects of frost on blossom. Fans can also be grown free-standing against posts and wires, but need a sheltered position.

Supports

Attach five to seven parallel wires set about 30cm (12in) apart to a wall or fence. They should be pulled taut and held at least 10cm (4in) or more away from the wall to allow air to circulate and prevent the tree from rubbing. The bottom wire should be about 45cm (18in) from the ground. If free-standing, the posts must be solidly set in the ground, 2–2.5m (6–8ft) apart.

Initial training

Start with a young feathered tree that has two suitable laterals just below the level of the first wire. In spring, cut the leader off just above the upper of the desired laterals. Cut back the two laterals to about 45cm (18in) from the base to an underside bud. Tie these laterals to individual long canes, which you fasten in turn to the wires at an angle of about 40 degrees. Shorten any other laterals to about two buds until the summer, then cut them off completely, tight to the trunk. Around mid-summer, tie in the new branch leaders to the canes. Select the best-placed side shoots and tie these in to the wires. Remove the rest, especially any vigorous vertical shoots. Try to encourage growth downward to fill the fan evenly. Continue to do this every summer until the fan framework has filled out.

ABOVE A plum fan trained against a wall, which helps to provide protection for the blossom against destructive winter frosts.

Established pruning

Every mid-summer, cut out any dead, diseased or damaged wood. You will also need to remove any vigorous growth along with any shoots that tend to crowd the framework, and any that point towards the wall or outward away from the plane of the fan. Leaders on all the branches and side shoots should be cut back to just a few leaves. In the spring (and not winter), it is important to thin out any new growth by pinching it back, retaining only those shoots that are required as replacements or to fill gaps.

LEFT This cluster of plums might have benefited from being thinned in the early summer, so that the remaining fruit grew larger.

TRAINING A PLUM FAN

Fans are probably the most complicated way of training plums. However, the result is a very decorative bush which produces fruit well. It should preferably be trained against a wall, but fences or free-standing post-and-wire structures are also suitable. Choose a tree that has two suitable laterals just below the level of the lowest wire.

In general, fan-trained plum trees are relatively short and so they can easily be pruned and picked without the need for ladders.

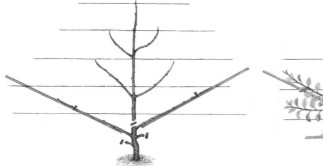

YEAR ONE, WINTER Plant a feathered tree in winter. In spring, cut off the leader just below the bottom wire. Cut back the two laterals to about 45cm (18in) and tie them to canes at about 40 degrees. Reduce the length of any other laterals to a few buds.

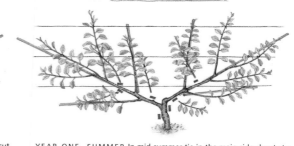

YEAR ONE, SUMMER In mid-summer tie in the main side shoots to canes as they develop, creating an even spread on both sides of the trunk. Select the best-placed side shoots and tie these in to the wires. Cut out any that cross or are badly placed. Continue this process every summer until the fan framework has filled out. Remove completely the remains of the cut-back laterals on the trunk.

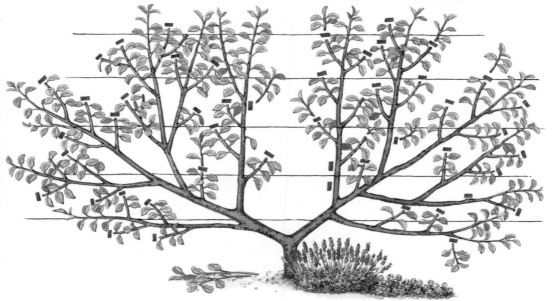

SUBSEQUENT YEARS As the fan becomes established, cut back the new growth of the main and side shoots to just two or three leaves in mid-summer. Remove completely any congested side shoots, keeping the shape relatively open so that sun reaches all the fruit. In spring, thin out any new growth, only retaining those shoots needed as replacements or to fill gaps.

CHERRIES *(Prunus* species)
Sweet cherry bush

Cherries have always been difficult for the home grower because until relatively recently there was no dwarfing stock, so the trees were too large for the average garden. The size not only made cherry trees difficult to prune and pick, but also to net, so that the birds got most of the fruit. Dwarfing stock has become easier to find, making it possible to grow dwarf bushes that are much more manageable. On the other hand, it is still possible to grow cherries as larger bushes or even as semi-standards although these are generally too large for small or even medium-size gardens. Another problem has been eased in that there are now more self-fertile varieties available. The basic pruning for the dwarf trees is the same as for the bushes given below. Cherries should only be pruned in the spring or early summer.

Varieties

Sweet		Acid
'Bradbourne Black'	'Merton Biggarreau'	'Kentish Red'
'Colney'	'Merton Favourite'	'May Duke'
'Early Rivers'	'Merton Glory'	'Montmorency'
'Governor Wood'	'Napoleon	'Morello'
'Greenstem Black'	Biggarreau'	'Nabella'
'Kent Biggarreau'	'Noir de Guben'	'Reine Hortense'
'Kentish Red'	'Stella'	'The Flemish'
'Lapins'	'Sunburst'	'Wye Morello'
	'Waterloo'	

Supports
Hammer a short stake into the hole where the tree will be planted, and spread the roots around it. Avoid planting the tree and then putting in the stake, as this might damage the roots underneath the ground. It is best to use a proprietary tree tie to connect the stake and trunk. In windy areas use two stakes, one on each side of the tree.

Initial pruning
Start with a feathered tree, staked. In early spring, cut back the leader at about 1.5m (5ft) from the ground, immediately above a bud which will produce the top branch. Reduce all laterals by about two-thirds to

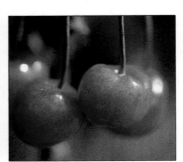

ABOVE A good crop of 'Lapins' cherries. It is advisable to pick cherries in the early morning before the heat of the day makes the leaves droop and hide them.

outward-facing buds. The next spring remove all laterals up to about 1m (3ft) from the ground, to produce a tree with a clear trunk. Also prune any branches that are misplaced, crowding or crossing others, either removing them completely or cutting them back to a bud which will make a better replacement. Also remove any shoots from the main branches that are misplaced or causing crowding, especially towards the centre of the tree. Cut back the tips of all remaining shoots by a half to two-thirds to outward-facing buds.

Established pruning
By the third year, the tree should have achieved its mature size. From now on prune only in early summer. Sweet cherries mainly flower on spurs on the older wood, so pruning chiefly consists of maintaining an open habit. In fact there is not a great deal to be done except to remove dead, diseased or damaged wood along with any weak or crossing stems. Also remove any upright growths (suckers) that appear on the main or subsidiary branches. Occasionally you may need to cut back main branches to keep the cherry within its allotted space. In this case, take them back to the first established side shoot.

ABOVE Hanging bunches of cherries are easy to harvest. Acid cherries such as these are best used for cooking purposes. You could use them to make jams or bottle them.

TRAINING A SWEET CHERRY BUSH

It is advisable to buy cherry trees on a rootstock that is suitable for growing as bushes: those that are grown as standards and semi-standards are generally too large for the average domestic garden and it is difficult to contain their size. Choose a feathered bush with strong laterals that spread out to cover an area of between 1.2–1.5m (4–5ft).

YEAR ONE, WINTER Plant a feathered tree in winter. In early spring, cut off the leader at the planned trunk height, about 1.5m (5ft) above the ground. Cut back all the laterals by about two-thirds of their length.

YEAR TWO, SPRING A year later, remove all laterals up to what will be the bottom branch, about 1m (3ft) from the ground. Cut out all misplaced shoots and reduce the rest by about half to two-thirds.

SUBSEQUENT YEARS Repeat until the tree has acquired its final shape and size. Future pruning should be done in early summer and only consists of removing any misplaced or over-vigorous wood.

ABOVE During the second year of training, cut back all shoots in the early part of the summer by half to two-thirds.

Sweet cherry fan

If you do not have enough room for cherry trees, you may nevertheless be lucky enough to have a wall or fence large enough to carry a fan. Although it needs a lot more pruning to keep it under control, it does have certain advantages over a tree. In particular, no ladder is necessary for pruning, picking or, very importantly, netting against birds.

Supports

If you have space on a wall or fence, attach five to seven parallel wires set about 30cm (12in) apart. Make certain that they are held at least 10cm (4in) or more away from the wall, to allow air to circulate and prevent the tree from rubbing. The bottom wire should be about 45cm (18in) from the ground. Alternatively, use free-standing posts, which must be solidly set in the ground, 2–2.5m (6–8ft) apart.

Initial training

Buy a young feathered tree that has two suitable laterals just below the level of the first wire. Plant in winter. The following spring, cut off the leader just above the upper of the desired laterals. Tie these laterals to individual long canes, and fasten the canes to the wires at an angle of about 40 degrees. Cut back the two laterals to about 45cm (18in) from the base to an underside bud. Shorten any other laterals to two buds, then cut them off completely in summer, tight to the trunk. Around mid-summer, tie in the new branch leaders to the canes. Select the best-placed side shoots and tie these into the wires. Cut out the remainder, along with any vigorous vertical shoots. Try to encourage downward growth that will fill in the fan. Continue to do this every summer until the fan has filled out.

ABOVE A sweet cherry fan in winter, clearly showing the structure of the tree. This cherry fan has been grown against a sunny fence, but it is also possible to grow the fan against a wall or in the open using a pole-and-wire structure.

Established pruning

In early summer, cut out any dead, diseased or damaged wood. Also remove any vigorous growth along with any shoots that tend to crowd the framework, and any which point towards the wall or outwards away from the plane of the fan. Leaders on all the branches and side shoots should be cut back to just a few leaves. In spring (not winter), thin out any new growth by pinching it back, retaining only those shoots that are required as replacements or

ABOVE A sweet cherry fan in summer, clearly showing the netting covering the tree. This is very important as it keeps the birds from eating all the fruit.

ABOVE A cherry fan demonstrating an even spread of blossom. This is what one should aim for when pruning.

to fill gaps. If a main lateral needs replacing, choose a suitably placed stem, tie it to a cane and then cut back the old branch. Try to keep the general shape of the fan as open as possible, while ensuring complete coverage of the space.

TRAINING A SWEET CHERRY FAN

Cherry fans should be started from feathered trees that have two good laterals which will eventually form the main branches from which the rest of the fan grows. Apart from the various stages of formative pruning, all pruning of cherries should take place in early summer to avoid disease entering winter wounds.

YEAR ONE, WINTER Plant a feathered tree in winter. In spring remove the leader just below the bottom wire. Tie in the two laterals to canes at about 40 degrees and then cut them back to about 45cm (18in). Shorten any laterals to two buds.

YEAR ONE, SUMMER In early to mid-summer, tie in the branch leaders to canes and the best-placed new side shoots to the wires, and cut out the rest. Cut off the laterals on the trunk completely.

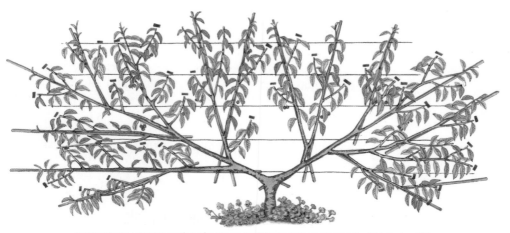

SUBSEQUENT YEARS Continue the process until the space is evenly covered with branches. Little pruning is required but, if necessary, cut out misplaced or over-vigorous shoots in early summer. Pinch back any new growth that is not required to fill a space.

Sour cherry bush

Sour or acid cherries are not as popular as they once were. They were used widely in cooking, especially for bottling for winter use. They were mainly grown as standards and semi-standards, but can now also be grown as bushes, although they are still rather vigorous and can grow too large for a small garden. 'Colt' rootstock can be used for bushes.

Supports
Knock a strong post into the ground to one side of the planting hole and spread the roots of the tree around it before backfilling. Do not hammer it in after the tree has been planted as this can severely damage the roots. Use a proprietary tree tie to secure the tree to the post, and check regularly to ensure that the tie does not become too tight as the tree grows.

Initial training
Unlike sweet cherries, sour cherries fruit on the previous year's wood. When pruning, the basic idea is to stimulate new growth by reducing

ABOVE Birds are very fond of cherries and you will need to protect your fruit from these marauders. Netting can be used, as here, to provide protection.

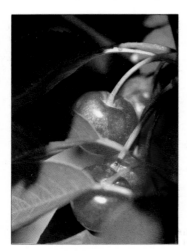

ABOVE Colourful cherries attract birds, as well as humans. Cherry bushes, like other types of fruit tree, can be grown in large fruit cages.

the amount of wood that has already produced fruit. Buy a feathered tree and plant it against a stake. In early spring, cut out the leader at about 1.5m (5ft) from the ground, just above a bud that will develop as the top branch. Shorten all laterals by about two-thirds, cutting to an outward-facing bud. The following spring, remove all laterals up to about 1m (3ft) from the ground to produce a tree with a clear trunk. Reduce all others by half to two-thirds. Also cut out any branches that are misplaced, crowding or crossing others, either removing them entirely or cutting them back to a bud that will produce a better replacement branch. Cut back the tips of all remaining shoots by a half to two-thirds, to outward-facing growth buds (not the plumper fruit buds). In summer, remove any shoots arising from the main branches that are misplaced or causing crowding, especially towards the centre of the tree. Try and keep the centre of the tree open.

Established pruning
In spring, cut out any dead, diseased or damaged wood. At the same time, remove some of the older branches to stimulate new growth. Always prune to the pointed growth buds and not the plumper fruiting ones. After fruiting, cut back all the shoots that have fruited that year to between one-quarter and one-third to a new shoot.

ABOVE Each type of cherry has its own distinctive flavour, so it is worth growing several, choosing ones that ripen at different times.

TRAINING A SOUR CHERRY BUSH

Dwarfing stock has been available longer for sour cherries, and it is relatively easy to find a young feathered tree that is suitable for growing as a bush. As with all cherries, pruning, after formative work is complete, should be confined to early summer.

YEAR ONE, WINTER Plant a young feathered tree in winter and then in early spring cut the leader off at about 1.5m (5ft). Reduce all the laterals by about two-thirds to an outward-facing bud.

YEAR TWO, SPRING The following spring, remove any laterals below what will be the bottom branch, at about 1m (3ft). Cut out any misplaced laterals and reduce all others by about half to two-thirds.

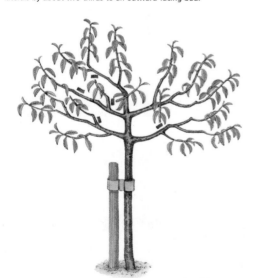

YEAR TWO, SUMMER In summer, continue to remove any misplaced side shoots, especially towards the centre of the bush, which should be kept open and uncongested.

ESTABLISHED PRUNING Once established and fruiting, cut back by a quarter to one-third all the shoots that have fruited that year to stimulate new fruiting wood for the following year. Once the tree is older, cut out one or two of the older sub-laterals to a good shoot on the main branch.

Sour cherry fan

Sour cherries are best grown as fans in a small garden, provided you also have enough wall or fence space – they will take up a length of up to 5m (15ft) of wall. A fan makes it much easier to prune, pick and net the fruit. Netting is essential for protection against birds, but is difficult on free-standing trees.

Supports

Firmly attach five to seven parallel wires, set about 30cm (12in) apart, to a wall or strong fence. They should be stretched taut and held 10–15cm (4–6in) away from the wall to allow air to circulate and prevent the tree from rubbing. The bottom wire should be about 45cm (18in) above ground level. If you want a free-standing fan, the posts must be solidly set in the ground, 2–2.5m (6–8ft) apart.

Initial training

Start with a feathered tree that has two strong shoots just below the proposed position of the bottom wire. Cut off the leader just above the upper one. Tie the laterals to canes, then attach these in turn to the wires at an angle of about 40 degrees. Shorten the side shoots back to about 45cm (18in) to a bud on the underside. This will help produce side shoots later that year. Shorten any other laterals to two buds, then cut them off completely in summer. Tie the laterals in against canes as they develop. The top bud will produce a new leader for each of the main arms and this should be tied in in the same direction, along the cane. Cut out any unwanted shoots, trying to keep the sides balanced. Remove any new growth arising from the main trunk. Cut back the tips of laterals on either side of the main stems so that they

TRAINING A SOUR CHERRY FAN

Fans are a very good way to grow sour cherries because they are easy to reach for pruning and picking as well as easy to cover with nets. Choose a feathered tree that has two good laterals at the correct height. It is advisable to check with your supplier to ensure that you are getting a suitable variety.

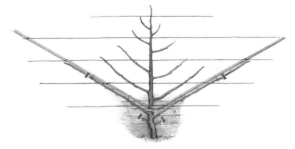

YEAR ONE, WINTER Plant a young feathered tree and in spring cut off the leader just below the bottom wire and above the two laterals that will form the main branches. Tie in the laterals to canes at 40 degrees and reduce them to about 45cm (18in). Shorten any laterals to two buds.

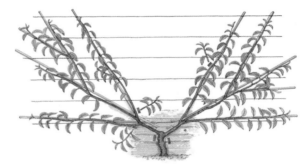

YEAR ONE, SUMMER Tie in the best-placed of the new shoots to canes and remove the rest so that an even framework starts to develop on either side of the trunk. Remove the laterals on the trunk and keep the centre of the tree open.

LEFT A sour cherry fan growing in a fruit cage against a post-and-wire support. Such a fan will give many years of productive use.

SUBSEQUENT YEARS, SUMMER Continue to develop the structure by cutting out the tips of the main shoots to encourage branching, and removing any shoots that are not required, especially those that cross or cause congestion.

ESTABLISHED PRUNING The main pruning, once the fan has matured and is fruiting, is to cut back the majority of the fruited shoots to a replacement shoot. Occasionally in early summer, as the tree ages, remove one or two of the older branches back to a replacement shoot.

in turn branch out. Remove any growth that projects forwards from the fan or in towards the wall. Over the next three years or so, gradually allow the fan to develop so that it branches more towards the periphery and covers the allotted space evenly.

Established pruning

Once the basic fan has been established, prune in early summer by cutting back the leaders to a suitable bud or shoot. As the fan matures, take out the occasional older branch to a strong new shoot to promote new growth. Always prune back to new shoots or to growth buds. After fruiting, prune back the fruited shoots to a replacement shoot. Keep established trees netted or in fruit cages, or the birds will take your crop.

PEACHES AND NECTARINES

(*Prunus persica* and *P. p.* var. *nectarina*)

Peach and nectarine bush

More and more gardeners are growing peaches and nectarines successfully in the open. The results are certainly rewarding. In cooler climates, where they will not fruit successfully as free-standing trees, fans are best, as they can be grown against protecting walls. There is no dwarfing stock as yet, but there is rootstock available that enables them to be grown successfully as bush trees.

Support

Put a stake in the ground before planting the tree so that you do not accidentally damage its roots. Use a proprietary tree tie to attach the tree to the stake, as alternatives can damage the bark.

Initial training

Plant a grafted feathered whip in winter. In the following early spring set about its formative pruning by

ABOVE Peach bushes are suitable for larger gardens, particularly in warmer areas. For small or cooler gardens the peach fan is probably better.

ABOVE A bed of young feathered peach trees just coming into bud. They can be purchased as bare-rooted specimens from nursery beds.

clearing the trunk of all laterals to about 1m (3ft) from ground-level. Select four or five well-placed laterals to form the main branches, then cut them back to about one-third of their original length. Cut back the main leader just above the top lateral. In summer, remove any new laterals that form on the trunk,

unless they enhance the overall shape. The centre should be kept open, so remove any sub-laterals that tend to fill it, along with any others that are crowding or crossing other branches and shoots. The following spring, reduce all the shoot leaders by about half, cutting back to an outward-facing bud.

Varieties

Peaches	Nectarines
'Amsden June'	'Early Rivers'
'Bellegarde'	'Independence'
'Duke of York'	'John Rivers'
'Dymond'	'Lord Napier'
'Peregrine'	'Pineapple'
'Rochester'	
'Redhaven'	
'Royal George'	

nectarines

peaches

TRAINING A PEACH OR NECTARINE BUSH

Peaches are usually purchased as feathered trees. Select one with strong laterals around the area where you want the branches to be formed. As with other members of the *Prunus* genus, such as plums and cherries, established pruning tasks are best carried out in summer to avoid disease which can enter through wounds in the tree.

YEAR ONE, WINTER Plant a feathered whip in winter. In early spring clear the bottom part of the trunk of laterals. Select four or five strong laterals to form the branches and then remove the leader just above the top one. Cut these laterals back by about two-thirds.

YEAR ONE, SUMMER During the following summer remove any misplaced or over-crowding shoots, making certain that the centre of the bush is kept relatively open.

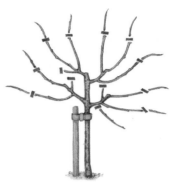

YEAR TWO, SPRING In the following spring remove all unwanted and misplaced shoots and cut back the remaining shoots by about half, to a strong bud.

Established pruning

From now on all pruning should take place in early summer. First remove any dead or damaged wood, and any shoots that are crossing or crowding other growth, especially towards the centre, which should be kept open. Fruits are produced on the previous year's wood, so remove some of the previous year's fruiting wood, preferably back to a point where there is new growth. Take out any shoots that appear on the main trunk below the bottom branch.

ABOVE There is nothing quite like eating a peach or nectarine fresh from the tree. This peach variety is called 'Redhaven'.

ESTABLISHED PRUNING Once established, as well as removing any misplaced or unwanted shoots, take out a large proportion of the wood that has fruited back to a new shoot.

Peach and nectarine fan

In many ways it is better to grow a peach or nectarine as a fan in cooler climates, provided you have a suitable wall or fence. It makes it easier to attend to the tree and to protect it against frosts and wet weather, by fixing what are in effect roller blinds of clear plastic which hang down from a frame over the plant. The wall also offers added warmth. Besides, fans always look especially attractive.

Supports

Attach parallel horizontal wires to the wall about 30cm (12in) apart, the bottom one about 45cm (18in) above the ground. The wires should be stretched taut and held about 10–15cm (4–6in) away from the wall. In warmer areas the fan can be supported on wires strung between strong posts, solidly set in the ground about 2–2.5m (6–8ft) apart.

Initial training

Start with a young feathered tree that has two suitable laterals just

ABOVE One advantage of peach and nectarine fans is that they are easier to protect from frosts than more conventional bush trees.

TRAINING A PEACH OR NECTARINE FAN

Fans are probably the best way of growing peaches and nectarines, especially if they are grown against a wall which helps keep the frosts away from the blossom. Fans are easier to reach when you are pruning and picking. They are also more decorative than conventional trees, especially if more than one is grown against a wall.

YEAR ONE, WINTER Plant a feathered tree in winter and then in spring cut back the leader to two strong laterals below the bottom wire. Tie these in to canes at 40 degrees and cut them back to about 45cm (18in). Cut back any other laterals to a few buds.

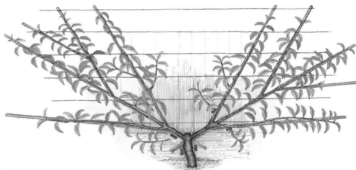

YEAR ONE, SUMMER Tie in the new branch leaders to canes and all the best-placed side shoots that you need to create an even spread to wires. Cut out any that are not needed or that are misplaced. Also remove the remains of the other laterals on the trunk.

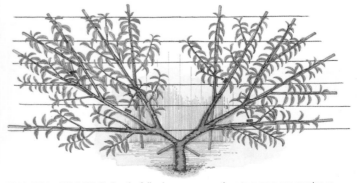

YEAR TWO, SUMMER During the following summer continue to remove any crossing or misplaced shoots, trying to ensure an even and balanced coverage on both sides of the trunk. Prevent the centre from becoming crowded.

PRUNING A PEACH FAN

1 In summer it can be an advantage to remove some of the shoots bearing leaves that shade the fruit, preventing them from ripening.

2 Some of the long shoots not bearing fruit can be cut back to one or two leaves of the new growth, opening up the fruit below.

3 The shade can be further reduced by taking out the tips of fruiting shoots. After fruiting, these will be cut back further.

below the level of the first wire. In spring, cut the leader back just above the uppermost of the desired laterals. Cut back the two laterals to about 45cm (18in) from the base to an underside bud. Tie these laterals to individual long canes, and fasten these in turn to the wires at an angle of about 40 degrees. Cut back any other laterals to two buds. In summer, cut them back completely, tight to the trunk. Around mid-summer, tie in the new branch leaders to the canes. Select the best-placed side shoots and tie these in to the wires. Remove the rest, especially vigorous, vertical shoots. Try to encourage downward growth that will fill the fan evenly. Do this each summer, tying the main shoots to canes until the fan has filled out.

Established pruning

Prune in mid-summer. Cut out any dead, diseased or damaged wood along with any vigorous growth, or stems that tend to crowd the framework and shoots which point towards the wall or project away from the plane of the fan. In late summer, after fruiting, cut back the wood that has carried fruit to a replacement shoot. Any older wood that is less productive can also be cut back to replacement shoots, which should be trained in to replace it.

ABOVE A peach fan grown against a wall. Note how easy it is for netting to be draped over the fan to protect the fruit from marauding birds.

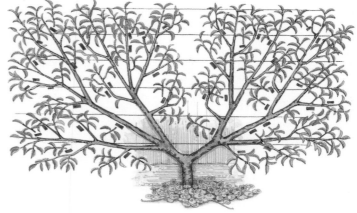

ESTABLISHED PRUNING, SUMMER Once established, cut back fruited shoots to a new shoot after fruiting. Also remove any crowding or misplaced shoots. After a few years remove the occasional old branch back to a replacement shoot.

APRICOTS (*Prunus armenica*)
Apricot fan

Apricots can be grown as bush trees, but these do not do very well in cooler climates. Grown against a wall, where they can be given winter protection, they are more successful. They can also be grown against fences, but walls provide better shelter. Glasshouses built against a wall are the ideal situation.

Varieties

'Alfred'   'Luizet'
'Bergeron'   'Moorpark'
'Breda'   'New Large Early'
'Early Moorpark' 'Polonais'
'Hemskerk'

Supports

Fix parallel horizontal wires to the wall, spaced at about 30cm (12in) intervals, the bottom wire about 45cm (18in) above ground-level. The wires should be stretched taut and held about 10–15cm (4–6in) away from the wall. In warmer areas, the fan can be supported by a strong fence or on wires strung between sturdy posts, solidly set in the ground about 2–2.5m (6–8ft) apart.

Initial training

Start with a young feathered tree with two suitable laterals just below the level of the first wire. The first spring after planting, cut the leader back just above the uppermost of the desired laterals. Tie them to individual long canes, and secure these to the wires at an angle of about 40 degrees. Cut back these two laterals to about 45cm (18in) from the base to an underside bud. Cut back any other laterals to two buds. In summer, cut them back completely, tight to the trunk. Around mid-summer, tie in the new branch leaders to the canes. Select the best-placed side shoots and tie these in to the wires. Remove the rest, especially any vigorous, vertical shoots. Try to encourage downward

ABOVE LEFT An apricot trained against a wall, showing the even spread of blossom over the whole fan. The wall will help to protect the blossom from frost.

LEFT A well-spread apricot fan on a wall. The two sides are slightly unbalanced but this will rectify itself as the left side catches up and some of the wayward shoots on the right are removed.

TRAINING AN APRICOT FAN

The only really successful way to grow apricots in cooler climates is with the protection of a wall, and the fan shape is the only practical way in which to do this. As with plums and cherries, the best time for pruning in order to prevent disease entering the wood is in the summer. A well-established apricot fan also has many decorative qualities.

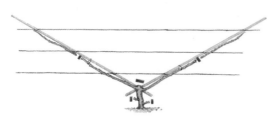

YEAR ONE, WINTER Plant a feathered tree in winter, and in spring remove the leader just below the bottom wire. Tie in two strong laterals to canes at 40 degrees and reduce their length to 45cm (18in). Cut back any other laterals to two buds.

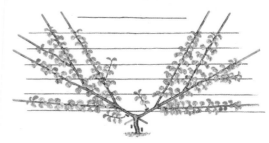

YEAR ONE, SUMMER Tie in the main side shoots as they develop, creating an even coverage of the wall and ensuring that the sides are balanced. Remove any unnecessary shoots, including the laterals on the trunk.

growth to fill the fan evenly. Do this every summer, tying the main shoots to canes, until the fan has filled out.

Established pruning

Once the fan is established, prune it in early to mid-summer only. Spring pruning can result in diseases entering the tree through the pruning wounds. Cut out any dead, diseased or damaged wood. At the same time, remove any vigorous growth, stems that tend to crowd the framework and shoots that point towards the wall or project away from the plane of the fan. New growth on all branch leaders and side shoots should be cut back to just a few leaves. Thin out any other new growth, retaining only those shoots that are required to fill gaps or to replace older stems. Periodically remove any old growth that is unproductive, cutting it back to a replacement shoot. Try to keep the centre reasonably open and clear of shoots. The canes can be removed and the shoots tied directly to the wires once the fan has reached maturity.

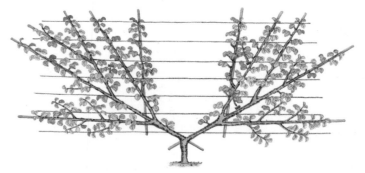

YEAR TWO, SUMMER During the following summer remove completely any vigorous vertical shoots and any misplaced ones, and tie in the rest to suitable spaces to ensure a good coverage.

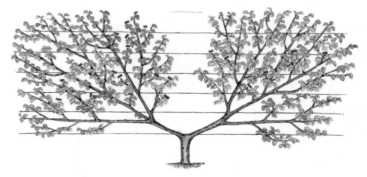

ESTABLISHED PRUNING, SUMMER Once established, continue to cut out any vigorous vertical growth and any unwanted shoots in summer. Cut back any new growth on branch leaders and all side shoots to one or two leaves. You can remove the canes when the fan is mature.

QUINCES *(Cydonia oblonica)*
Quince bush

Quinces are not grown as widely as they should be. Admittedly, the fruit cannot be eaten directly off the tree, but it is most delicious when cooked. Quinces can be grown as fans, but are best grown in the open as trees. They are also successful as multi-stemmed trees if they are kept well pruned, but bush trees are easier to maintain and produce a more reliable crop.

Varieties

'Champion'
'Dutch'
'Lusitanica'
'Maliformis'
'Meech's Prolific'

Supports

Knock a short stake into the ground inside the planting hole and then plant the tree, spreading the roots around the post. Do not knock the post in after planting as this can damage the roots. Use a proprietary tree tie to support the trunk.

Initial training

Start with a young feathered tree. Clear the trunk of any laterals up to about 60cm (2ft) from ground level. Another 30cm (1ft) or so above this, cut back the leader just above a strong bud. Remove the tips of the remaining laterals, shortening them by up to two-thirds at an upward-facing bud. The following winter, cut back the new main leader just above a strong lateral about 30cm (1ft) above the previous winter's cut. This lateral will now become the top branch. Shorten the tips of all the other laterals by one-third to half of the previous year's growth.

Established pruning

Once the basic shape of the quince bush is established, it will continue to throw out new shoots. Unless they are filling in a gap, these should be removed, especially if they are crossing or crowding other branches and shoots. Keep the centre relatively open to allow in plenty of light and circulating air. As the tree ages, remove some of the older spurs to thin out congested clusters and new growth low down. Remove the tips of the leaders to promote spur production. If any laterals appear low down on the trunk, or suckers from its base, these should be removed.

LEFT Most quinces are grown on relatively small trees and this, along with their very decorative blossom and fruit, makes them an attractive tree for the small garden.

RIGHT A young quince in its second or third year. The laterals have been cut back to outward-facing buds so that it has bushed out nicely. One or two of the crossing and more vigorous shoots will have to be removed shortly.

TRAINING A QUINCE BUSH

Quinces are usually grown as bush trees, although they can be trained into other forms such as fans. They can grow as multi-stemmed trees but are best if they can be trained with a single trunk. They have a tendency to sucker and these should be removed. The suckers may appear from below ground or from the base of the trunk.

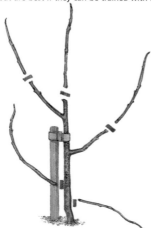

YEAR ONE, WINTER Plant a young feathered tree and cut off the leader at about 1m (3ft). Select two or four strong laterals at the top of the trunk and then remove all the other ones. Cut back the remainder by up to two-thirds.

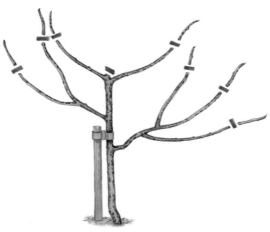

YEAR TWO, WINTER/SPRING Next winter or spring, cut out the new leader at about 30cm (1ft) above the previous cut and choose two more good laterals, making around five or so, removing any others. Cut back the branch leaders by one-third to half of the previous season's growth.

YEAR THREE, WINTER By the following winter the general shape should be becoming apparent. Remove any crossing, rubbing or misplaced shoots and keep the centre as open as possible.

ESTABLISHED PRUNING, WINTER In the established tree cut out any vigorous vertical growth along with any new shoots that are not required to fill an empty space. Remove the tips of the leaders.

FIGS *(Ficus carica)*
Fig bush

Figs form distinctive-looking trees. In warm areas, they can be grown as free-standing bushes, although it is quite common to see bushes trained against walls. These, however, are often fans that have grown wild through lack of pruning. A bush will grow up to about 4m (12ft) tall and the same across, and is worth having if you have the space and can provide the appropriate conditions.

Supports

Knock a sturdy post into the ground in the planting hole and spread the roots of the tree around it. Avoid knocking in the post after planting, as this can damage the roots. Use a proprietary tree tie to fasten it to the trunk. Restrict root growth by planting in a large bottomless container or sinking four 60cm

(2ft) paving slabs on edge into the ground around the root system. This helps to dwarf the tree and encourages it to bear fruit rather than putting on too much leafy growth.

Initial training

Plant a two-year-old tree in spring. Remove all the lower laterals below the ones you wish to keep as your lowest branch – probably around 60cm (2ft) from ground-level. Retain around six or seven branches and cut back the leader immediately above the top branch. This should be at about 1.2m (4ft). The next spring, remove any laterals that cross or crowd one another. In summer, pinch out the tips of all new shoots, restricting them to five or so leaves. This will expose the developing fruits to sunlight and so encourage them to open.

Varieties

'Bourjasotte Grise'
'Brown Turkey'
'Brunswick'
'Rouge de Bordeaux'
'San Pedro Miro'
'White Marseilles'

Established pruning

The main pruning should take place in early spring. Figs reshoot readily, so can be heavily pruned (even back to the ground) if necessary to restrict growth. The main aim is to keep the bush open. Remove any crossing or overcrowded stems, if possible cutting to upward-pointing shoots so that the tree grows upright rather than spreading. Cut out any dead or damaged wood. In summer, take out shoot tips as described.

TRAINING A FIG BUSH

In warmer districts, figs can be grown as bush trees in the open. When planting, it is important that you restrict their roots by planting in a large bottomless container sunk into the ground, as this helps to restrain the tree's growth. It is best to start the bush with a well-balanced feathered tree, as this will save at least a year over a maiden whip.

YEAR ONE, SPRING Plant the young feathered tree. Cut off the leader at about 1.2m (4ft), above the desired top branch. Cut off all laterals below the desired bottom branch, about 60cm (2ft) above the ground.

YEAR TWO, SPRING The following spring cut out all the crossing shoots and those not needed to form the framework of the tree. In the summer, cut back all new growth to five or six leaves.

ESTABLISHED PRUNING, SPRING Once established, prune in spring, cutting out any crossing or unwanted shoots. If necessary, the bush can be cut back quite hard if it is becoming overgrown or taking up too much space. In summer, take out the shoot tips.

Fig fan

In cool areas figs grown as fans stand a better chance of producing a good crop of fruit, as the warmth of a wall will help to protect them. Figs are quite vigorous, even if the roots are restricted, so it is important to keep on top of the pruning and not let the fan degenerate into a tree.

Supports

Attach five to seven parallel wires, set about 30cm (12in) apart, preferably to a wall, though a solid fence will also do. Make certain that they are held at least 10cm (4in) away from the wall to allow air to circulate. The bottom wire should be about 45cm (18in) from ground-level. Restrict root growth by sinking 60cm (2ft) paving slabs on edge into the ground around the root

system. This helps to dwarf the tree and encourages it to bear fruit rather than putting on too much leafy growth. Alternatively, grow the fig in a large container.

Initial training

In the early spring, plant a two-year-old fig. The plant should have two strong laterals, the upper one around 38cm (15in) above ground-level, or just below the bottom wire. Train these shoots sideways, attached to canes tied in at an angle of about 40 degrees to the horizontal. Cut back the laterals to about 45cm (18in). Cut off the leader just above the higher of the two laterals. The following spring, cut back the new growth on the main branches and any new sub-laterals to about half

their length. During the summer, tie in new growths to canes as they develop. The following winter, repeat the previous spring's steps, and reduce the lengths of all new growths. Remove any that grow towards or away from the wall, and take out any growth that will cause overcrowding. Aim for an even, relatively open spread. Stop all growths when they have filled the allotted space.

Established pruning

In spring, cut back shoots that have fruited to one bud. Prevent the tree from being overcrowded by removing crossing or crowding branches and shoots. Take out any dead or damaged wood. Remove the tips of any new branches that are extending beyond the allotted space.

TRAINING A FIG FAN

For most gardens situated in cooler areas the best way in which to grow figs is as a fan. They grow best against a wall, but can also be trained against a fence. Restrict the roots by planting in a bottomless container sunk into the ground. This will restrain the fan's growth. If the roots are allowed to grow freely, the fan may become too vigorous.

YEAR ONE, SPRING Plant a two-year-old feathered tree in early spring and cut the leader out just above two strong laterals. Tie the laterals to canes at 40 degrees and cut them back to about 45cm (18in).

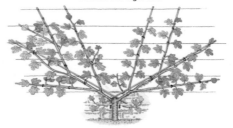

YEAR TWO, SPRING In spring, cut back all new growth to about half. In summer, tie the new growth to canes. In winter, repeat the previous spring's steps and reduce the length of all new growths. Remove unwanted growth.

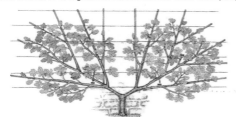

SUBSEQUENT YEARS Continue to follow this regime until the whole space is evenly filled with shoots. Keep the centre relatively clear and take out any vigorous vertical shoots.

ESTABLISHED PRUNING, SPRING Once established, the main pruning in spring is to cut all fruited shoots back to one bud. As usual, also cut back any misplaced new shoots.

MEDLARS (*Mespilus germanica*)
Medlar tree

Medlars are grown mainly for their ornamental qualities and historical associations. They cannot be eaten directly from the tree but need, in effect, to be rotten before they become edible.

Support
Before planting, knock a short stake into the ground where the medlar is to be planted.

Initial training
Plant a young feathered tree and remove completely any laterals on the trunk up to a height of about 1.2m (4ft) above ground-level. Reduce the other laterals, below what

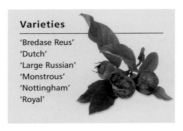

Varieties
'Bredase Reus'
'Dutch'
'Large Russian'
'Monstrous'
'Nottingham'
'Royal'

will be the lowest branch, by about half. The following winter, select the laterals that you want to form the basis of the crown of the tree, then remove the rest. If the tree has reached the height you wish the trunk to attain (probably about 2m/6ft), cut back the leader just

above the top lateral. If not, let it grow unpruned for another year. Remove any unwanted laterals. Also cut out any shoots that are crossing or crowding, especially any that are dominating the centre of the tree, which should be left open.

Established pruning
This is one of the easiest fruits to prune, as there is virtually nothing to do once the tree has matured. If necessary, remove any dead or damaged wood during late summer. Do not shorten, or tip-prune the horizontal branches, as this is likely to result in a lot of sucker growth, which will spoil the shape of the tree.

TRAINING A MEDLAR TREE
Because of their ornamental value, young medlar trees are still relatively easy to buy. Once established, they do not need much in the way of pruning and so are simple to look after. Start with a young feathered tree. Medlars make attractive specimen trees and can be planted in a decorative part of the garden rather than with other fruit or vegetables.

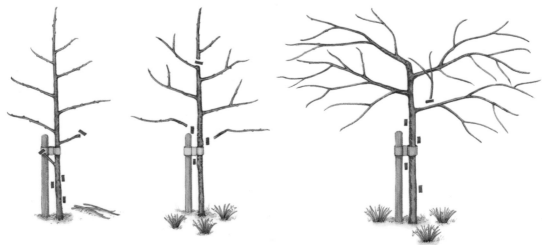

YEAR ONE, WINTER Plant the young tree in the winter and remove the lowest laterals. Reduce the other laterals, below what will eventually be the lowest branch, by about half.

YEAR TWO, WINTER In the second winter select the laterals that you wish to have as the branches. Cut the leader off above the top one and remove all other laterals below the bottom one.

ESTABLISHED PRUNING, WINTER By the third year the basic shape should have been formed, and established pruning only involves the removal of any misplaced wood and any shoots that appear on the trunk. If necessary, remove any dead or damaged wood in late summer.

MULBERRIES (*Morus* species)
Mulberry tree

Mulberries are in a category all on their own in that most will outlive the person who planted them — they can live for hundreds of years.

Supports

Hammer a strong stake into the ground to hold the tree straight in its early years. Put the stake in before planting so that you do not damage the roots.

Initial training

For an ornamental tree with a gnarled look, little needs to be done after planting, but for a more productive, better-shaped tree a little formative training helps. Prune only in the early part of winter, as any cuts will bleed if made at other times

Varieties

'Chelsea'
'King James'
'Large Black'
'Wellington'

of year. Plant either a maiden whip or a feathered tree. Remove the lower laterals up to about 1.2–1.5 (4–5ft) above ground-level once the tree has grown large enough and has several branches developing above the cleared trunk. A year later, cut the leader back above the lateral that you want to become the top branch. If you want it to grow into a tall tree, leave the main leader intact. The tree can now be left to develop naturally.

Established pruning

In general, there is no pruning to do on an established mulberry tree, other than cutting out any dead or damaged wood, which should be done in early to mid-winter. Any other branches that you have to take off for any reason should also be removed at this time of year. Very old mulberry trees often have a pronounced lean, and wooden props under at least one branch may be needed in order to prevent collapse. This lean can sometimes be apparent even at a relatively young age, and you may find that you have to put a stout prop under one of the branches yourself. However, far from being unsightly, this only adds to its venerable appearance.

TRAINING A MULBERRY TREE

Mulberries have become generally available once more and are not especially difficult to find. They are easy to look after because there is little pruning needed once they have been established, although in their old age they may well need some form of support, which usually takes the form of a prop because these trees have a tendency to lean.

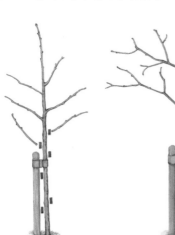

YEAR ONE, WINTER Plant a feathered tree in winter and tie it to a firm stake. Remove any laterals below what you want as your lowest branch.

YEAR TWO, WINTER In the following winter cut out the leader just above what you want as the top branch. Leave it another year or two if you want a taller tree.

ESTABLISHED PRUNING No pruning of established trees is generally required, but very old trees may need to have stout props put under some of their sagging limbs to prevent them breaking or the tree collapsing entirely.

CITRUS FRUITS (*Citrus* species)

In recent years there has been a surge of interest in growing citrus fruit. Some gardeners grow the trees solely for their decorative value, while others hope to produce edible fruit. Nurserymen have responded to this and citrus plants are now commonly available in cooler regions. Oranges, tangerines, mandarins, lemons, limes and kumquats are the most commonly available to the average gardener.

Climate

Citrus are trees of sub-tropical or tropical origin and are generally suited only to hotter climates, but as long as they are kept to a small size they can easily be grown in containers in a warm conservatory. They can be moved outside for the summer, or indeed left inside under glass if you prefer. Generally they will not tolerate frosts and so are unsuitable for growing outside except in warmer areas where these rarely occur. Below about 13°C (55°F) the trees become dormant, so it is essential that they are placed where they will have long periods of sustained warmth. Even when moved outside in summer, they should be given a sheltered position, away from any cold winds. There are some varieties that are more tolerant of cold conditions. Check before buying whether they are best kept under glass or can be moved outside.

Where citrus fruit is grown commercially in areas with potential frost, soil is heaped up around the trunks to the level of the lower branches in the winter as protection. Even if the topgrowth is killed by frost, new growth regenerates from the trunk once the soil is cleared away in spring. This is a major task and is normally carried out only for the first four years, but you may feel

Varieties

Calamondins
Grapefruits
Kumquats
Lemons
Limes
Mandarins
Oranges
Tangerines

oranges

lemons

it worth attempting in the garden in order to grow trees outside. If potted trees are left outside they are far more prone to frost damage as the rootball can easily freeze through the sides of the container. Always move these inside whenever frost is forecast.

Supports

If citrus trees are grown in pots, they are small enough not to need staking in any way. However, outdoors they can easily blow over, so it may be

ABOVE Most citrus fruit can be grown on small trees in containers that can be kept inside during the colder months and moved outside during the summer. They provide decoration as well as fruit.

necessary to anchor the container in some way. If you grow citrus as standards then you will need a cane in the pot to support the tall stem.

Initial training

Generally, citrus trees are sold in containers and have already been shaped by the nursery or grower, leaving little to do. However, it is possible to buy citrus as unbranched trees, which are much cheaper than mature plants and possibly essential if you intend to grow them outside (container plants are usually too small). These will need some preliminary training to establish the desired habit. Generally, training is as for other bush trees. Allow the trunk to develop to the desired height, then stop it above a bud. In the case of container plants, this may be 30–60cm (12–24in); it will be higher for planted trees. Standard trees grown in containers can be treated in the same way except that they must be allowed to reach their final height before the tip is removed. Choose the top three or four branches during the following winter and shorten these to 25cm (10in) in the case of container trees and 30–35cm (12–14in) in the case of outdoor trees. Remove any other side shoots that appear below this. The following winter shorten all leaders of all main shoots back by about one-third and remove any side shoots that are growing towards the centre of the plant and causing congestion. Continue to do this until the tree matures.

Established pruning

Little pruning is usually necessary on mature plants. However, frosted wood will die back, and must be removed. If containers are kept in inadequate light levels, growth will

TRAINING A CITRUS STANDARD

In cooler countries the only way that citrus fruit can be overwintered is by growing them in containers and keeping them under glass. Most trees sold in these countries are suitable for just that, but it is worth checking with your supplier that they are intended for that purpose. Citrus plants can often be purchased in the container in which they will grow.

YEAR ONE, WINTER If not already trained by the nursery, allow the leader to develop to the desired height and then remove the tip at a bud. Remove any unneeded laterals.

SUBSEQUENT YEARS, WINTER Continue to cut back the new growth on the shoots to make them branch into a bush shape. Once established little pruning is necessary, other than to pinch back the leader growth to a couple of buds and remove any misplaced shoots.

YEAR TWO, WINTER In the following winter shorten the branches to about 25cm (10in) and reduce the new leader to about two leaves.

become drawn. This can be redressed by removing the top by up to one-third, preferably in mid-winter when the plant is dormant. Remove some of the resulting shoots if the tree becomes too dense and overgrown, thus reducing the light reaching the lower branches. Aim to avoid legginess by improving the light conditions. Sometimes a container-grown tree is too large, and difficult, to move in and out of its winter home. In this case it may be necessary to remove some of the outer branches to reduce its size, a job best tackled in mid-winter. Finally, remove any crossing branches and any other shoots that crowd the bush. If the top growth of a tree is killed by frost, the rootstock may throw up new shoots. But these will be rootstock, not the upper grafted part that bears the fruit. If the tree is purely ornamental, this may be acceptable. Select one main shoot, then proceed as for initial training. For a fruiting tree, however, you will need a replacement.

COBNUTS *(Corylus avellana)*
Cobnut tree

Cobnuts and filberts have a dual function: they are grown both for their decorative appearance and for their nutritious nuts. A third function can also be added: a well-developed cobnut makes a very pleasant tree to sit under. Decide what you want the tree to do. In nature, hazel tends to be a multi-stemmed tree and this form is the most decorative in the garden. Nuts will be produced on such a tree, but for greater numbers the trees are usually grown on a single, short stem, from which the main branches appear.

Supports

Generally no supports are required except for the initial planting if the site is exposed. Should that be the case, a short stake with a proprietary tree tie will suffice until the tree has become established.

Initial training

For a multi-stemmed bush, there is little else to do than to put in a young plant and let it develop, but for a tree a little more attention is required. It can be formed in the same way as many other bush fruit trees. Start with a one-year-old

ABOVE A cluster of developing cobnuts. They will need netting if there are any squirrels in the vicinty, or they will all disappear.

sapling. Cut back the tip to about 60cm (24in) above ground-level, just above a bud. The following year, a number of laterals will form. Select the top three or four of these and remove the rest to create a clear trunk of about 45cm (18in). Cut back each of the chosen laterals to about 25cm (10in) at a strong bud. In the third winter, remove the tips of all the main shoots to encourage further branching.

Established pruning

Keep the trunk below the main branches clear of growth. In late summer, snap all the new long, strong growths in half, being careful

Varieties
'Cosford Cob'
'Kentish Cob'
'Red Filbert'
'Webb's
     Prize Cob'

to break them only partially so that they hang down (a process known as "brutting"). This is not a particularly attractive method and is not recommended for ornamental varieties, but is an effective way of increasing the fruiting capacity of the tree. In early spring, as soon as you can see the small clusters of tiny red female flowers (much smaller than the yellow catkins that appear at the tips of the fruiting buds), cut back all the shoots, including the broken ones, to the first bunch of catkins or the first cluster of female flowers. If the shoot contains catkins only, leave until the catkins fade then remove it entirely. Also take out any dead, crossing or congested wood, keeping the centre of the tree open. As the tree matures, cut some of the older wood back to where there is suitable young growth.

PRUNING A COBNUT TREE

1 An old established cobnut tree, showing the ideal open goblet shape that you should aim for when pruning.

2 Some of the older growth can be removed to stimulate new growth and to open up the centre of the tree.

3 Remove growth that is going to cross and rub against other branches. Also remove any growth that is likely to cause congestion.

4 Inward-facing branches should be removed completely so that the open goblet shape of the tree is maintained.

TRAINING A COBNUT TREE

Cobnuts can be bought in their first year as maiden whips, without any side shoots. Care is needed to ensure that they are properly trained otherwise they may develop into multi-stemmed shrubs rather than trees. This will not be a disaster, but for nut production, trees are better. Multi-stemmed shrubs are in turn much easier and more decorative to grow.

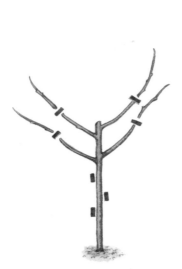

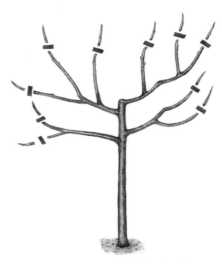

YEAR ONE, WINTER Plant a sapling in the winter and cut off the leader at the height where you want the top of the trunk to be, at about 60cm (24in).

YEAR TWO, WINTER In the second winter decide which laterals you want to create the branches, and remove the rest. Cut back the chosen laterals to about 25cm (10in) or so.

SUBSEQUENT WINTERS In the following winters until the tree is fully developed, cut out the tips of the shoots to provoke further branching.

BRUTTING, SUMMER It is normal to "brut" established trees in late summer. Snap all the long growth in half, but do not break them completely. Leave them hanging, although they might look untidy.

BRUTTING, SPRING In early spring, prune these broken stems back to just above the first tiny red flower you can see. If the shoot has only catkins, wait till they fade and then remove the shoot completely.

WALNUTS (*Juglans* species)
Walnut tree

Walnuts were often grown as hedgerow plants, the only attention given being the gathering of the walnuts once they were shed. Today, they are grown by discriminating gardeners who have enough room for them. Walnut trees tend to grow large but are extremely decorative.

Varieties

'Broadview'
'Buccaneer'
'Franquette'
'Mayette'

Supports

Support is needed only for the first couple of years until the tree is well established, after which it can be dispensed with. A stake knocked into the ground and a proprietary tree tie are all that is required.

Initial training

Walnuts can be purchased as feathered trees in containers for planting in late autumn to early winter. The best time for all pruning is autumn to early winter, after the wood has matured. Pruning at other times results in copious sap bleeding from the wounds. In the autumn after planting, remove some of the lower laterals. A year later, if the tree has grown enough, remove all the laterals from the trunk below those that will form the lowest branches. For a tree with a leader, the most commonly grown form, allow this to continue to grow unpruned. For a more rounded tree, remove the leader above the required topmost branch. Often the leader is stopped by frost or wind damage. In this case, two leaders will probably now develop. Left as they are, the tree will not grow quite so tall, but if you want to continue with a central leader, rub out one of the two buds beneath the damaged tip (if they have already started growing, cut out one of the new replacement shoots). Other than removing any crossing or congested wood, allow the tree to develop in its own time.

Established pruning

Very little is required other than to remove any dead, diseased or damaged wood and to cut back any crossing wood.

TRAINING A WALNUT TREE

Walnuts are usually grown as standard trees, either tall with a leader, or as a more rounded shape with branches radiating from the top of the trunk. They bleed easily, so pruning should take place in autumn to early winter.

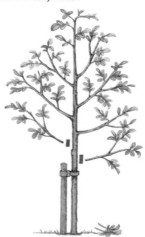

YEAR ONE, AUTUMN/WINTER Plant a feathered tree in late autumn to early winter and the following autumn remove the lower laterals to form a clear trunk up to 60cm (2ft).

YEAR TWO, AUTUMN A year later, in autumn, repeat the exercise and remove a few more laterals, up to 1.2m (4ft). The lowest remaining ones will now form the lowest branches.

ESTABLISHED PRUNING Once established, very little pruning is required except to remove any dead or damaged wood. Any crossing wood can also be removed.

SWEET CHESTNUTS (*Castanea sativa*)
Sweet chestnut tree

The other nut tree that is commonly grown in cooler climates is the sweet chestnut. However, it is grown mainly for its timber, the nuts being incidental. The best nuts are to be found on trees that are grown in hotter regions. However, a number of cultivars that reliably produce fruit are now available.

Supports
Generally none is required, but a single stake may be advisable for the first couple of years in more exposed positions, while the tree is establishing.

Initial training
When buying, ensure that you ask for sweet chestnut (*Castanea sativa*) and specify that you want it for the

Varieties

'Laguépie'
'Marron de Lyon'
'Marron de Redon'
'Marigoule'

nuts so that you get a good cultivar – some particularly decorative forms produce inferior nuts. Generally, sweet chestnut trees are allowed to develop into a central-leader standard. Allow a feathered tree with a strong leader to develop, removing the lower laterals at the height you wish the lower branches to be. Other than removing any crossing or unwanted laterals as the tree establishes, it can be left to develop on its own.

Sweet Chestnut timber

Chestnut produces very good timber for stakes and poles for garden use, or larger poles for constructing arbours or fences. If the tree is trained as a multi-stemmed stool, it will produce a number of poles every few years. Cut these to within 30cm (12in) or so of ground-level. More shoots will then develop.

Established pruning
Little pruning is required once the tree is established other than to remove any dead or damaged wood. The trees will start to produce fruit in quantity after about ten years. In maturity, a sweet chestnut can shed limbs, and any such breakages should be neatly trimmed.

TRAINING A SWEET CHESTNUT

Sweet chestnut trees are usually planted for timber in cooler countries but increasingly stock suitable for fruiting trees is being offered. This is usually in the form of feathered trees. Once established, the tree needs little in the way of pruning.

YEAR ONE, WINTER Plant a feathered tree in winter. Remove the lowest branches, up to about 60cm (2ft), and cut back the higher ones, up to 1.2m (4ft), by about half of their length.

YEAR TWO, WINTER In the following winter cut out completely those laterals that were cut in half last winter. If the trunk is still not tall enough, cut more laterals in half, up to the desired lowest branches.

SUBSEQUENT YEARS Once the height of the cleared trunk has been reached, remove any remaining stubs. The tree will grow for many years and need very little pruning, other than to keep the shape balanced.

Climbing Fruit

Some fruit is produced on climbing plants. For most gardeners, the main fruiting climber is a grapevine. Vines are increasingly popular among home gardeners, whether you are looking to grow just a few grapes for the table or for making a couple of bottles of wine, or are intending to plant up the whole garden and turn it into a vineyard. As with other aspects of gardening, it is very easy to become hooked on growing grapes.

A plant that is not necessarily thought of as a fruit is the hop. For centuries, this has been grown on a large scale for making another beverage: beer. However, as the number of commercial hop gardens diminishes, there is a corresponding increase in gardeners who are growing hops themselves for a spot of home-brewing.

Although the detail is different, the basic principles behind the training and pruning of climbing fruit are the same as any other kind of pruning: the purpose is to maximize cropping and to keep the plants in a reasonably tidy condition, especially if they double as ornamental plants.

LEFT A pleasing sight: bunches of your own grapes that will soon be ready for wine-making or eating. Fresh fruit straight from the plant is always the tastiest.

GRAPES *(Vitis vinifera)*
Basic pruning

Grapes are generally grown outside, but, in cooler climates, dessert types are usually best under glass. Wine grapes can easily be grown outside in cooler regions, provided the ripening fruits have adequate exposure to sunlight.

Rootstocks

After the incidence of phylloxera, a disease that ravaged French vineyards in the late nineteenth century, grape vines have nearly always, with a few minor exceptions, been grafted on to a resistant rootstock. This means that it is almost certain that you will be offered grafted plants. There are a number of different rootstocks, but it is likely that you will be supplied with those that are most suited to your region. If in doubt, check with your supplier, who can usually also recommend the most suitable variety of grape for your area.

Growing methods

Grapes need well-drained soil and a position exposed to the sun. They are trained on systems of posts and wires. Since grapevines have a long

Varieties

Outdoor varieties
'Brant' black, wine
'Chardonnay' white, wine
'Chasselas' ('Royal Muscadine') white, dessert
'Léon Millot' black, wine
'Madeleine Angevine' pale green, dual-purpose
'Madeleine Silvaner' white, wine
'Müller-Thurgau' white, wine
'Noir Hatif de Marseilles' black, wine
'Perlette' black, dual-purpose
'Pirovano 14' red-black, wine
'Précoce de Malingre' white, wine

white grapes

'Riesling' white, wine
'Siegerrebe' golden, dual-purpose
'Triomphe d'Alsace' black, wine

Indoor varieties
'Alicante' black, dessert
'Buckland Sweetwater' white, dessert
'Foster's Seedling' white, dessert
'Gros Maroc' black, dessert
'Reine Olga' red-black, dessert
'Schiava Grossa' ('Black Hamburgh') black, dessert
'Seyval Blank' white, wine

black grapes

life, it is essential to make certain that these supports are solid structures. Posts can be wooden but must be treated against decay. Metal posts are more usual. The wires often have some method of tensioning them so that they can be

tightened as they slacken over time. Generally, most systems require one line of posts and wires, but some of the lesser-known methods involve two parallel rows. The various systems train the rods (or fruiting stems) up, along or down the wires.

Pruning and training

There are two basic systems of pruning and training. In one, the fruiting shoots are allowed to develop from scratch each year and are removed after fruiting. This is know as rod renewal. The other is rod-and-spur in which the stems are cut back to one or two buds once the fruit is produced. It is from these spurs that the following year's fruiting growth develops. The method depends on the variety, so it is best to ask your supplier whether the vine is spur-producing or not. The main pruning takes place in the

ABOVE Grapes grown against a wall. Walls provide warmth and help both to protect the blossom and to ripen the fruit.

ABOVE All methods of training involve pruning back the previous year's fruiting growth to one or two buds.

ABOVE Some growers like to leave tying up the vines as late as possible as the fruiting buds develop more easily on arched stems.

middle of winter, but it is also necessary to do a little pruning during the growing season, mainly pinching out growth and unwanted flower bunches.

Pruning cuts

As with most pruning, angle the cuts so that water runs off. On vertical shoots, make the cuts at 30 degrees to the horizontal. On horizontal shoots, cut straight across the stem. The cut should be above a bud, but not so close that you damage the swollen node on which the bud rests. Summer pruning is normally a simple matter of pinching out the soft growth with finger and thumb.

Thinning fruit and leaves

For dessert grapes, it is necessary to thin out the number of grapes in a bunch to produce larger fruit. With a pair of fine-pointed scissors, remove about a quarter to one-third of the fruit from the bunch, leaving the remainder room to develop fully. In autumn, once the fruit begins to ripen, remove any leaves covering the bunches so that sun and light can reach the grapes.

BASIC TECHNIQUES FOR GROWING GRAPES

There are some basic techniques which apply to all methods of growing grapes. Some may not apply to large-scale grape production in commercial vineyards, but the home-grown crops will benefit if you use them.

FOLIAGE THINNNG Once bunches of grapes begin to ripen, it is a good idea to remove some of the leaves that are covering the bunches, to let in sun and light.

SUMMER PRUNING Some vines will grow too vigorously. Any shoots that are not required should be pinched out as soon as they appear.

THINNING THE FRUIT If you want to use the grapes for dessert purposes, it may be necessary to thin them out so that they fill out well.

ROD RENEWAL METHOD The basic pruning cut is to remove the old fruited stem back to one or two buds, from which springs the new fruiting growth.

ROD-AND-SPUR METHOD There comes a point in the life of the vine when the stubs become overcrowded and it is necessary to remove some of them.

The Guyot system

There are in fact two Guyot systems, the single and the double. The double is the most commonly used. The single is very similar but uses only one rod (or fruiting stem) on one side instead of two rods, one on either side. Both methods are widely used for wine grapes grown outside.

Supports

Set well-anchored posts in the ground about 4–5m (13–16ft) apart, with four or five horizontal wires at 30cm (12in) intervals. The bottom wire should be about 45cm (18in) above the soil. The main stem of each individual vine is supported by a wooden stake.

Initial training

Plant a one-year-old vine next to the post in autumn or early winter.

ABOVE The Guyot system is particularly well suited to wine-grape production, which usually gives larger bunches of small grapes, as here.

Around mid-winter, cut it right back to about 15cm (6in) above the ground, retaining two buds. During the summer, allow the main stem to grow and pinch out any side shoots. The following mid-winter, cut back this stem to about 40cm (16in) from the ground, leaving three good strong buds just below the bottom wire. During the following summer, tie in vertically the three shoots that develop from these buds. In mid-winter, gently pull down the two outer shoots to the horizontal and tie them in to the bottom wire on either side of the main stem. Take out the tips of each of these shoots to a bud about 60cm–1m (2–3ft) from the main stem. Cut back the central shoot, leaving three strong buds to develop for the next year.

ABOVE Although vines are normally grown against wires, if only one or two are involved a more permanent support can be used.

ABOVE The Guyot system can be modified for growing dessert grapes under glass in a cool greenhouse or conservatory.

Established pruning

During the following summer, a series of vertical shoots will form on the horizontal arms. Tie these in as they develop and pinch out any side shoots that develop on them. Allow the three buds on the central stem to develop and tie them in, again removing any side shoots that are produced on them.

Fruit is produced on the vertical shoots. Cut out these shoots during the following winter, except for the three central shoots. These are treated the same way as the previous winter, the two lower ones being tied down to the horizontal wires and the central one shortened to three buds. This procedure is repeated every year.

GROWING GRAPES USING THE GUYOT SYSTEM

The Guyot system is very popular among those who grow large quantities of vines for wine-making. It is a relatively simple system and produces good crops, which is the whole purpose of growing grapes in the first place.

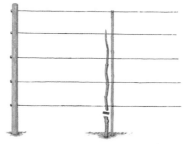

YEAR ONE, WINTER Plant a one-year-old vine and about mid-winter cut back to two buds about 15cm (6in) above the ground.

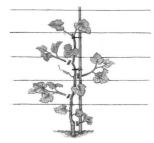

YEAR ONE, SUMMER During the following summer allow the leader to grow. Tie it in and pinch out the side shoots.

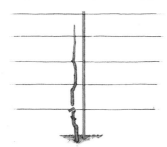

YEAR TWO, WINTER In the following winter cut back the leader to three strong buds just below the bottom wire.

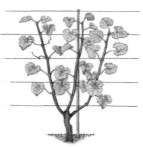

YEAR TWO, SUMMER As the three shoots grow from these buds, tie them in vertically to the stake.

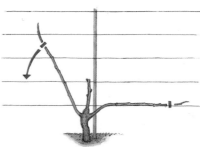

YEAR THREE, WINTER Gently pull down the two outer shoots and tie them horizontally. Cut the central one back to three buds.

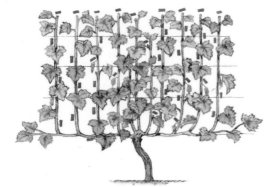

ESTABLISHED PRUNING, SUMMER During the summer tie in the vertical shoots, including the three from the centre, as they develop, pinching out any side shoots. Fruit is produced on the vertical shoots.

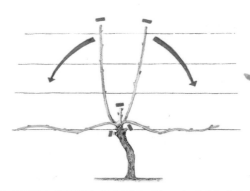

ESTABLISHED PRUNING, WINTER In winter, cut out all the fruited shoots apart from the three central ones. Again, pull down the lower shoots and cut back the central one to three buds. Repeat the last two operations every year.

Grape cordons

Some grape types, especially the dessert varieties, are better pruned using the rod-and-spur system. This method allows rods to grow each year from the same spur as the previous year, rather than being renewed as in the Guyot system. Check when you are buying your grape-vines as to which system is required for growing them. This system is useful for vines grown under glass.

Supports

Using strong supporting posts, run six or more parallel wires between them about 25cm (10in) apart, with the bottom one about the same distance above the ground. Place a post or cane into the ground where each vine is to be planted. Some growers like to put tension screws at the end of the wires so that they can be tightened if the wires begin to go slack. Alternatively, the wires can be tightened manually.

ABOVE Dessert grapes are best pruned using a rod-and-spur system, which is suitable for greenhouses as well as growing in the open.

GROWING GRAPES AS CORDONS

Growing grapes using the cordon method is popular among home growers. It is relatively labour-intensive, but, on the other hand, not a particularly difficult process. Grape cordons have the advantage of not taking up too much space in the garden – no more than, say, blackberries or loganberries.

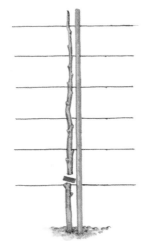

YEAR ONE, WINTER Plant a one-year-old vine in early to mid-winter and cut it back just below the bottom wire to two strong buds.

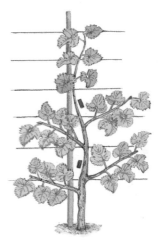

YEAR ONE, SUMMER Tie in the main shoot and tie in any laterals level with the wires. Pinch out any side shoots that form on these stems and any side shoots not level with the wires.

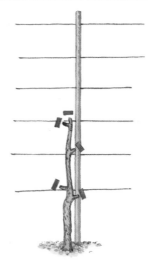

YEAR TWO, WINTER The next winter, prune back all the laterals to just one bud. Cut back the new growth of the main shoot to half.

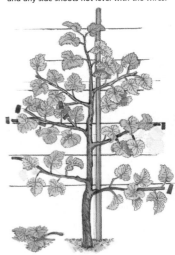

YEAR TWO, SUMMER Continue the previous summer's treatment, except now prune back any sub-laterals to one leaf and take out the tips of the laterals themselves.

Initial pruning

Plant a one-year-old vine in early to mid-winter, and cut it back to two strong buds roughly at the level of the bottom wire. During the following summer, allow the main shoot to develop and tie it in. Allow any side shoots to develop that are level with the wires, so that one can be trained on either side. Pinch out any others. Also pinch out any side shoots that form on the stems that are retained. The following winter, prune back the laterals heavily to just one or two buds on each. Cut back the main shoot to about half its length, choosing a bud on the other side of the stem to the previous year's cut. Continue this cycle until the vine has rods trained on to all the wires.

Established pruning

The bottom arms will be established before the top ones have been produced. The procedure is basically the same as the initial training. Pinch out all side shoots on the lateral arms in summer. If the grapes are for dessert use, reduce the number of bunches of flowers to one on each so that only one bunch of grapes develops on each arm. More can be allowed on wine grapes, as the berries do not need to grow so large. Pinch back the tips of the laterals to about 60cm (2ft) or longer if they are wine grapes, in which case tip them just beyond the last bunch of flowers. The following winter, cut back all rods to just one or two buds. Gently bend the top of the main stem to the horizontal and tie it down. This will encourage the buds on the lower rods to produce shoots. Once the buds start to burst, release the top of the main stem and tie it in vertically again. Repeat this procedure every year.

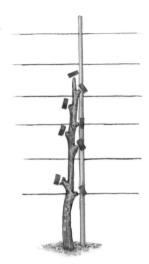

YEAR THREE, WINTER Continue to cut back each winter all laterals to one or two buds and the new growth of the leader by about half.

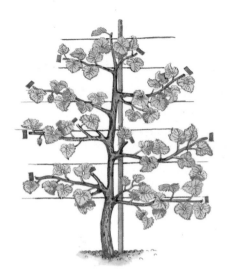

SUBSEQUENT YEARS Repeat both previous summer and winter pruning until the leader consists of mature wood right up to the top wire. From now on, cut the leader back to about six leaves each summer.

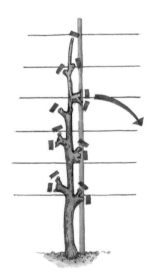

ESTABLISHED PRUNING, WINTER Each winter after becoming established, cut back all main laterals and the leader to one or two buds. Gently pull the top half of the leader down to the horizontal and tie it in.

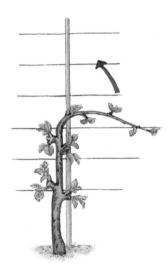

ESTABLISHED PRUNING, SPRING In spring, once the bottom buds start to break, take the leader up to the vertical. In summer cut back the laterals and leader to about 60cm (2ft) and all side shoots to one leaf.

Single curtain system

This is a system widely used in commerce for spur-pruned vines. It is less labour-intensive than other methods as there is no tying-in.

Supports

Insert sturdy posts into the ground at 4–5m (13–16ft) intervals. Stretch five wires tightly between them, spaced 45cm (18in) apart. Insert a post or cane in the ground where the vine is to be planted.

Initial training

Plant one-year-old vines against each of the canes and tie them in. In the first winter, cut the stems hard back to about 15cm (6in), leaving at least one strong bud. In summer, tie in the new leader as it develops. Next winter, cut back the leader again, removing about half of the previous year's growth. Tie in the new leader as it develops. During the third winter, remove all laterals on the main stem except for two just below the top wire (or one lateral and the leader if there are not two well-placed laterals). Bend these outwards and tie them down to the top wire. Next summer shoots will appear along these laterals that will initially be upright, then hang down. Allow them to develop at about 30cm (12in) intervals along the laterals, removing any in between. Also pinch out any side shoots that appear on them, as well as any shoots that appear on the underside of the main laterals.

Established pruning

From now on the main pruning should be carried out around mid-winter, before the sap rises. Cut back all the hanging shoots to one or two upward-facing buds. Remove completely any downward-pointing ones. Next, allow one shoot to develop on the previous year's spurs and remove any others.

GROWING GRAPES USING THE SINGLE CURTAIN SYSTEM

This is a system that, like that of using cordons, produces a rod-and-spur system, but there is not as much labour required.

This means that it is easier for large numbers of vines. The basic principles are the same as for other methods.

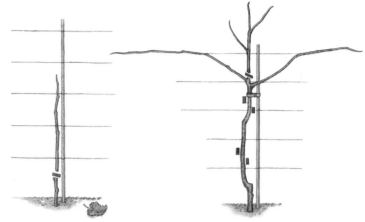

YEARS ONE AND TWO, WINTER AND SUMMER Start with a one-year-old vine planted in winter and cut through the leader about 15cm (6in) above ground-level. In summer, tie in the new leader as it develops. The following winter, cut back the leader again, this time removing about half of the previous year's growth. Again, tie in the leader as it develops. Continue this process until the top wires are reached.

YEAR THREE, WINTER In winter remove all the laterals on the main stem except for two just below the top wire. Bend these out and tie to the top wire.

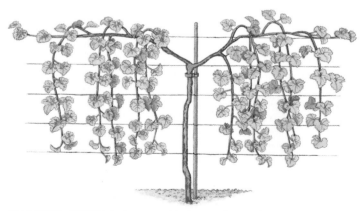

YEAR THREE, SUMMER In the summer, side shoots on these two laterals will develop and hang down. Allow them to develop at 30cm (12in) intervals. Pinch out any side shoots that appear on them, as well as any that appear on the underside of the main laterals. Once established, prune in the winter, cutting back all the hanging shoots to one or two upward-facing buds and allowing one shoot to develop on the previous year's spurs.

Double curtain system

Also known as the Geneva Double Curtain, this was the original curtain system from which the single system and other minor variations were developed. The advantage for the home grower is that it saves space. Although each row is slightly wider, the method allows more vines to be grown in the same length of row.

Supports

There are two possible methods of wirework. One involves two parallel rows of wire stretched taut between sturdy posts. The rows are about 60cm (2ft) apart and the wires are held 1.5m (5ft) from the ground. The alternative is to use one row of posts, each with a crossbar at the top from which the two rows of wires are suspended. Posts to support the vines are placed down the middle of the two rows (or at either side/to one side of the single row) at each planting position, roughly 1.2m (4ft) apart.

ABOVE In cooler countries dessert grapes are best grown under glass, where a good crop can be expected.

Initial training

This is exactly the same as for the single system, except that the top laterals are first tied across the rows and then turned in opposite directions along the wires. You will first need to plant one-year-old vines against each of the planting posts. The first winter, cut the stem hard back to about 15cm (6in) above ground-level, leaving at least one strong bud. In the summer, tie in the new leader as it develops. In the second winter, cut back the leader again to remove about half of the previous year's growth. Again tie in the new leader as it develops. During the third winter, remove all laterals that have developed on the main stem except for two just below the wire (or one lateral and the leader if there are not two conveniently placed laterals). Bend these outwards until they meet the wires and then turn them along the wires, one in each direction, tying them down to the wires. The next summer, shoots will appear along these laterals that will initially be upright, then hang down. Allow them to develop at about 30cm (12in) intervals along the laterals, removing any in between. Also pinch out any side shoots that appear on them, as well as any shoots that appear on the underside of the main laterals.

Established pruning

The main pruning should be carried out around mid-winter, before the sap rises. Cut back all the hanging shoots to one or two upward-facing buds. Remove completely any downward-pointing ones. The next summer, allow one shoot to develop on the previous year's spurs and remove any others. Repeat these procedures every winter and summer.

GROWING GRAPES USING THE DOUBLE CURTAIN SYSTEM

This system is very similar to the previous method, the single curtain system, except that it is spread over two rows about 60cm (2ft) apart. This allows more vines to be grown in a small space than with the single method.

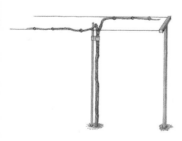

YEAR THREE, WINTER The vine is grown in the same way as for the single curtain system except that each lateral is bent in an L-shape and spread along alternate wires.

ESTABLISHED PRUNING Again the system is the same as for the single curtain sytem, with the side shoots now hanging from the laterals in two rows instead of one.

HOPS *(Humulus lupulus)*

Hops are well suited to cooler climates and have been grown for centuries for beer-making as well as other uses such as dye production. Commercial production is in decline as tastes in mass-produced beers change, but home-brewing is on the increase and many gardeners are turning to growing their own hops, albeit in small quantities.

Varieties

'Fuggles'
'Hip-Hop'
'Prima Donna'
'Wye Challenger'
'Wye Northdown'

Supports

Traditionally, hops are grown up poles or strings supported by a wirework, with bines often growing to 3.6–4.25m (12–14ft) high. A full-scale wirework-supported system is uneconomic and rather impractical for a garden. New dwarf varieties have recently been introduced that grow only to around 2m (6ft) or less. These are ideal for the garden as they can be grown in a row using a support structure such as is used for runner beans. This can consist of two wires supported by firmly planted poles at about 3m (10ft) intervals. One wire is about 15–20cm (6–8in) above the ground and the other is 2m (6ft) high. Commercially, a plastic wide-mesh netting is suspended between the two wires for the hops to climb up. Pea netting can be substituted in the garden, but

ABOVE Hops can be grown decoratively over archways and still produce enough hops for use in brewing or indoor decoration.

this will have to be replaced every year as it is difficult to untangle the bines. With small-scale production in a garden, you can also use strings tied between the wires at 30–45cm (12–18in) intervals. You can grow hops up individual poles with the tops tied together for mutual support, either as tripods or in a row. Use bean poles for the shorter varieties. If you want to grow the traditional taller ones, 3m (10ft) chestnut poles firmly embedded in the ground at 1.2m (4ft) intervals can be used. These need a sheltered position, as a tall pole covered with hops can easily blow over.

Training

Hops are perennials that die back below the ground each year and subsequently throw up new shoots each spring, putting on a

USING VERTICAL POLES Hops can be trained using several different methods in the garden, depending on the size of crop required. For a larger crop, taller varieties using poles and strings may be best. An even older method is to grow the hops up vertical poles, which is possible in larger gardens. The poles support each other by being tied with horizontal strings.

ABOVE Bunches of hops which are made up of clusters of bracts (leaves) hiding the flowers and eventually the seed.

phenomenal amount of growth. Traditionally hops were planted in spring, but now it is more common to plant in autumn. It takes a year or more for a hop to become large enough to produce its full growth, but there is no special training during that period, other than the following routine, which keeps the plant neat and tidy. In the spring, once growth has started, a number of new shoots are produced. Two or three should be selected for each string. Encourage these to grow up the string or support. The shoots are delicate and can easily snap, so handle them with care. They should

be twisted clockwise around the support (a process delightfully known as "twiddling"). Once the main shoots are twiddled, cut off any remaining ones. Repeat this a few weeks later to ensure that all the bines are still growing up strings and twiddle in any that are hanging loose. With nets, make certain that the shoots are spread out evenly across the netting rather than being bunched up together. On taller hops, lower, unproductive side shoots can be removed, as they tend to become whippy. On netting, hops are mainly

self-supporting, but it is still worth removing any weak growth and twiddling in any wayward shoots. Harvest the hops in autumn. On netting you can pick the hops as they hang. Cut the bines off close to the ground around mid-winter, before the new growth starts. If you are using another method, cut the bines down or pull up the poles to facilitate harvesting, cutting the bines at about 45cm (18in) above the ground. In mid-winter go round and cut off the remaining stems, close to the ground.

TENDER CLIMBING FRUITS

Passion fruit
Passion fruit are grown mainly as ornamentals in cooler areas but they do produce edible fruit, especially if grown against a warm wall. Attach horizontal wires to the wall, or free-standing posts in warmer areas, and grow the young plant against it, training the top two laterals on either side along the top wire. Remove all other side shoots on the main stem. Side shoots will appear on the top two laterals and they will hang down as they grow. In windy areas, they should be tied in to the wires. After fruiting, cut back the fruiting shoots to a couple of buds.

Kiwi fruit
Actinidia kolomikta is a widely grown ornamental, but its close relative *A. deliciosa*, the kiwi fruit, is also becoming popular, even in cooler areas. It can easily be grown against a warm wall, which will provide protection. The best way to grow a kiwi is as an espalier, in a similar fashion to that used for training pears. In warmer areas, they can be trained on free-standing posts and wire supports and treated in the same way.

TOP RIGHT Passion fruit are increasingly grown as decorative and fruiting plants.

MIDDLE AND BOTTOM RIGHT Kiwi fruit is a new fruit to grow for most gardeners, but is well worth the challenge.

ABOVE The traditional method of growing hops is up string supported by wires. This is on too large a scale for gardens.

Soft Fruit

Soft fruit has always been one of the mainstays of the garden, even the small one. One reason for this is that while tree fruit can be stored and easily transported, soft fruit tastes much better eaten straight from the bush, or at least within a short time of picking. Shop-bought fruit can never compare with your own. Even a few canes of raspberries, for example, will provide a surprising amount of fruit, and there is often enough to freeze some for the future, or to make into jam.

Soft fruit is relatively easy to look after as long as pruning takes place regularly. If neglected, the bushes or canes can become an unproductive, tangled mess. Pruning them is not arduous or complicated once you have grasped the basic principles. There are two important aspects that must be given equal attention if you are to succeed. The first is to control weeds, which are not a problem that usually affects tree fruit. They must be kept at bay and prevented from climbing up through the plants. The other problem is birds, who are as fond of raspberries and blackberries as we are. Some form of protection is necessary if you are to get a good crop.

LEFT Luscious blackberries that make your mouth water simply by looking at them. As with most fruit, they always taste that much better when freshly picked.

Growing soft fruit

Soft fruit is not difficult to grow, nor is the initial training and subsequent pruning tricky. The canes and bushes can be easily purchased and will usually produce at least some fruit in the first year. Siting and conditions are important, most requiring a reasonably rich, moisture-retentive but not waterlogged soil. Although all need sun, few require great heat and they can easily be grown in cooler areas.

ABOVE Tayberries are one of the several hybrid berries that are worth experimenting with for new tastes. They are not difficult to grow.

ABOVE Blackberry canes can use spaces that might otherwise be wasted. Here they are supported on a fence by an old shed.

Buying

All soft fruit is readily available from garden centres or specialist nurseries. The latter give a much larger range of choice and often better advice. If, for example, you wanted to grow raspberries from early summer through to late autumn, then a specialist nursery will be able to advise on which varieties are most suitable to give you a constant flow of fruit. Although it is possible to propagate your own from existing stock, it is generally better to start

with fresh, certified stock every few years to prevent the build-up of disease.

Planting

The canes or young bushes are usually supplied in late autumn for winter or early spring planting. (Frequently, those from specialist nurseries are bare-rooted. If they cannot be planted straight away, heel them into the soil until they are required.) The soil should be well dug, with plenty of well-rotted organic material incorporated into it.

For fruit bushes that need support, raspberries and blackberries for example, it is best to erect the wirework first to avoid damaging the newly planted canes. Look for the soil mark on the stems and plant to the same depth as they were grown in the nursery beds.

Supports

Cane fruit will need support, usually provided in the form of wires tightly stretched between posts. Over time these can slacken as the wire stretches, so it is advisable to make the wires adjustable, using bottle-screw tighteners, for example. The posts are likely to be in place for a number of years, so if they are wood,

ABOVE A selection of delicious fruit from the garden. From top left: red currants, strawberries, blackcurrants, raspberries, blackberries and gooseberries.

ABOVE Most soft fruit needs to be pruned back once it has been planted. The stems on sold plants are generally too long.

GROWING SOFT FRUIT ON POSTS AND WIRES

ABOVE A large garden is not necessary for fruit-growing. This method of growing red currants produces a good crop that is bird-proofed.

1 Use strong posts to form the framework for supporting soft fruit. Knock the posts firmly into the ground using a mallet so that they do not wobble.

2 A brace set at an angle of 45 degrees will help to keep the post stable as well as prevent it from tipping under the strain of the wires.

3 The wire can be initially drawn tight by hand and partially stapled into position. It should then be tightened with a strainer and the staples hammered home.

4 Soft string can be used to tie in the canes. This should preferably pass between the wire and the stem in order to prevent any chafing which will damage the plant.

treat them first to prevent them rotting. Bush fruit generally does not need supporting unless you are training it into a decorative form such as a fan or a standard. In the case of the former, wires supported by a wall or sturdy fence are best. A standard needs a stake or strong cane to support it, at least during the formative years and often throughout its life.

ABOVE When cutting out the dead canes from raspberries and blackberries, cut as low as possible and try not to leave too many snags.

Initial training

Cane fruit is usually trained from the start as it will go on being trained. Most bush fruits are generally grown as open bushes, which need to be of good shape and relatively open with no cross-overs or congested growth. Many can also be trained in more decorative ways, such as cordons, espaliers, fans and even, in some cases, standards. These require a bit more attention to keep them in shape. Individual requirements will be given for each type of fruit.

Established pruning

Dead canes should be removed every year and new ones tied in to the supports. Bush fruit also needs a little attention each year to ensure that the bushes stay healthy and productive. The techniques vary for each type of fruit as is detailed on the following pages.

The pruning cuts are the same as already discussed for all other plants. They should be made just above a bud so there is no snag, and should preferably slope away from the bud at about 30 degrees.

CANE FRUITS
Raspberries (*Rubus idaeus*)

Raspberries are not difficult to grow and with the right selection of varieties the fruit is produced over a long season, often continuing until the first winter frosts. It is possible to grow just a few canes tied together at the top, with a net thrown over them to keep the birds off, but they are more often grown in rows, preferably in a fruit cage.

Varieties		
Raspberries	Mid-season	'Augusta'
Early	'Glen Lyon'	'Leo'
'Delight'	'Glen Prosen'	'Malling'
'Glen Coe'	'Julia'	'Malling Joy'
'Glen Cova'	'Malling Jewel'	
'Glen Moy'	'Malling Orion'	Autumn
'Malling Exploit'		'Autumn Bliss'
'Malling Promise'	Late	'Fallgold'
'Sumner'	'Admiral'	'Heritage'
		'Norfolk Giant'
		'September'

Supports

Raspberries are usually planted in rows. Each cane is supported against horizontal wires, which are held in place by sturdy posts at 2.5–3m (8–10ft) intervals. The bottom wire is at about 60cm (2ft), with two more wires above that at the same intervals of 60cm (2ft). The wires should be stretched as tight as possible and should have bottle screws or some other method of tightening them in case they start to slacken. Rows should be 2m (6ft) apart. Plant the young canes at 60cm (2ft) intervals, in well-prepared soil, between late autumn and early spring. Usually, the canes will have been cut back to about 60cm (2ft)

when you buy them. If not, trim them back and tie into the bottom wire so that they do not blow over while the roots are establishing.

Summer-fruiting raspberries

In spring, new canes are produced. Tie these into the wires in an upright position. Once the new canes have started growing, the old canes from the previous year can be cut back to the base. If the canes are extra long, bend them over and tie their tips down. At the end of winter, cut off the arching tips, leaving about 15cm (6in) above the top wire. During the summer, these canes will fruit, and at the same time a new

set of canes will arise from the base. Once they canes have finished fruiting, cut these off at the base and tie the new ones in their place in a continuous cycle. Remove any new suckering growth between the rows.

Autumn-fruiting raspberries

Autumn-fruiting raspberries are dealt with differently. If they are treated in the same manner as summer-fruiting types they will fruit in the same way. However, they are normally pruned in the spring to produce an autumn crop. The newly planted canes will produce growth during their first summer that will produce fruit in the autumn. As they grow, tie them in to the wires, although some of the shorter forms are almost self-supporting. Towards the end of winter, cut all canes to the ground. New ones will appear and these should be tied in. Fruit will appear on these in autumn and they can be cut back again the following late winter, in a continuous cycle. Some new varieties of autumn-fruiting raspberry fruit both in the autumn and again in the following summer on the same canes. Leave these canes unpruned until after their second crop, which means in effect that they are trained and pruned like summer-fruiting raspberries. Check when you buy which type you have.

PRUNING AUTUMN RASPBERRIES

1 Autumn raspberries are pruned differently from summer raspberries. As with ordinary raspberries, during the winter they consist of a mixture of fruited and new canes.

2 Regardless of what they are, the canes are all cut to the ground and completely removed.

3 Once the canes have been cut back, new growth quickly appears. Once the canes are tall enough, they should be tied in to supporting wires.

TRAINING RASPBERRIES

Some of the shorter autumn varieties can be grown without wire supports, but all other raspberries are best given a post-and-wire support, and grown in open ground rather than against a fence or wall. Raspberries are best planted in winter from plants that have been newly purchased because unlike existing canes, these will be disease-free.

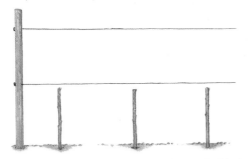

YEAR ONE, WINTER Often the canes will have been cut back by the nursery. If not, cut back to 60cm (2ft) and tie them to the bottom wire.

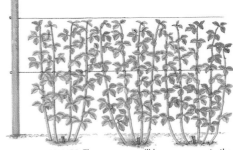

YEAR ONE, SUMMER The new canes will have grown up to the top wires, and should be tied to the supports.

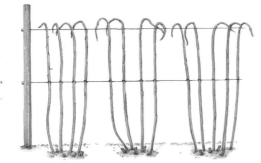

SUMMER-FRUITING RASPBERRIES, YEAR TWO, WINTER
In the early winter cut out the remains of the old stems. Pull the tips of the new canes over and tie them to the wires.

AUTUMN-FRUITING RASPBERRIES, YEAR TWO, WINTER Cut all canes to the ground. The result may look drastic, but the tufts of new growth will soon appear and produce a crop through to late autumn.

AUTUMN-FRUITING RASPBERRIES, YEAR TWO, SUMMER
New canes will have grown up to the top wires and should be tied to the supports.

ABOVE A ripening crop of 'Glen Rosa' raspberries. When picking raspberries, gently squeeze them between finger and thumb and ease away from their stalk, the remains of two of which can be seen here.

Blackberries (*Rubus fruticosus*) and hybrid berries

Blackberries and hybrid berries are usually grown in the same way. They both occupy considerable space. Although derived from wild blackberries, cultivated varieties usually produce larger and sweeter fruit. The hybrid berries, such as loganberries and tayberries, have usually been crossed with another similar fruit. Some varieties are thornless, which is a great advantage when harvesting.

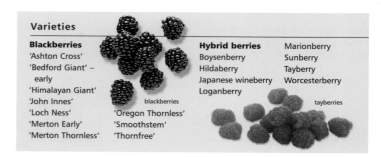

Varieties

Blackberries		**Hybrid berries**	
'Ashton Cross'		Boysenberry	Marionberry
'Bedford Giant' – early		Hildaberry	Sunberry
'Himalayan Giant'		Japanese wineberry	Tayberry
'John Innes'		Loganberry	Worcesterberry
'Loch Ness'	'Oregon Thornless'		
'Merton Early'	'Smoothstem'		
'Merton Thornless'	'Thornfree'		

blackberries

tayberries

Supports

A sturdy post-and-wire system is required, with the posts being set at about 3m (10ft) intervals. Four or five wires, about 30cm (12in) apart, should be stretched between them, the lowest being about 45cm (18in) from the ground. They can also be grown against fences, making a useful impenetrable barrier.

Initial and subsequent training

There are several ways to train blackberries and hybrid berries, all essentially similar but differing in detail. Basically, the previous year's growth (on which the fruit will be carried) is tied in to the wires, while the current year's growth is kept separate. After fruiting, all fruited wood is cut out and the current year's wood tied in to replace it. One of the easiest methods is the one-way or alternate bay system. The canes are trained along the wires either to the right or left of the plant, but only in one direction. Depending on the number of canes, each wire will support one or more. As it grows, the current year's growth is tied in to the wires on the opposite side of the plant. After fruiting, all the

TRAINING METHODS FOR BLACKBERRIES AND HYBRID BERRIES

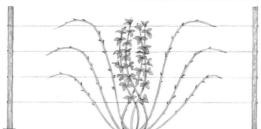

FAN TRAINING The new canes are temporarily tied vertically and along the top wire, while the fruiting canes are tied in singly along the wires. Any excess canes are removed. After fruiting, these canes are taken out and the new growth tied in their place.

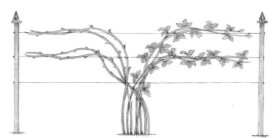

ALTERNATE BAY One way in which you can train blackberries is to tie all the new growth to one side of the wirework. After fruiting, remove the previous year's growth from the other side and then use this for the next year's new growth. Repeat each year.

Thornless blackberry blossom

Blackberries

Hildaberry flowers

canes on the fruited side are cut out and during the second year the new growth is tied in to replace them. This is a good method for prickly varieties, as the canes only have to be handled once.

For cultivars that produce long, vigorous stems, the canes can be woven along the wires on either side in a snakelike manner, either running parallel to each other or alternating. The new growth is tied in two bundles along the top wire. After fruiting, the old canes are cut off at the base and the bundles are untied for weaving in a similar manner to the previous year's canes.

With less vigorous varieties, the fruiting canes can be tied in a straight line against the wires (no weaving), with the following year's canes tied in a column at the centre.

ABOVE New shoots should be tied in as they grow, otherwise they will thrash around and cause damage to themselves and other plants.

After fruiting, the old canes are removed and the new ones tied in their place.

Established pruning

As the years pass, the plants may produce more canes than there is space for, so you may need to thin the current year's growth. Take out

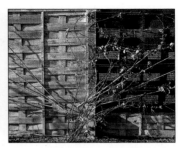

ABOVE Tayberries tied in using the alternative bay method, with all the new shoots tied to the right and last year's removed from the left.

any thin or weak canes. Try to ensure that the canes are tied in properly for the winter or they may thrash around in the wind and be damaged. They should be tied in all year round, as any tips that touch the ground may well root, creating another clump. Blackberries form thickets if not kept under control.

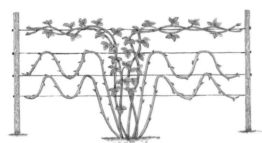

WEAVING This is a good method of training blackberries where space is short. The current year's fruiting growth is woven up and over two or three wires, while the following year's fruiting canes are all temporarily tied in to the top wire.

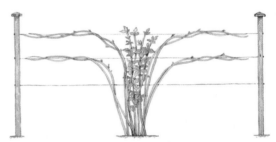

ROPE TRAINING A second way to train blackberries is to temporarily tie in all new growth vertically to the wirework and along the top wire. The current fruiting canes are tied in groups horizontally. These are removed after fruiting and the new growth tied in their place.

Japanese wineberry

Hildaberries

Tayberries

BUSH FRUITS
Blackcurrants *(Ribes nigrum)*

Blackcurrants are a popular garden fruit because of their high vitamin content. One bush is often sufficient to provide enough fresh fruit and some left over for the freezer. Although red and white currants appear similar, apart from the colour of the fruit, they have a different pruning regime, so do not apply the same techniques to them all.

Supports

Blackcurrants do not need supports. However, the bushes need netting to prevent birds stealing the fruit. One or two bushes can be netted individually but it is more practical to grow blackcurrants in a fruit cage.

Initial training

Plants are often sold bare-rooted. If you cannot plant them in their final position straight away, heel them in temporarily in some spare ground. Plant to the same depth, or fractionally lower, as they were grown

ABOVE A trug of freshly picked blackcurrants. Even one bush will produce a surprising quantity of currants.

in the nursery (look for the soil mark on the stems), then cut them back to a bud roughly 5cm (2in) above ground-level. This will result in the production of strong new shoots in the following year. These

Varieties	
Blackcurrants	'Ben Sarek'
'Baldwin'	'Boskoop Giant'
'Ben Connan'	'Malling Jet'
'Ben Lomond'	'Mendip Cross'
'Ben More'	'Wellington XXX'

can be left unpruned, but you will need to cut out any weak ones. Fruit will appear on these shoots in their second year, and new growth will begin to develop from the base of the plant. In winter, cut out about one-third of the old fruited wood and any weak shoots.

PRUNING A YOUNG BLACKCURRANT ON PLANTNG

1 A newly planted blackcurrant bush before it is pruned.

2 First remove any weak growth, cutting it right out and removing old wood if necessary.

3 Finish by cutting back the longer shoots by half to a strong outward-facing shoot.

ABOVE It is important that you always cut out any dead or diseased wood, using a saw for thicker material.

ABOVE Cut out up to four of the oldest stems each year and cut the remainder of the fruited branches back to a new shoot.

ABOVE The remaining previous year's growth must be thinned out slightly to provide an open bush so that air and light can enter.

Established pruning

The fruit of blackcurrant bushes is carried on the previous year's or older wood. Older wood, however, progressively loses its ability to fruit well, so some of the oldest fruited wood should be removed every year to ensure that new wood will be produced and the bush revitalized.

Each year, between fruiting and the following spring, cut out two or three of the old branches completely. You also need to cut back some of the remaining older wood to vigorous new side shoots. Remove any branches or side-branches that are close to the ground and thin out the centre of the bush so that light enters and air can freely circulate.

PRUNING BLACKCURRANTS

With blackcurrants the fruit is carried on the previous year's or older wood. For this reason, it is important not to over-prune or all the fruiting wood will be removed. However, it will be necessary to prune out older wood.

YEAR ONE, WINTER After planting, completely cut out any weak wood and reduce the other shoots to about 5cm (2in) or so above ground-level.

YEAR ONE, SUMMER The following summer, growth will spring from these reduced shoots, as well as completely new growth from the base. Cut out any weak shoots.

YEAR TWO, WINTER In the winter, cut out one-third of the old wood and any weak or damaged shoots to the base.

ESTABLISHED PRUNING, WINTER Once established, cut out up to four of the oldest branches each winter and then cut back the remaining fruited branches to a strong shoot.

Jostaberries

The jostaberry is an interesting hybrid between blackcurrants and gooseberries. It is treated in exactly the same way in terms of training and pruning as blackcurrants.

Red and white currants (*Ribes sativum*)

Red and white currants are variations of the same fruit. They are pruned in the same way, but differently to blackcurrants. As well as bushes, you can train red currants into decorative forms, such as cordons, espaliers, fans and standards.

Supports

Bush forms do not need any support but the more decorative forms need training, using wires against a wall or fence, or stretched between posts. Standards need a stake or a stout cane.

Initial training

Choose a strong-growing one-year-old plant with four good main branches on the main stem, about 10–12cm (4–5in) above the soil. Remove any other branches and

reduce these four by about half their length, cutting to an outward-facing bud. In the second winter, prune back all the new leaders by about half. Choose the best outward shoots on each of the main branches and cut these back by a half. Reduce any remaining shoots to a couple of buds. Any badly placed shoots that cross or are congested should be removed.

Established pruning

Remove the tips of all the main leaders and, once the framework of the plant has developed, you will need to cut back all subsequent side shoots to one bud. Every few years, remove a couple of main branches that have become unproductive, cutting back to a strong shoot.

Varieties

Red currants	White currants
'Jonkheer van Tets'	'Versailles Blanche'
'Junifer'	'White Dutch'
'Laxton's Number 1'	'White Grape'
'Red Lake'	'White Pearl'
'Redstart'	
'Rondom'	
'Rovada'	

red currants   white currants

Decorative forms

Red and white currants can be grown in a number of decorative forms. Cordons, espaliers and fans are trained and pruned in a very similar way to the method used for spur-producing apples. The aim is to create single or multiple cordons with one, two or three uprights bearing spurs rather than branches. Fans are slightly

more complicated but basically similar. Develop two strong laterals from near the base and spread these out at an angle of about 40 degrees. Allow more shoots to develop from these until an even covering of the wall or fence is achieved. Reduce all other side shoots to one bud to produce fruiting spurs, and

prune to maintain this. A standard can be achieved by grafting a red currant bush on to the stem of a vigorous currant stock. Treat the resulting top growth in the same way as you would for a normal bush, but keep it more compact. Remove any side shoots that appear on the main stem.

MULTIPLE CORDON This has two or more vertical stems. Start by cutting back a shrub to three shoots and train two horizontally and one vertically. Then treat as individual cordons.

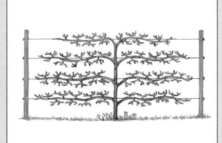

ESPALIER This is produced in the same way as an apple or pear espalier. Once the espalier is formed the individual arms are treated in the same way as the cordons.

STANDARD This is best bought ready formed, or it can be created by grafting a red currant on to a flowering currant rootstock and treating it as a bush currant.

TRAINING A RED CURRANT BUSH

Red currants are different to blackcurrants because they are spur-fruiting and so a permanent framework has to be built up.

This can be done in bush or cordon form or in a more decorative way (see the panel on the opposite page). Red currants are best

grown in a fruit cage in order to prevent marauding birds removing the delicious crop of currants.

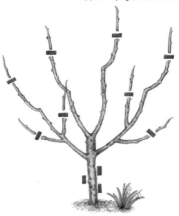

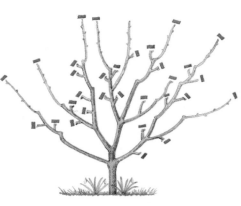

YEAR ONE, WINTER Plant a new bush. Select four well-placed branches and remove the rest. Reduce the remaining branches to half their length.

YEAR TWO, WINTER In the second winter, prune back the new growth on all the leaders by about half, cutting back to an outward-facing bud.

ESTABLISHED PRUNING, WINTER Once established, each winter cut back the tips of all the leaders and cut back any side shoots to one or two buds.

TRAINING A RED CURRANT CORDON

Red and white currants grown as cordons can save a great deal of space and so are particularly good for a small

garden. They are easier to net as individual plants and so do not necessarily need a fruit cage.

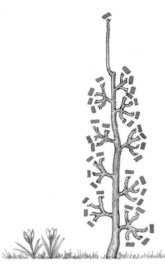

YEAR ONE, WINTER Start with a two-year-old plant and cut back all the side shoots to two buds. Then cut the new growth of the leader back by a half.

YEAR ONE, SUMMER In the summer take out the tips of the side shoots, cutting back to about five or six leaves.

YEAR TWO, WINTER In the following winter, cut back all the side shoots to one or two buds. Repeat the process every year.

Gooseberries *(Ribes uva-crispum)*

Although quite different in bush and fruit, gooseberries are often bracketed with red currants, as they are treated in the same way. There are a number of dessert varieties, but most gardeners grow them for culinary use. They have vicious thorns that can catch on skin, hair and clothes, so it is essential to wear tough gloves when pruning.

Varieties

'Bedford Red'	'Lancashire Lad'
'Broom Girl'	'Leveller'
'Careless'	'Whinham's
'Early Sulphur'	Industry'
'Greenfinch'	'White Lion'
'Invicta'	'Whitesmith'
'Jubilee'	'Yellow Champagne'

Supports

Gooseberries are normally grown as free-standing bushes, but they can also be grown as cordons, fans or standards. The first two methods need wires attached to walls or fences or stretched between stout posts.

Initial training

As with red currants, the first task when training gooseberries is to create a basic framework consisting of three or four main branches with several side branches, creating a well-clothed but not too dense shrub. Choose a good plant with a short (10–12cm/4–5in) leg from the top of which emerge three or four strong shoots. Cut these back to about half their length to upward-facing buds. The following winter, cut back all the new leaders and any strong side shoots that you want to keep for the framework by about

Decorative forms

Gooseberries can be grown as cordons and fans, which are not only decorative but also kinder on the hands when it comes to picking the fruit, as you do not have to thrust your hand into the bush. The different forms are developed in the same way as for apples, with single or multiple stems for cordons and an array of branches, all starting from two initial stems that are spread out at an angle of 40 degrees or so, for fans. Once the cordon stems or the branch structure of the fan have been developed, prune all shoots back to one bud to create a spur system.

Standard gooseberries are produced by grafting a bush on to a tall, vigorous currant stem. Once the bush has developed, it is pruned in the same way as for a free-standing bush, although it is best to keep it more compact to prevent wind rock.

SINGLE CORDON Cordons can be created in much the same way as red and white currant cordons, building up a spur stytem.

MULTIPLE CORDON This can be created in exactly the same way as a single cordon, except that at the outset you will need to allow three shoots to develop, two of which should be trained horizontally and one vertically.

FAN This is a very decorative method of growing gooseberries. A gooseberry fan can be trained in the same way, although on a smaller scale, to a pear fan. Again, the basic idea is to form a good structure of spurs.

STANDARD It is best to buy standards already formed, but you can graft a gooseberry on to a flowering currant stem and then treat the top growth as an ordinary gooseberry bush, keeping the main stem bare.

ABOVE Start picking gooseberries before the first berries are fully ripe in order to give the remainder an opportunity to ripen.

TRAINING GOOSEBERRIES

The main point to remember about gooseberries is the vicious thorns; you will need to wear a pair of stout leather gloves when tackling them. It is easiest to start with a two-year-old bush. Keep the bush open in order to make it easier to pick the fruit without pricking your hands. Growing gooseberry bushes is similar to the method for growing red currants.

YEAR ONE, WINTER Plant the gooseberry bush in the winter. Select three or four well-placed branches and remove the rest. Cut back the remainder of the branches by about half their length.

YEAR TWO, WINTER In the following winter, cut back all the new growth on the leaders and any new shoots you want to keep by one-third. Cut back the rest to one bud.

ESTABLISHED PRUNING Once established, keep the shrub as open as possible. Cut back all new growth to one bud in order to build up the spurs and, once it begins to age, remove some of the older growth to rejuvenate the bush.

one-third, also to upward-facing buds. Cut back the rest to one bud. Remember that you will have to put your hand right into the plant to harvest the fruit, so keep the bush relatively open with the minimum amount of congestion.

Established training

Once established, the simplest way of pruning is to cut back all new growth every winter to one bud, so that a system of spurs is built up similar to that of apples. Cut out any congested or crossing growth and occasionally take out an old branch back to a strong shoot. Some gardeners prefer to remove all the older wood to promote new growth, allowing the fruit to appear on this once it is two years old. It is important that you always try to keep the centre of the bush open. This will not only allow in light and air, but will also make it easier to pick and prune.

RIGHT Gooseberries make excellent cordons. Train them up canes that are supported by horizontal wires.

Blueberries (*Vaccinium corymbosum*)

Blueberries are becoming ever more popular, and several varieties are now available. They form multi-stemmed bushes which, once established, will provide masses of fruit. The type that is most commonly grown is known as the highbush blueberry. Blueberries must have acid soil, but can be grown in containers filled with ericaceous compost if your garden soil is alkaline.

Supports

No supports are necessary but some means of netting plants is essential if you hope to get to the fruit before the birds do. The ideal is to grow them in a fruit cage, but it is possible to drape a net over individual bushes while they are in fruit.

Varieties

'Berkeley'
'Bluecrop'
'Bluejay'
'Bluetta'
'Duke'
'Goldtraube'
'Herbert'
'Patriot'
'Spartan'

ABOVE In general, blueberries are left to grow in their natural state with little pruning when they will provide clusters of delicious berries.

Initial training

Blueberry bushes are sold as one- or two-year-old plants that have been grown from cuttings. There is little to do after planting and for the first few years. Let them develop naturally, restricting pruning and taking out any weak growth or stems that cross or create congestion. Also remove any shoots that develop horizontally. Aim to produce an upright plant.

Established pruning

Remove a few of the oldest stems to rejuvenate the plant. Also cut out any spreading branches, or those that cross and create congestion.

TRAINING BLUEBERRIES

Blueberries are very easy to look after and need little pruning, even during their formative stage. They are usually bought as one- or two-year-olds and planted in the winter or early spring. Blueberries need an acid soil. If they are grown in chalky or limestone areas, then they should be grown in containers rather than in the open ground.

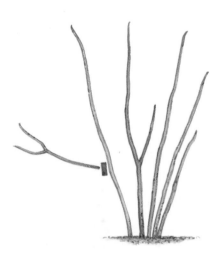

YEAR ONE, WINTER Plant the new blueberry bush in the winter and remove any weak, damaged or obviously wayward shoots. Otherwise allow to develop naturally.

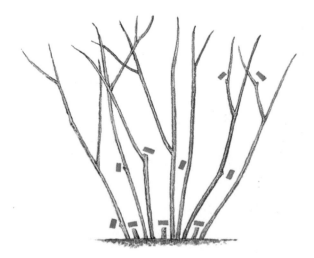

ESTABLISHED PRUNING, WINTER Once established take out one or two of the oldest stems to rejuvenate the plant and perhaps cut back any crossing or misplaced stems. Do not let the bush become too dense.

Cranberries (*Vitis macrocarpon*)

Cranberries are less widely grown than blueberries, but have become popular on account of their vitamin content as well as their culinary use. Several different varieties are available. Like blueberries, they thrive only on acid soils, but suitable conditions can be created in raised beds or in containers.

Support

Cranberries are low plants that are adapted to windy situations, so no support is required.

Initial training

After planting, allow the bushes to develop naturally. Cut out any dead or damaged wood as it appears.

Established pruning

Little attention is needed beyond keeping the site weed-free. Cranberry bushes send out runners and can create large colonies, but an excess of these reduces productivity. Prune out excess runners in spring, leaving just enough to extend the colony and fill gaps. Also remove some of the old uprights. If you have a large planting of cranberries, shears can be used for this, as long as you do not remove too much of the plant.

Varieties

'Early Black'
'Franklin'
'Hamilton'
'MacFarlin'
'Pilgrim'

The bilberry or whortleberry (*Vaccinium myrtillus*) and the European cranberry (*V. oxycoccos*) can be grown in the same way.

ABOVE Cranberries are popular because of their health-enhancing properties. They can be eaten as fruit or in juice and used in cooking.

ESTABLISHED PRUNING Little pruning is required other than shearing over the plant to remove some of the old uprights. The runners can also be removed to prevent congestion.

ABOVE Cranberries are healthy to eat and make an attractive plant in the kitchen garden.

ABOVE Commercial wet harvesting of cranberries. The plants are submerged in water and then the plants beaten so that the berries float off. They are then rounded up.

Glossary

Acclimatization The need to allow new trees and shrubs to get used to cooler or moister conditions if they have been stored inside.

Adventitious buds Dormant buds waiting to be stimulated into growth. They frequently cannot be seen.

Aerial roots Roots that emerge from trunks or other stems above ground.

Alternate Said of leaves or buds when they are not directly opposite one another on a stem, but staggered.

Apex The tip of a stem or shoot.

Axil The upper angle that a leaf stalk makes with the stem.

Axillary buds Buds that are formed in the axils, i.e. between the leafstalk and the stem.

Bare-rooted Plants that are bought or otherwise acquired that are not in a container, and have had the soil removed from their roots.

Basal Leaves or shoots growing at the base of a plant.

Blind shoots Shoots that have failed to produce a flower.

Bracts Petal-like modified leaves that often appear around a flower. Frequently coloured.

Branch leader The main shoot of a branch that is increasing its length.

Break Shoots, leaves or blossom starting to grow from their buds.

Brutting The partial breaking of shoots on a cobnut tree.

Bush tree A compact tree on a short trunk.

Canopy The main part of the tree above the trunk.

Central leader The main, central shoot of a tree or shrub.

Chainsaw A motor-driven saw for cutting through large branches or trunks.

Climber A shrub, perennial or annual that grows through other plants, or needs walls or a framework for support.

Coppicing Regular cutting back to ground or near ground-level of trees and shrubs, done to stimulate new growth.

Cordon A single-stem method of growing fruit trees and bushes in a confined area.

Crown The main part of the tree above the trunk.

Cultivar A variation originating in cultivation of a wild plant.

Deadheading The removal of fading or dead flowers or their resulting seed pods.

Deciduous Plants in which the leaves die during their dormant period.

Defoliation Loss or removal of leaves.

Die-back The dying of shoots or other wood from either the tip or point of cutting.

Dormancy A period when a plant is inactive, most frequently in winter.

Double cordon A two-stemmed cordon forming a "U"-shape.

Dwarfing rootstock Rootstock that produces small trees.

Epicormic shoots Shoots that appear on the stem, often on the trunk of mature trees as a result of wounds.

Espalier A decorative form of training with tiered layers of side branches either side of a central trunk.

Evergreen A plant that does not lose its leaves at the end of its growing season.

Fan A decorative training method where branches radiate out from a short trunk.

Fastigiate Describing narrow trees and shrubs with almost vertical branches.

Feathered Trees with branches or shoots on either side of a main trunk.

Feathered maiden A one-year-old tree with a main stem and side shoots.

Framework The permanent structure of branches.

Graft Joining one type of plant on to another plant's rootstock.

Graft union The junction between the top (scion) and the bottom (rootstock) of a grafted plant.

Internode The piece of shoot between to nodes, i.e. between two side-shoots, leaves or buds.

Lateral Side shoot.

Leader A main stem.

Long-arm pruners Secateurs (pruners) on a long pole that can be operated from the lower end while reaching up into trees or shrubs.

Long-handled pruners Secateurs (pruners) that have long handles for cutting thicker stems.

Maiden A tree in its first year.

Maiden whip A tree in its first year without as yet any side shoots.

Mulch A ground-covering material to conserve moisture and prevent weeds.

Multi-stemmed A tree or shrub with more than one main stem or trunk.

Multiple cordon. A cordon that has three or more vertical stems.

Petiole A leaf stalk.

Pinching out To prune by pinching out a soft shoot between finger and thumb.

Pleaching Training adjacent trees so that their branches are interwoven to form a screen.

Pollarding Cutting back all of the branches or shoots of a tree from the top of its trunk.

Pot-bound A container-grown plant in which the roots have outgrown the available space and are wound round each other.

Prostrate Growing along the ground.

Pruning saw A special saw designed specifically for pruning.

Pyramid trees Small trees in the shape of a cone or round pyramid.

Rambler A climbing plant that scrambles though other plants.

Repeat flowering Of a plant that has more than one flowering period.

Replacement shoot A strong shoot that is used to replace the one being removed.

Reversion A process whereby variegated leaves return to their original green state.

Ripe wood Wood that has hardened.

Root-bound A container-grown plant in which the roots have outgrown the available space and are wound round each other.

Rootball The collection of roots, still with their soil, as found in a container or when a plant is dug up.

Rootstock The rooted section of a grafted plant.

Rubbing out Removal of soft shoots by rubbing with the hand.

Secateurs (pruners) Hand tools that are somewhat like strong scissors for pruning thin stems.

Scion The upper part of a grafted plant, from which the plant takes most of its character.

Secondary growth Late summer growth after pruning.

Semi-evergreen A plant that retains some of its leaves while discarding others during its dormant period.

Semi-standard A tree that is half-way between a bush tree and a full standard. The clear trunk is usually about 1.2m (4ft).

Shears A cutting tool like large scissors for trimming hedges.

Side shoot A shoot that appears on the side of a more major stem.

Snag A short length of stem between a bud and a pruning cut.

Spindle bush A small fruit tree in which the branches are artificially lowered to the horizontal.

Spur A short shoot that bears the fruit buds.

Spur-pruning Pruning to encourage the development of spurs.

Spur-thinning Reducing the number of spurs in one place when they become overcrowded.

Standard (1) A full-size tree usually with a clear trunk. (2) A shrub grafted on to a single stem to appear like a miniature tree.

Stepover A low fruit tree form with one or two wide branches that can be stepped over.

Stool A cluster of stems all rising from the same place at ground-level. Coppicing often produces them.

Stopping Pinching out a shoot to make it branch out.

Stub The remaining portion of a shoot when the rest has been cut off.

Sub-lateral A side shoot on a shoot that is already a side shoot itself.

Sucker (1) Shoots that arise from around the base of a plant or from its roots. (2) Vigorous vertical growth from the branches of a fruit tree.

Terminal The tip of a shoot.

Thinning Reducing the number of shoots, spurs or fruit.

Tip-bearing Fruit trees that bear mainly at the ends of their shoots.

Tip-pruning Removing the tip of a shoot to make it branch out.

Topiary A decorative way of shaping a bush.

Trunk The main stem of a tree.

Variegated Foliage that consists of more than one colour.

Water shoots Quick-growing shoots that can appear on the trunks of certain trees, often stimulated by wounds.

Weeping Trees or shrubs that have branches that hang down.

Whip A young tree before it develops any side shoots.

Wirework Wires attached on posts used to support plants.

Suppliers

Hand tools A range of tools for pruning are available from local garden centres and hardware stores. In country areas, agricultural merchants also carry a wide selection.

Power tools Power tools for most purposes are available from garden centres and hardware stores. More powerful machines are also available from garden and farm machinery outlets. Better deals may be had by sourcing from the internet, but local suppliers may also service the machinery. One of the biggest suppliers is Stihl and a search of their webside (www.stihl.com) will give a list of worldwide suppliers. They can be bought locally and have a network for servicing and repairs.

Tree ties, stakes, string, netting and other sundries These are available from garden centres, hardware stores and agricultural merchants.

Fruit cages Smaller units are generally available from local garden centres. For larger ones and for competitive prices a search of the internet is recommended.

Index

Acknowledgements

The Publisher would like to thank the following gardens and garden owners for kindly allowing photography to take place on their premises:

Andrew Mikolajski, Northamptonshire; Bedgebury Pinetum, Kent; Batsford Arboretum, Gloucestershire; Brogdale Horticultural Trust, Faversham, Kent; Chenies Manor, Buckinghamshire; Chiffchaffs, Dorset; East Lambrook Manor, Somerset; Elsing Hall, Norfolk; Headland Garden, Cornwall; Fiona Henley Design; Lamport Hall, Northamptonshire; Merrist Wood, Surrey; Pine Lodge Gardens,

Cornwall; Renishaw Hall, Sheffield; RHS Chelsea Flower Show 2004; RHS Hyde Hall, Essex; RHS Gardens Rosemoor, Devon; RHS Gardens Wisley, Surrey; Rodmarton Manor, Cirencester; Spinners, Devon; Westonbirt Arboretum, Gloucestershire; Wollerton Old Hall, Shropshire; Writtle College, Essex; Wyken Hall, Suffolk; Yalding Organic Gardens, Kent

A special thank you goes to STIHL Ltd. who kindly lent some of the tools and equipment used in the book. A list of worldwide suppliers that stock Stihl products can be found on their website: www.stihl.com

In addition, the Publisher would like to thank the following people for acting as models in photography sessions:

Jeff Clayton; Nick Robinson; Peter Sedgewick; Robin Whitehead; Stephen Coling

The Publisher would also like to thank the following picture libraries for kindly allowing their images to be reproduced in this book:

t = top b = bottom c = centre
l = left r = right

Science Photo Library
39bl (Paul Shoesmith); 189tl (Dan

Sams); 189tr (Keith Seaman); 189bl (M F Merlet); 190b (Ed Young); 192bl (Roger Standen); 192br (K Wise); 196bl (John Marshall); 200t (G Newport); 200 br (BSIP Chassenet); 249bl (Helmut Partsch)
The Garden Picture Library
14t (Marie O'Hara); 14bl (Jane Legate); 14br (David England); 37bl (Jane Legate); 166bl (Ellen Rooney); 198b (John Glover); 199tl (John Glover)

Garden World Images
169tr; 190t; 202b; 248tr

Holt Images
168t; 204t; 208c; 233bl; 233tr; 249br